SRA Corrective Reading

A Direct Instruction Program

Series Guide

Siegfried Engelmann

Susan Hanner

Gary Johnson

Mc
Graw
Hill
Education

Acknowledgments

The senior author of all *Corrective Reading* programs is Siegfried Engelmann.

Coauthors of *Corrective Reading* programs are:

Decoding Strand
- **Decoding A:** Linda Carnine, Gary Johnson
- **Decoding B1:** Linda Carnine, Gary Johnson, Linda Meyer, Wesley Becker, Julie Eisele
- **Decoding B2:** Gary Johnson, Linda Carnine, Linda Meyer, Wesley Becker, Julie Eisele
- **Decoding C:** Gary Johnson, Linda Carnine, Linda Meyer

Comprehension Strand
- **Comprehension A:** Phyllis Haddox, Susan Hanner
- **Comprehension A Fast Cycle:** Phyllis Haddox, Susan Hanner
- **Comprehension B1:** Steve Osborn, Susan Hanner
- **Comprehension B1 Fast Cycle:** Steve Osborn, Susan Hanner
- **Comprehension B2:** Steve Osborn, Susan Hanner
- **Comprehension C:** Susan Hanner, Phyllis Haddox

12 ©Chairat/RooM the Agency/Corbis, BlueMoon Stock/SuperStock, Marty Honig/Getty Images, ©Pixtal/age Fotostock; 171 (r)JUPITERIMAGES/ Comstock Images/Alamy; 172 ©hywit dimyadi/Alamy; 173 (r)JUPITERIMAGES/ Comstock Images/ Alamy; 174 ©hywit dimyadi/Alamy; 214 Media Bakery; 216 (tr)Media Bakery; 220 Media Bakery; 36 ©Best View Stock/ age fotostock, Design Pics/Bilderbuch, Purestock/SuperStock, Purestock/SuperStock, Ken Eis/WeatherVideoHD.TV, Design Pics/Bilderbuch; cover (l to r, t to b)©Pixtal/age Fotostock, (3)©Chairat/RooM the Agency/Corbis, (4)©Best View Stock/age fotostock, (5)Design Pics/Bilderbuch, (6)BlueMoon Stock/SuperStock, (7)Ken Eis/WeatherVideoHD.TV, (8)Marty Honig/Getty Images, (9)©Pixtal/age Fotostock, (11)©Chairat/RooM the Agency/Corbis, (12)©Best View Stock/age fotostock, (13)Design Pics/Bilderbuch, (14)BlueMoon Stock/SuperStock, (15)Ken Eis/WeatherVideoHD.TV, (add by hand)Marty Honig/Getty Images.

MHEonline.com

Send all inquiries to:
McGraw-Hill Education
8787 Orion Place
Columbus, OH 43240

ISBN: 978-0-07-611248-7
MHID: 0-07-611248-9

Printed in the United States of America.

14 15 QLM 19 18

Contents

Contents

Contents

OVERVIEW
SRA's *Corrective Reading* Series

SRA's ***Corrective Reading*** series is designed to accommodate the full range of problem readers. These students may be deficient in decoding skills (misidentifying words), comprehension skills (not understanding what they read), or both decoding skills and comprehension skills. The series consists of two independent strands. Each strand requires one full period every day. The program is not designed to be presented three days a week or on any schedule other than daily. Each daily period is 35 to 55 minutes. So, if one strand is implemented, the commitment is for one daily period devoted exclusively to that strand. If both strands are implemented, two daily periods are required. (Periods do not have to be consecutive.)

The Decoding and Comprehension strands both comprise four levels: A, B1, B2, and C. Level A addresses the most basic skills, and Level C, the most sophisticated skills.

The ***Corrective Reading*** Placement Tests indicate whether individual students need work in decoding, comprehension, or both. Students who need instruction in both strands do not necessarily start on the same level in each strand. For example, a student may place in **Decoding B1** and in **Comprehension A.** This independent placement for Decoding and Comprehension assures that the material students read in both strands is appropriate for their skill levels.

Single Strand

Comprehension A	Comprehension B1	Comprehension B2	Comprehension C
Comprehension A Fast Cycle	Comprehension B1 Fast Cycle		

OR

Decoding A	Decoding B1	Decoding B2	Decoding C

Double Strand

Comprehension A	Comprehension B1	Comprehension B2	Comprehension C
Comprehension A Fast Cycle	Comprehension B1 Fast Cycle		

AND

Decoding A	Decoding B1	Decoding B2	Decoding C

Choose Decoding, Comprehension, or Both

1

Decoding Programs

help students who have trouble identifying words, who don't understand how the arrangement of letters in a word relates to its pronunciation, and whose reading rate is inadequate.

2

Comprehension Programs

help readers who do not follow instructions well, lack vocabulary and background knowledge needed to understand what they read, and have poor thinking skills.

Decoding Strand

Level A
Word-Attack Basics
Decoding A (65 lessons)

Decoding A teaches sound-spelling relationships explicitly and systematically and shows students how to sound out words.

Students are first taught the connection between sound-spelling relationships through regularly spelled words. Then irregular words are introduced. Later, sentence- and story-reading activities are used to teach students to apply their newly learned strategies in real contexts.

After completing **Decoding A,** students can be expected to read basic sentences and simple stories composed mostly of regularly spelled words. They can accurately read many words that typically confuse poor readers and can read quickly enough to comprehend what they read.

Teaches:	Basic reading skills: phonemic awareness, sound-symbol identification, sounding out regular and irregular words, word reading, sentence and story reading, rate building, Workbook applications

Outcomes:	60 wpm, 98 percent accuracy, reading at about a 2.0 grade level

Level B
Decoding Strategies
Decoding B1 (65 lessons)
Decoding B2 (65 lessons)

In **Decoding** Levels **B1** and **B2,** word-attack skills are refined and applied to more sound-spelling patterns and difficult words. These skills are applied in stories designed to correct mistakes the poor reader typically makes.

Students are introduced to new words and word types, phonemic relationships, long and short vowel sounds, new sound combinations, and new word endings. They apply their discrimination skills by reading stories of increasing length and with more complex syntax and then answering comprehension questions both orally and in writing.

After completing **Decoding B1** and **B2,** students show great improvement in both reading speed and accuracy.

Teaches:	Pronunciation, sounds of letters and letter combinations, word endings, word reading, critical word discriminations, understanding literal and inferential comprehension questions, rate building, Workbook applications

Outcomes:	**B1:** 90 wpm, 98 percent accuracy, reading at about a 3.0 grade level; **B2:** 130 wpm, 98 percent accuracy, reading at about a 4.0 grade level

Decoding Strand

Level C
Skill Applications
Decoding C (125 lessons)

Decoding C bridges the gap between advanced word-attack skills and the ability to read textbooks and other informational material.

Students are introduced to the meaning of 600 new vocabulary words and read a variety of passages, from narrative to expository, with fairly sophisticated vocabulary. To prepare them to read in all content areas, **Decoding C** introduces sentence types and conventions that are typical of textbook material.

After completing **Decoding C,** students can read an average of 150 words per minute at 98 percent accuracy. They can read materials with a wide range of syntax, vocabulary, format, and content. They can learn new information and apply it after only one reading.

Teaches:	Letter combinations, affixes, vocabulary development, accurate reading of story selections and informational passages, understanding literal and inferential comprehension questions, rate building, Workbook applications
Outcomes:	Over 150 wpm, reading at about a 6.0–7.0 grade level

Comprehension Strand

Level A
Thinking Basics

Comprehension A (65 lessons)

Comprehension A Fast Cycle
           (30 lessons)

Comprehension A teaches basic reasoning skills that form the framework for learning information. It also fills in crucial gaps in students' background knowledge.

Students are taught thinking operations they can use to solve problems in any content area. They practice organizing groups of related facts and develop basic logic skills such as making inferences. They also learn common information they may be lacking, as well as word meanings.

At the end of **Comprehension A,** students are able to complete simple analogies, identify synonyms, recite poems, and follow simple instructions. They have mastered some higher-order thinking skills and established a foundation upon which to build.

Teaches:	Oral language skills: deductions, inductions, analogies, inferences, vocabulary building, statement repetition, common information

Outcomes:	The ability to apply some higher-order thinking skills and use many word definitions

Level B
Comprehension Skills

Comprehension B1 (60 lessons)

Comprehension B1 Fast Cycle
           (35 lessons)

Comprehension B2 (65 lessons)

The **Comprehension B1** and **B2** programs teach the many separate skills necessary to read content-area textbooks, learn new information, and respond to written questions that involve deductions and rule applications.

Lessons focus on developing the background knowledge, vocabulary, and thinking skills needed to construct meaning from written text. Reasoning and analysis strategies are taught in content-rich contexts, enabling students to transfer these strategies to many subject areas. Games help students master important facts and vocabulary.

By the time they finish the Level B programs, students have learned basic strategies that allow them to read for information in academic subjects and learn new facts and vocabulary.

Teaches:	Literal and inferential skills, reading for information, writing skills, following sequenced instructions, analyzing contradictions, common information

Outcomes:	The ability to apply a variety of comprehension skills in all school subjects; the ability to read information and learn new facts and vocabulary

Comprehension Strand
Level C
Concept Applications
Comprehension C (140 lessons)

Comprehension C teaches students to use thinking skills independently. They move from basic reasoning tools to higher-order skills.

Students learn to infer definitions from context, read for basic information, write precise directions, recognize the main idea of a passage, draw conclusions from basic evidence, and identify contradictions and faulty arguments.

By the end of **Comprehension C,** students can evaluate advertisements and editorials and recognize contradictory information in newspaper and magazine articles. They have learned to evaluate sources of information and know how to use information resources.

Teaches:	Critical thinking skills in analyzing arguments, organizing and utilizing information, using sources of information, communicating information
Outcomes:	The ability to apply analytical skills to real-life situations and answer literal and inferential questions based on passages read

Who Needs *Corrective Reading?*

The following tables describe characteristics of students who benefit from the Decoding strand, the Comprehension strand, or both. Note that the Placement Tests for Decoding and Comprehension provide a more detailed profile of what students need to learn and which level of the program is most appropriate for them.

Decoding A

For students in grades 3 through 12 who read so haltingly or inaccurately they can't understand what they read

Decoding B1

For students in grades 3 through 12 who do not read at an adequate rate and who confuse words

Decoding B2

For students in grades 3 through 12 who do not read at an adequate rate and who confuse words

Decoding C

For students in grades 4 through 12 who have trouble decoding multisyllabic words and typical textbook material

Comprehension A

For students in grades 4 through 12 who cannot understand orally presented concepts that underlie much of the material being taught

Comprehension A Fast Cycle

For students in grades 4 through 12 who are weak in comprehension skills but not as weak as students who place in regular **Comprehension A**

Comprehension B1

For students in grades 4 through 12 who have difficulty with conclusions, deductions, and contradictions

Comprehension B1 Fast Cycle

For students in grades 4 through 12 who lack important comprehension and reasoning skills but who will probably learn these skills faster than students who place in regular **Comprehension B1**

Comprehension B2

For students in grades 4 through 12 who have difficulty with conclusions, deductions, and contradictions

Comprehension C

For students in grades 5 and up who can't comprehend grade-level textbooks, do not learn well from material they read, or have trouble thinking critically

Features of the Series

Each level of SRA's *Corrective Reading* series has features that have been demonstrated through research studies to be effective in improving student performance. The programs directly address all the critical reading components identified by the National Reading Panel (2002)—phonemic awareness, phonics, fluency, vocabulary, and comprehension. Note that vocabulary and comprehension are not major objectives of the Decoding strand but are thoroughly addressed by the companion Comprehension strand.

■ All details of the series are designed to provide **differentiated instruction** that is appropriate for each learner. The Placement Tests assess each learner's skills and indicate the appropriate level for different students. The daily lessons are designed so the teacher is able to respond to the performance of each student in the group. The Mastery Tests assess the progress of each student in all the skills the program teaches. The teacher who teaches students to mastery provides instruction that is tailored to each student.

■ Each program is a core program, not ancillary material. Each program contains all the material you need and provides students with all the practice they need to learn the skills.

■ All skills and strategies are taught through DIRECT INSTRUCTION. This approach is the most efficient for communicating with the students, for evaluating their performance on a moment-to-moment basis, and for achieving student mastery. Students are not simply exposed to skills. Skills are taught.

■ Students are taught everything that is required for what they are to do later. Also, they are not taught skills that are not needed for later skill applications. The programs concentrate only on the necessary skills, not the nuances.

■ Each program is based on cumulative skill development. Skills and strategies are taught, with lots of examples. Once a skill or strategy is taught, students receive practice in applying that skill until the end of the program. This type of cumulative development has been demonstrated by research studies to be the most effective method for teaching skills so they become well learned or automatic.

■ Because of the cumulative development of skills, the difficulty of material increases gradually but steadily.

■ Each program is divided into daily lessons that usually can be presented in a class period (35 to 55 minutes of teacher-directed work and independent student applications).

■ Each program provides detailed data on student performance. Students see documentation of their improvement as they progress through the program.

- All levels of **Corrective Reading** contain in-program Mastery Tests. These tests are criterion-referenced performance measures that provide detailed information about student performance and that indicate remedies for groups of students who have not mastered specific reading skills. The Mastery Tests also show the students how their performance is improving as they progress through the program.

- Each program includes an effective management system. Students earn points for performance on each part of the daily lesson. Records of this performance may be used for awarding grades and documenting progress in specific skill areas.

- Each program specifies both teacher and student behavior. The lessons are scripted. The scripts specify what you do and say as well as appropriate student responses. The scripted lessons assure that you will (a) use uniform wording, (b) present examples in a manner that communicates effectively with students, and (c) be able to complete a lesson during a class period.

- The **Corrective Reading** Decoding Placement Test and the Comprehension Placement Test provide detailed information for the accurate placement of students in SRA's **Corrective Reading** Decoding and Comprehension programs. The Decoding Placement Test measures each student's decoding accuracy and rate of oral reading. The Comprehension Placement Test measures performance on analogies, similarities, recitation behavior, vocabulary, knowledge about basic information, deductions, and other skills assumed in complex comprehension activities.

The Materials

The teacher's materials for each level of **_Corrective Reading_** consist of a Teacher's Guide and one or two Teacher Presentation Books. The Teacher's Guide contains basic information about the program and specific information for presenting exercises and correcting mistakes. The Teacher's Guide also includes a copy of a Placement Test, a Scope and Sequence Chart, a list of Behavioral Objectives, a Skills Profile Chart, and forms for keeping records of student performance. (**Note:** The Teacher's Guides for **Comprehension A Fast Cycle** and **B1 Fast Cycle** are in the Teacher Presentation Books.)

The Teacher Presentation Books contain a script for each lesson. Scripts specify what you say and do and how students are to respond. The Teacher Presentation Books also include reproductions of the student pages with answers.

All levels of **_Corrective Reading_** have a consumable student Workbook that contains activities for each lesson. Some activities are teacher directed; others are independent. All Workbook activities are integral parts of the lessons. The Workbook also contains charts on which students record points earned for their performance on the parts of each lesson.

Some levels also have a nonconsumable Student Book with activities such as word lists, story selections, and informational articles for each lesson.

Decoding 2008	Teacher's Guide	Teacher Presentation Book	Consumable Workbook	Nonconsumable Student Book
Decoding A	1	2	1	
Decoding B1	1	1	1	1
Decoding B2	1	1	1	1
Decoding C	1	2	1	1

Comprehension 2008	Teacher's Guide	Teacher Presentation Book	Consumable Workbook	Nonconsumable Student Book
Comprehension A	1	2	1	
Comprehension A Fast Cycle	*	1	1	
Comprehension B1	1	1	1	
Comprehension B1 Fast Cycle	*	1	1	
Comprehension B2	1	1	1	
Comprehension C	1	2	1	1

*incorporated in the Teacher Presentation Book

THE PROGRAMS

SRA's **_Corrective Reading_** series is designed to help a wide range of students in grades 3 through 12. The programs are designed to meet the needs of students who are performing below grade-level expectations in reading and perhaps other subjects, too. Some students will require a great deal of remedial work; other students will have far fewer skill deficiencies. The goals of the Level A programs, which deal with very basic skills, are relatively modest in number, while the objectives of the Level C programs are manifold. Students who initially are placed in a Level C program have mastered the basics and are ready to master a wider range of skills.

Corrective Reading is appropriate for students who speak and understand basic conversational English and whose scores on the Placement Tests indicate that they belong in one of the programs. The programs are not meant to be used with students who do not speak English or with students whose grasp of English is quite weak.

Corrective Reading works effectively with students in both general-education and special-needs programs. As long as students demonstrate the skill level necessary to enter a program, they may be placed in that program.

The Decoding Programs

The illustration below shows the four Decoding programs in SRA's **_Corrective Reading_** series.

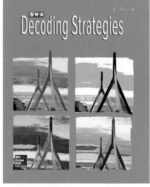

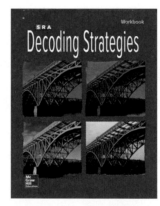

Decoding A
65 lessons

Decoding B1
65 lessons

Decoding B2
65 lessons

Decoding C
125 lessons

The Decoding Programs and the Problem Reader

The Decoding programs are designed to change the behavior of the problem reader. The specific decoding tendencies of this student suggest what a program must do to be effective in changing the student's behavior.

■ The problem reader makes frequent word-identification errors. The student makes a higher percentage of mistakes when reading connected sentences than when reading words in word lists. Often the student reads words correctly in word lists and misidentifies the same words when they are embedded in connected sentences.

■ The specific mistakes the reader makes include word omissions, word additions, and confusion of high-frequency words (such as **what** and **that, of** and **for, and** and **the**). The student also reads synonyms (saying "pretty" for **beautiful**). The student often guesses at words, basing the guess on the word beginning or ending. And the student is consistently inconsistent, making a mistake on one word in a sentence and then making a different mistake when rereading the sentence.

■ The student doesn't seem to understand the relationship between the arrangement of letters in a word and the pronunciation of the word. Often the student is confused about the word meaning (a fact suggested by synonym reading, opposite reading, and word guessing). The strategy seems to be based on rules the student has been taught. The problem reader follows such advice as: "Look at the beginning of the word and take a guess," "Think of what the word might mean," and "Look at the general shape of the word." The result is a complicated strategy that is often backwards: The student seems to think that to read a word, one must first "understand" the word and then select the spoken word that corresponds to that understanding.

■ Although the problem reader may use a strategy that is meaning based, the reader is often preempted from comprehending passages. The reason is that the student doesn't read a passage with the degree of accuracy needed to understand what the passage actually says. (Omitting the word **not** from one sentence changes the meaning dramatically.)

■ The student's reading rate is often inadequate, making it difficult for the student to remember the various details of the passage, even if they were decoded accurately. Often the problem reader doesn't have an effective reading comprehension strategy because the student's poor decoding and slow rate don't make the material sensible.

■ Initial relearning may be very slow and require a great deal of repetition. For a seventh grader—who chronically confuses **a** and **the**—to read words at 98 percent accuracy when they appear in passages, the student may have to read these words more than 800 times when they appear in sentences. Furthermore, the student must receive feedback. The only way to provide the necessary practice and feedback is through a presentation format that requires lots of oral reading. Until the 800 practice trials are provided, the high rate of accuracy will not occur.

■ Finally, the problem reader is not a highly motivated student. For this student, reading has been punishing. The student often professes indifference: "I don't care if I can read or not." But the student's behavior gives strong suggestions that the student cares a great deal.

The student's ineffective reading strategies and negative attitudes about reading become more ingrained as the reader gets older. To overcome them requires a very careful program, one that systematically replaces the strategies with new ones and that provides lots and lots of practice.

Decoding Procedures

The procedures that are used in the program derive directly from the difficulties that students have with particular tasks. Based on the problems students have, we can identify two major levels of difficulty. The less difficult level is reading isolated words. The more difficult level is reading words that are in a connected-sentence context.

Isolated words are easier because they do not prompt the student to use inappropriate guessing strategies that the student applies when reading connected sentences. When the student reads word lists, therefore, the student is not as likely to guess on the basis of the order of the preceding words or on the basis of images that are prompted by preceding words. Not all word lists are the same level of difficulty.

Less difficult lists require reading words that have similar parts. *More difficult lists* require reading words that do not have similar parts. This type of list is sometimes called a "mixed list" because all types of words appear in it.

Reading words in connected sentences is more difficult than reading words in isolation. The task of reading a particular passage can be made relatively more difficult or less difficult.

Passage reading is less difficult if the student has read the passage and received feedback on all errors.

Passage reading is more difficult if the student is reading the passage for the first time.

Lessons in **Corrective Reading** Decoding programs are designed within the skill limits of the student, which means that an appropriately placed student will not be overwhelmed with difficult tasks or bored by tasks that are too easy.

Each lesson presents words in isolation and gives students practice with easier lists and more difficult lists. When new words are introduced, they often appear in lists of words that have similar parts. In later lessons, these same words appear in mixed lists for which the students must rely more on the decoding skills taught earlier. Except for the early lessons in Level A, all lessons provide students with practice in reading familiar words in sentence contexts.

The procedures require the students to read sentences or passages and then reread them. In Levels B1, B2, and C, students keep a record of their performance on the Fluency Assessment, called an Individual Reading Checkout. Their improved performance on timed reading provides students with evidence of their ability to retain and apply the decoding skills they have been taught. Students who read more fluently have better reading comprehension because what they read is more like natural speech.

The structure of the lessons addresses skill deficiencies directly but positively, in a manner that provides the type of practice students need to relearn fundamental strategies and to learn new skills. The teaching is designed so that it does not overwhelm students with material or rules that result in a high rate of errors.

The Problems

An effective corrective reading program must address the specific needs of the problem reader.

1 The learner must learn to look at the order of letters in a word and learn that this order suggests the general pronunciation of the word. Furthermore, the student must learn that the game is simple: First figure out how the letters suggest to say the word. Then see if the word you say is one that you recognize, one that has meaning. (Note that this strategy is basically the opposite of the one the typical problem reader uses.)

2 The problem reader must receive practice in reading connected sentences that are composed of words that have been taught in isolation. Merely because the student reads words in lists does not imply transfer to written sentences.

3 An effective corrective reading program provides a great deal of daily fluency practice. The demands for fluency become greater as students move through the Decoding strand. In **Decoding A** there is much more emphasis on accuracy than fluency. By **Decoding C,** students are expected to read fluently, accurately, and with expression.

4 The student must receive strong reinforcement for working on reading because the task is very difficult and frustrating for the student. The student has received a great deal of evidence that reading is a puzzle that can't seem to be solved.

5 Finally, the student must receive practice in reading a variety of passages. If the student practices reading only narrative passages, the student will not "automatically" transfer the reading skills to textbooks, articles, or other forms of expository writing. Therefore, different styles must be introduced.

The Solutions

SRA's **_Corrective Reading_** Decoding programs are successful with problem readers because they provide the careful integration, the practice, and the management details the student needs to succeed.

- ■ **The student receives daily practice in oral reading with immediate feedback.** (Only through oral reading can we discover what the student is actually reading.)

- ■ **The student reads word lists with information about how to pronounce various letter combinations,** such as **th** and **or.** The student also reads sentences and passages composed of words that have been taught. The sentences and passages are designed so that they are relatively easy if the student approaches words as entities that are to be analyzed according to the arrangement of letters but difficult if the student guesses on the basis of the context or syntax of the sentence. (The sentences are designed so that guesses often lead to an incorrect identification of the word.)

- ■ **Together, the Mastery Tests and checkouts in the series assure that the student observes progress in reading rate and reading accuracy.** Students become increasingly motivated by their progress in timed reading, as their records show improvement in reading rate and accuracy.

- ■ **Stories and story-comprehension activities assure that students attend to the content of what they read.** Initially in the Decoding series, the comprehension activities are deliberately separated from the decoding activities so that the student's misconceptions about reading are not exaggerated. The comprehension activities, however, show the student that what is read is to be understood. When students progress through the series, reading longer selections, they answer comprehension questions presented before, during, and after the selections. Comprehension items also appear in the Workbook.

- ■ **Finally, the series addresses the problem reader's poor self-image.** The series is designed so the student can succeed on real reading tasks. Furthermore, a point system that is based on realistic performance goals assures that the reader who tries will succeed and will receive reinforcement for improved performance.

In summary, the series uses a two-pronged approach. Each level teaches effective reading skills to replace the student's ineffective approach to reading. Each level also contains an effective management system that turns students on to reading. This turn-on is not achieved by "seducing" the reader with entertaining topics but by rewarding the reader for steady improvement in reading performance. The approach **works.**

Use of Decoding Programs with English-Language Learners

The test of where English-Language Learners should be placed in the Decoding strand is: Would they be able to understand all details of the story if somebody orally read it to them? If the answer is no, the students should not be placed in the Decoding program. They should be placed in an oral language program. Programs that are particularly effective with English-Language Learners are **Language for Learning** and, for more advanced students, **Language for Thinking.**

If a school uses only a single-strand Decoding sequence with older students who are not proficient in English, the best option is to present the stories they will read in the Decoding program as oral stories before those stories are presented as reading stories. The procedure is to read to students the stories that are at least twenty lessons beyond where students are placed in the program and work on the content the stories present. The instructor (a parent, an aide, or an English-speaking student) reads the story to the students and asks the story questions specified in the Teacher Presentation Book. The instructor models the answers as needed.

Students should not read a story until at least twenty school days have passed since the oral presentation of that story. For example, if the students are placed at Lesson 1 in **Decoding B1,** the plan would be to present story 21 as an oral story, with comprehension questions, and at a different time present story 1 as a reading story in the regular lesson. On the next day, story 22 would be presented as an oral story and story 2 as a reading story, and so forth.

Progress Through the Decoding Programs

The programs are designed so that there is a careful progression of skill development from level to level. There are **four** entry points.

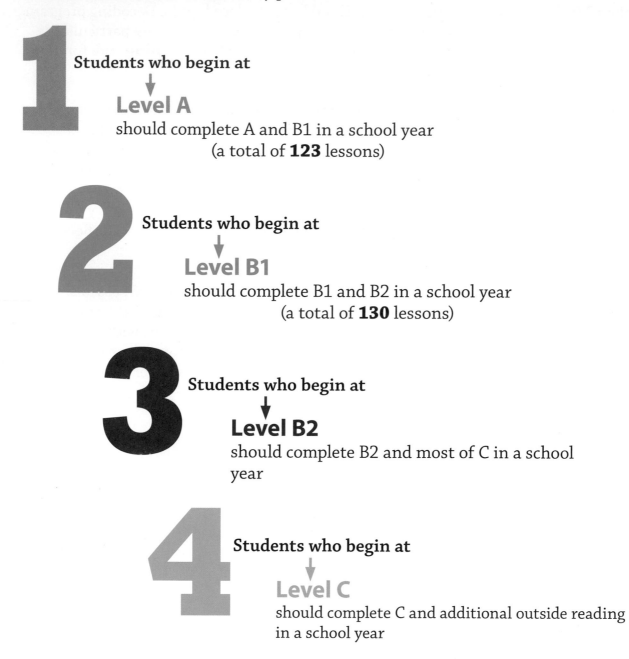

1 Students who begin at

Level A

should complete A and B1 in a school year (a total of **123** lessons)

2 Students who begin at

Level B1

should complete B1 and B2 in a school year (a total of **130** lessons)

3 Students who begin at

Level B2

should complete B2 and most of C in a school year

4 Students who begin at

Level C

should complete C and additional outside reading in a school year

A summary of the programs follows. For each program, the summary describes (a) the reading behavior of students typically placed in that program, (b) what is taught, and (c) what students should be able to do at the end of the program.

Decoding A—Word-Attack Basics

Who It's For

Decoding A is appropriate for very poor readers in grades 3 through 12. These students read so inaccurately or haltingly that they cannot comprehend what they read.

What Is Taught

Decoding A is a phonics program, which means it teaches the alphabetic principle (phonemic awareness and using letter sounds to sound out and say fast unknown words).

The following skills are taught in **Decoding A:**

- Identifying the sounds of letters

- Sounding out words that are presented orally and then saying them fast

- Sounding out and identifying written words that are spelled regularly

- Decoding irregularly spelled words

- Reading words "the fast way"

- Reading sentences

- Reading short selections

- Spelling

Related skills such as matching, word completion, and symbol scanning are included in the student Workbook pages.

The basic objective in **Decoding A** is to teach students that there are regularly spelled words, words that are pronounced by blending the sounds of the letters in them. Once students understand that the identification of a word is related to its spelling, irregularly spelled words, such as **said** and **what,** are introduced. These words are spelled one way but pronounced in a different, "irregular" way. However, the primary focus is on those elements of the reading code that are regular. Therefore, emphasis is not on sight words of any kind but on uniform procedures for decoding regularly spelled words, including words that have difficult consonant blends (for example, **truck, block, mast, cats, dent, greet**).

The sentence-reading exercises give students practice in reading words that are presented within a context. Usually students who qualify for this program do not understand what decoding is. This problem is magnified when they try to read sentences. Usually their sentence-reading strategy involves guessing based on the syntax or the position of words within the sentence. For instance, they guess that the first word is **the.**

The objective of the sentence-reading activities is to retrain students in how to read words in sentences. Although work on isolated words (in lists) teaches word-attack skills, practice in reading sentences ensures that students apply these skills.

The sentences in this program are designed so that there is low probability of guessing a word correctly. If students guess the next word in a sentence on the basis of the preceding words, they most likely will be wrong. The low-probability feature provides students with consistent evidence that guessing is not effective. A guess equals a mistake; therefore, students quickly abandon the guessing approach and use the decoding skills being taught.

The story-reading exercises give students practice in decoding material similar to what they will encounter at the beginning of **Decoding B1** and in answering comprehension questions about what they have read.

Outcome Behavior

Upon completion of **Decoding A,** students should be able to do the following activities:

- Read sentences, such as **She was a master at planting trees.** These sentences are composed primarily of regularly spelled words (containing as many as six sounds).

- Read short selections, such as the following:

    Ten men got in a truck.
    They went to the creek and set up a tent.
    How can ten men fit in the tent?
    They can not.
    Six men will sleep under a tree.

- Read short selections at a rate of approximately 60 words per minute.

- Read common irregular words, such as **what, was, do, said, to, of,** and **you,** with only infrequent errors.

- Read words that begin with difficult letter combinations, such as **st, bl, sl, fl, pl, sw, cl, tr,** and **dr.**

- Read words that end with difficult letter combinations, such as **nt, nd, st, ts, mp, ps, cks, ls, ms, th, er, ing, ers,** and **y.**

- Pronounce commonly confused word parts, such as the **k** sound in **trick,** the **e** sound in **set,** and the **s** ending sound in **mats, runs,** and **clocks.**

- Spell simple words that have a clear sound-symbol relationship, including words that contain **th, wh, sh, ch,** and various other letter combinations.

- Independently perform various simple activities, such as matching sounds and completing words with missing letters.

What's New in the 2008 Edition—Decoding A

1 Improved and uniform management system. In the earlier editions, the management system for **Decoding A** was different from that used in **Decoding B1, Decoding B2, and Decoding C.** While B1, B2, and C students were able to earn 20 points for each lesson, this was not the case for A. In the current edition, students in A are able to earn 20 points per lesson.

2 Simplified Mastery Test system. In earlier editions, some of the Mastery Tests were not specified in the teacher's presentation material. In the current edition, procedures for administering Mastery Tests appear in the teacher's presentation material. Also, the schedule for presenting Mastery Tests has been modified to give the teacher more timely information about different types of decoding problems students may be experiencing. The timely identification of problems leads to more timely remedies.

3 Improved schedule and criteria for checking students' daily reading fluency and accuracy. The rate requirements have been graduated so that students read at about 30 words in 45 seconds (40 words per minute) in Lessons 46 through 50 and gradually increase in rate to over 60 words per minute near the end of the program.

4 Lesson Objectives. Preceding every five lessons in the Teacher Presentation Books, a one-page summary of Lesson Objectives lists the skills and activities for those five lessons.

5 Minor changes designed to make the teacher and student material easier to use.

6 More efficient transition procedures for students who complete **Decoding A.** Because these students frequently read better than students who initially place in B1, students who complete A do not start on Lesson 1 of B1 but on Lesson 8.

Decoding B1—Decoding Strategies

Who It's For

Decoding B1 is appropriate for many problem readers in grades 3 through 12. Students who place in **Decoding B1** have some appropriate reading behaviors but also exhibit much confusion. They guess at words. They have trouble reading words like **what, that, a,** and **the** when the words appear in a sentence context. They add or omit words. They often read synonyms for printed words and are generally inconsistent in their reading behavior (reading a word correctly one time and missing it the next time).

What Is Taught

The typical **Decoding B1** lesson is divided into four major parts.

1 Word-Attack Skills

2 Group Reading

3 Individual Reading Checkouts

4 Workbook Exercises

Word-Attack Skills take about 10 minutes. Students practice pronouncing words, identifying the sounds of letters or letter combinations, and reading isolated words composed of sounds and sound combinations they have learned. Students earn points for performance in the word-attack portion of the lesson.

Group Reading follows immediately after Word-Attack Skills. This part of the lesson takes approximately 15 to 20 minutes. Students take turns reading aloud from their Student Book. Students who are not reading follow along. During Lessons 1 through 10, students read isolated sentences (a total of about 30 to 95 words per lesson). Stories begin in Lesson 11 and are divided into parts. If the group reads a part within the error limit, all students earn points for that part. Stories increase in length from about 200 words in Lesson 11 to over 600 words by Lesson 65.

Individual Reading Checkouts begin in Lesson 6. They follow Group Reading and take about 10 minutes. In Lessons 1 through 10, individual students read to the teacher. Starting in Lesson 11, students work in assigned pairs, and the teacher observes and provides feedback as students read one story passage to each other. Starting in Lesson 16, the assigned pairs of students read two passages as a Fluency Assessment. The first is from the lesson just read by the group; the second is from the preceding lesson. Each member of the pair first reads the passage from the current story and then the passage from the preceding lesson. A student can earn points for both passages. Points for the first passage are earned if the student reads within a specified error limit. To earn points for the second passage, the student must read the passage within a specified rate criterion and also a specified error criterion. (For instance, the student must read 85 words in 1 minute, with no more than 2 errors.)

Workbook Exercises are presented as the last part of the lesson. Some of these activities are teacher directed and are very important to the students' skill development. Other activities are independent. The Workbook Exercises take about 10 minutes. Students earn points by staying within an error limit in the Workbook for the lesson.

The following activities are included in Word-Attack Skills:

- Pronouncing words with consonant blends **(slam, cast, flip),** orally constructing words with endings (adding **ed** to **show** to pronounce **showed**), and identifying the component sounds of orally presented words

- Identifying the long and short sounds of the vowels **o, e, a,** and **i**

- Identifying the sounds of consonants

- Identifying the sounds of letter combinations **(th, ee, sh, or, ol, ch, wh, ing, er, oo, ea, oa, ai, ou, ar, oul, ir, igh, al)** and reading words with those combinations

- Reading lists of regularly spelled words, such as **mat** and **trip,** and irregularly spelled words, such as **what** and **said**

- Reading words that contain difficult consonant blends **(drop, splash, slip)**

- Reading words with endings **(dropping, rested)**

- Reading silent-**E** words **(save, times, hoped)**

- Reading compound words **(herself, anybody)**

- Practicing pattern drills that demonstrate consistent phonic relationships **(big, bag, beg, bug)**

The **stories** in **Decoding B1** increase in length, difficulty, and interest. All stories are composed of words that have been taught in the series or words the students can already read. After new words and word types are introduced in Word-Attack Skills, the words are incorporated in stories. Furthermore, the introduction of words in stories is cumulative, which means that once words have been introduced, they recur in the stories.

The syntax and structure of the stories are designed to correct the mistakes the problem reader typically makes. Early stories are low-interest stories because the poor reader must concentrate on a new game—looking at words and identifying them, without guessing. With high-interest stories, the reader becomes preoccupied with the content of the story and reverts to habitual, inappropriate decoding strategies, which means that errors increase greatly. Later in the program, after students have practiced the game of accurate decoding, the stories become more interesting. Although the content "distracts" the reader, appropriate strategies are now strong enough for the reader to read with acceptable accuracy.

Comprehension questions are presented before students read the story, after students read each part of the story, and after students have completed the selection. Most story questions are about details of each story part students read. Questions that occur before students read a selection have to do with summarizing events of the preceding story and predicting what may occur in the current selection. Questions that occur during and after the story reading address story characters, setting, problems and solutions, sequence of events, cause and effect, and comparisons or contrasts.

The daily **Individual Reading Checkouts** provide each student with a lot of practice in reading connected sentences. Starting in Lesson 11, the students work in pairs and read one passage to each other. Starting in Lesson 16, the student pairs read two passages to each other, and the entire checkout doesn't take very long—about 10 minutes for both checkouts. The daily timed reading checkouts help students gradually develop acceptable reading rates (from 55 words per minute at the beginning of Level B1 to 90 words per minute at the end of Level B1).

The **Workbook Exercises** are carefully integrated with the word-attack activities and with the stories the students read. From lesson to lesson, there is a careful development of skills in the Workbook. Students also write answers to a variety of comprehension items in the Workbook that require recall of story events, sequencing, and characters.

> It is very important for the students to do the Workbook Exercises as part of each lesson.

Each Workbook lesson is one page. The different activities provide students with practice in writing sounds, copying, answering comprehension questions, spelling, and transforming words. Many of the activities deal with word details because these are the details the problem reader tends to ignore.

Outcome Behavior

Upon completion of **Decoding B1,** students' progress can be seen in both improved accuracy and improved rate. Following is one part of the story from Lesson 65. Students can read this passage with 98 percent accuracy and at a minimum rate of 90 words per minute.

4

Stop the Drams

Jean was trying to think of everything that had happened just | 11
before the drams went to sleep. She remembered how she had been | 23
running with the drams biting her. She ran and fell into a hole in the | 38
floor. She remembered getting out of the hole and running again. | 49

But were the drams biting her then? "Think, think." | 58

"No," Jean said to herself. "I don't remember being bitten | 68
after I fell into the hole. Something must have happened before | 79
I fell into the hole." | 84

Jean tried to think of <u>everything</u> that happened before she | 94
fell into the hole. She looked at the beach. More drams were | 106
marching closer to the barracks. They were marching over the | 116
sleeping drams. "Bzzzzzzzzzzzz." | 119

[2]

Lesson 65, part 4, Decoding B1 Student Book

What's New in the 2008 Edition—Decoding B1

1 The transition from **Decoding A** to **Decoding B1** is more seamless than it was in the 2002 edition. Those students who go through **Decoding A** learn and use sounding-out techniques to decode regularly spelled words. In the 2008 edition of **Decoding B1,** students practice sounding out in the first ten lessons. These lessons have a slower rate of introducing new skills and provide explicit instruction with teacher-directed practice.

■ The 2008 edition also makes the first lessons easier for the students who have not gone through **Decoding A** and assures that students are firm on the pronunciation of the vowel sounds in words they will decode in Lesson 10.

■ The number of irregularly spelled words **(of, was, you)** has been reduced in the first ten lessons so that students receive more practice with regularly spelled words **(ram, clock, glass).**

■ The earlier lessons provide practice in catching errors the teacher makes while reading sentences aloud. This practice is important for preparing students to identify errors when they do peer checkouts with a partner.

2 **Decoding B1** contains expanded comprehension items and activities that meet state and district standards for comprehension. Students

■ summarize the events of the previous story.

■ answer questions about characters, setting, events, and problems and solutions.

■ identify sentences that express the main idea of a selection.

■ identify causes and effects.

■ compare and contrast characters.

■ identify sequences of events.

3 Comprehension questions are displayed in a way that makes them easier to present. These questions appear just after the story part that answers them (rather than at the end of the entire selection).

4 Running word counts are displayed in blue in the right column of the Student Book. These word counts make it easy for students to count the number of words they read during the Fluency Assessment. The target word (for example, the 60th word in Lessons 16 through 19) is underlined in the Student Book.

5 The system for awarding points to students who do well has been modified so that

■ the data translates more easily into letter grades for individual students.

■ the data may still be used to convert into rewards the number of points students earn.

6 New Workbook activities provide students with increased practice identifying the base part of words that have endings **(like, liking).**

7 **Decoding B1** has Mastery Tests every ten lessons. The directions for administration, scoring procedures, and test remedies are specified in the Teacher Presentation Book. The test forms are in the back of the Workbook.

8 Preceding every five lessons in the Teacher Presentation Book, a one-page summary of Lesson Objectives lists the skills and activities for those five lessons.

Decoding B2—Decoding Strategies

Who It's For

Decoding B2 is appropriate for students in grades 3 through 12 who have some decoding problems, who do not read at an adequate rate, who still tend to confuse words with similar spellings, and who tend to make word-guessing mistakes.

What Is Taught

Decoding B2 follows the same format as **Decoding B1.** Each lesson is divided into four major parts.

1 Word-Attack Skills (10 minutes)

2 Group Reading (15–20 minutes)

3 Individual Reading Checkouts (10 minutes)

4 Workbook Exercises (10 minutes)

The following activities are included in **Word-Attack Skills:**

- Identifying the sounds of letter combinations **(tch, ir, ur, er, wa, oi, ce, ci, tion, ea, ge, gi, kn)** and reading words with those combinations

- Reading lists of regularly spelled words, such as **risks,** and irregularly spelled words, such as **league**

- Reading words that contain difficult consonant blends **(flip, drop, splash)**

- Reading words with endings **(dropping, rested)**

- Reading silent-**E** words **(fine, taped)**

- Reading compound words **(greenhouse)**

- Practicing pattern drills that demonstrate consistent phonic relationships **(sigh, sight, night, fight, flight)**

The **stories** in **Decoding B2** increase in length, difficulty, and interest. All stories are composed of words that have been taught in **Decoding B2** or words the students can already read. The syntax and structure of the stories are designed to correct the mistakes the problem reader typically makes. Story length increases from about 600 words in Lesson 1 to nearly 900 words by Lesson 65.

Comprehension questions are presented before students read the story, after students read each part of the story, and after students have completed the selection. Most story questions are about details of each story part students read. Questions that occur before students read a selection have to do with summarizing events of the preceding story and predicting what may occur in the current selection. Questions that occur during and after the story reading address story characters, setting, problems and solutions, sequence of events, cause and effect, and comparisons or contrasts. Students also write answers to a variety of comprehension items in the Workbook that require recall of story events, sequencing, and characters.

The daily **Individual Reading Checkouts** help students develop both accuracy and reading rates (from 90 words per minute at the beginning of Level B2 to 130 words per minute at the end of Level B2).

The **Workbook Exercises** are carefully integrated with the word-attack activities and with the stories the students read.

> It is very important for the students to do the Workbook Exercises as part of each lesson.

Outcome Behavior

Upon completion of **Decoding B2,** students' progress can be seen in both improved accuracy and improved rate. Following is one part of the story from Lesson 53. Students can read this passage with 98 percent accuracy and at a minimum rate of 120 words per minute.

4 **Digging for Gold**

Tony's hands were sore. His back was sore. So were his legs. 12
He was beginning to realize that Salt had been right when he'd 24
said that the real work was just beginning. For the past three 36
hours, Tony had hauled rocks from the pile. At first the pile had 49
been about six feet high. Now it was only about one foot high. 62

Tony bent down and grabbed another rock. When he picked 72
it up, he saw something below it. "Hey, Rosa," he said. "What's 84
that?" 85

Rosa tossed a rock into the underbrush. Then she wiped the 96
sweat from her eyes. She bent down and looked where Tony 107
was pointing. "It looks like a knife handle," Rosa said. "I'll 118
pull it out." 121

[1]

Lesson 53, part 4, Decoding B2 Student Book

What's New in the 2008 Edition—Decoding B2

1 Additional exercises in Lessons 1 through 5 give students practice in reading words with a silent **E.** The students learn a simple rule that is taught in the **Decoding B1** program: If there's a **final E** at the end of a word, the vowel says its name. They practice reading lists of word pairs (such as **ride** and **rid** or **hop** and **hope**) that require students to figure out the sound of the medial vowel before reading the word.

2 Story comprehension questions are displayed in the Teacher Presentation Book in a way that makes them easier for the teacher to present. The questions are displayed after each part of the story, not at the end of the entire selection.

3 Expanded comprehension items and activities meet state and district standards for comprehension. Students

■ summarize the events of the previous story.

■ answer questions about characters, setting, events, and problems and solutions.

■ identify sentences that express the main idea of a selection.

■ identify causes and effects.

■ compare and contrast characters.

■ identify sequences of events.

4 Teacher-observed Fluency Assessments occur in Lessons 2 through 65. Minimum reading rates are increased from those in the 2002 edition. Students read at a minimum rate of 90 words per minute at the beginning of the program and 130 words per minute at the end.

5 Running word counts are displayed in blue in the right column of the Student Book. These word counts make it easy for students to count the number of words they read during the Fluency Assessment. The target word (for example, the 100th word in Lessons 10 through 19) is underlined in the Student Book.

6 The system for awarding points to students has been modified so that

■ the data translates easily into letter grades for individual students.

■ the data also can be used to convert into rewards the number of points students earn.

7 Mastery Tests are administered after Lessons 10, 20, 30, 40, 50, and 65 and provide documentation of students' performance. The directions for administration, scoring procedures, and test remedies are specified in the Teacher Presentation Book. The test forms are in the back of the Workbook.

8 Preceding every five lessons in the Teacher Presentation Book, a one-page summary of Lesson Objectives lists the skills and objectives for those five lessons.

Decoding C—Skill Applications

Who It's For

Students who complete **Decoding B2** demonstrate considerable improvement in reading accuracy and rate, but in that program they are not confronted with either the vocabulary or the sentence forms that appear in textbooks. The passive voice, the use of parenthetical (nonrestrictive) clauses, the longer multiclause sentences, and similar constructions are deliberately avoided in **Decoding B1** and **B2. Decoding C** is appropriate for problem readers in grades 4 through 12 who have mastered many basic reading skills but who have trouble with multisyllabic words and typical textbook material.

What Is Taught

Decoding C teaches word analysis skills (letter combinations, affixes, parts of multisyllabic words), vocabulary development, accurate reading of story selections and informational passages, understanding literal and inferential comprehension questions, rate building, and Workbook applications.

The following activities are included in **Word-Attack Skills:**

- A review of words containing letter combinations such as **th, oa, ea, ai, ou, ar, ir, er, ur, igh, oi, tion, ce, ci, ge, gi**

- Introduction of the sounds for the letter combinations **ure, aw, au, tial, cial**

- Introduction of the meaning of about 600 vocabulary words

- Introduction of the affixes **ex, ly, un, re, dis, pre, tri, sub, less, ness, able**

- Practice in reading words containing various letter combinations and affixes

- Practice in identifying the parts of multipart words **(re/spond/ed, ex/clama/tion, en/large/ment)** and reading those words in sentences

- Practice in writing complex words as root words plus affixes

The following activities provide practice in **Selection Reading skills:**

- Reading selections that give specific factual information on a particular topic

- Reading selections that are fictional

- Reading selections that contain a high percentage of new words

- Reading informational passages that are similar to selections in magazines, newspapers, and textbooks

The following activities provide practice in reading **comprehension skills:**

- Orally answering literal and inferential questions about the selections that are read

- Writing answers to a variety of comprehension items, including both literal and inferential items that require recall of story events, sequencing, and characters

Decoding C Program Goals

One goal of **Decoding C** is to **maintain and consolidate the skills** that were taught in **Decoding B1** and **B2. Decoding C** is designed to provide continued practice on skills taught earlier so that the correct application of the skills becomes habitual.

Another goal is to **fill the gap between tightly controlled syntax and vocabulary presentations and presentations typically encountered in traditional reading materials.** The presentation of new reading vocabulary is simplified in **Decoding C.** Little prompting is provided; most new words are introduced by a simple test statement: **What word?** In **Decoding B1** and **B2,** new words are taught in the Word-Attack Skills exercises for several lessons before they appear in stories. In **Decoding C,** new words may appear only once in word-attack exercises before being included in the stories. The purpose of this accelerated strategy is to develop students' ability to learn new words quickly.

To bridge the gap between students' performance level at the end of **Decoding B2** and the level required to read textbooks and other informational material, **Decoding C** introduces several sentence types and conventions that characterize text material. Qualifiers such as *nevertheless, indeed,* and *frequently* receive considerable use in **Decoding C.** The use of passive voice, nonrestrictive clauses, sentences that define words, and other mechanical features of nonfictional discourse are also introduced.

Another goal is to **present the meaning of words frequently encountered in text materials.** Vocabulary exercises are presented so students will be introduced to new words before reading them. Many of the 600 words included in the vocabulary exercises are words students have already encountered; however, students frequently have only a vague or incorrect notion of their meaning.

Another goal is to **provide reinforcement of a broad variety of comprehension-question types.** The types include literal comprehension, vocabulary, new information facts, and inferential reading.

Another goal of **Decoding C** is to **help students apply the decoding skills taught in the program to reading material encountered outside the program.** Because the procedures used in *Corrective Reading* instruction are unique, students sometimes fail to realize that the skills are applicable to material outside the program. After all, for years these students have not been able to handle material in various subject areas successfully. Unless they receive pointed demonstrations that undermine the I-can't-do-this attitude, students may continue to read successfully in the *Corrective Reading* group and still not apply these skills to other reading situations. To achieve this goal, **Decoding C** presents a series of twenty-nine information passages on topics that are related to what students might encounter in newspapers, magazine articles, or history textbooks.

The final goal of this program is to **decrease students' dependence on highly structured presentations** and to expose students to a wider range of content than lower levels of *Corrective Reading* Decoding programs provide.

Outcome Behavior

Students who complete **Decoding C** are fluent readers who make only occasional decoding errors when they read materials that contain a fairly broad vocabulary and a variety of sentence forms. They can read the following passage with 98 percent accuracy or better and at a minimum rate of 150 words per minute.

---

5   **Galen's Theories**

    Around 1500, some doctors began to question the medical theories   10
that had been accepted for hundreds of years. These doctors exhibited   21
a great deal of courage because most people were suspicious of   32
anybody who challenged established theories.   37

    But a few doctors had the courage to record what they observed,   49
even though their observations were in conflict with long-standing   58
theories and with the accepted medical practice of the time. The basic   70
theory of medicine around 1500 had been accepted for over a   81
thousand years. It had been developed by a man named Galen, a   93
Greek who tried to explain how the body worked and how to cure its   107
ailments. ❶   108

    During Galen's time, doctors were not permitted to dissect (cut up)   119
dead bodies. Galen realized, however, that doctors could not work   129
with the human body unless they understood the anatomy of the   140
body. (The study of anatomy deals with the structure of the body—   152
the bones, muscles, nerves, and organs.) Galen wrote an elaborate   162
work on anatomy. He drew conclusions about human anatomy by   172
studying the anatomy of different animals. Since he couldn't work on   183
human bodies, he dissected animals, such as pigs and apes. ❷   193

    Galen proclaimed that human hipbones looked like those of an   203
ox—a conclusion based upon his dissection of oxen. Galen thought   214
that different human organs were identical to those found in the hog,   226
the dog, the ox, or the ape. He made these mistakes because his   239
conclusions about human anatomy were based upon animal anatomy   248
instead of human anatomy.   252

Lesson 119, part 5, Decoding C Student Book

Students who complete **Decoding C** are capable of reading with enough accuracy so that their comprehension will no longer be distorted by misreading the words. They are able to decode at a rate sufficient to facilitate comprehension of what they read.

The students can demonstrate accuracy and rate capabilities across a range of syntax, vocabulary, format, and content. They have the ability to learn new information rapidly and well enough to apply it after one reading of an informational selection.

Although students may have comprehension deficits that affect their overall reading performance, their decoding problems may be considered remedied when they successfully complete **Decoding C.**

What's New in the 2008 Edition—Decoding C

1 Additional exercises in Lessons 6 through 25 give students practice reading multipart words. The "parts" of these words are not necessarily syllables but simply the first part, middle part, and last part. Students first read multipart words in isolation and then in sentences that are more challenging than sentences in the program's daily reading selections for those lessons.

2 All lessons in the program follow a regular sequence of four parts: Word-Attack Skills, Selection Reading, Fluency Assessment (Individual Reading Checkouts), and Workbook Exercises. In the previous edition, Workbook Exercises were assigned as homework for Lessons 55 through 124, but this homework procedure was difficult for some teachers to implement because of time constraints and the need to keep Workbooks in their classrooms. In the 2008 edition, students complete all four parts of a lesson during the regular lesson time.

3 Starting with Lesson 56 of the previous edition of **Decoding C,** students read outside material in most lessons. They were to select material from newspapers, magazines, and other textbooks. Most teachers did not have time to read and prepare materials for this part of the lessons. The 2008 edition of **Decoding C** replaces these activities with fourteen "bonus" selections that students read after they complete the regular parts of the lesson. The bonus selections have a carefully controlled vocabulary and are written so that the sentence structures are more complicated than those that occur in the regular reading selections. The selections present information that is interesting (why dinosaurs vanished from Earth, the story of the Hubble Space Telescope, facts about the most dangerous occupations), and they provide practice in reading passages that have difficult words. These "bonus" information passages are in addition to the short information passages students read for the regular reading selection in every fifth lesson starting at Lesson 55.

4 Expanded comprehension items and activities meet state and district standards for comprehension. Students

- summarize the events of the previous story.

- answer questions about characters, setting, events, and problems and solutions.

- identify sentences that express the main idea of a selection.

- identify causes and effects.

- compare and contrast characters.

- identify sequences of events.

5 Teacher-observed Fluency Assessments (2-minute timed reading checkouts) occur in Lessons 2 through 125. Minimum reading rates are increased from those in the 2002 edition. Students read at a minimum rate of 100 words per minute at the beginning of the program and 150 words per minute at the end.

6 Running word counts are displayed in blue in the right column of the Student Book. These word counts make it easy for students to count the number of words they read during the Fluency Assessments. The target word (for example, the 240th word in Lessons 21 through 50) is underlined in the Student Book.

7 The system for awarding points to students has been modified so that

- the data translates easily into letter grades for individual students.

- the data also can be used to convert into rewards the number of points students earn.

8 Mastery Tests are administered after Lessons 30, 60, 95, and 125 and provide documentation of students' performance. The directions for administration, scoring procedures, and test remedies are specified in the Teacher Presentation Book. The test forms are in the back of the Workbook.

9 Preceding every five lessons in the Teacher Presentation Books, a one-page summary of Lesson Objectives lists the skills and objectives for those five lessons.

The Comprehension Programs

The illustration below shows the six Comprehension programs in SRA's *Corrective Reading* series.

Comprehension A

5 preprogram lessons

60 program lessons

7 Fact Games

5 Mastery Tests

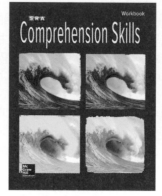

Comprehension A

Fast Cycle

30 lessons

3 Fact Games

3 Mastery Tests

Comprehension B1

60 lessons

6 Fact Games

6 Mastery Tests

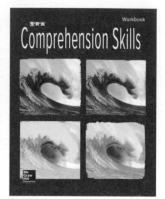

Comprehension B1

Fast Cycle

35 lessons

3 Fact Games

4 Mastery Tests

Comprehension B2

65 lessons

6 Fact Games

7 Mastery Tests

Comprehension C

140 lessons

9 Fact Games

14 Mastery Tests

What's New in the 2008 Edition

Here are the features that are new in the Comprehension strand of the 2008 edition of SRA's *Corrective Reading.*

1 Fast Cycle programs for Comprehension A and B1. Many older students who place in Comprehension A or B1 master the content much faster than younger children. For this reason, the Comprehension strand now includes two fast-cycle programs, Fast Cycle A and Fast Cycle B1. These programs cover the same content the regular programs cover, but they do it at an accelerated rate. Fast Cycle A is 30 lessons long (compared to 65 for regular A). Fast Cycle B1 is 35 lessons long (compared to 60 lessons in regular B1). Appendix A of the Teacher's Guides for all the Comprehension programs specifies criteria for placing students in the fast-cycle programs. This information can also be found on pages 252 and 253 of this guide.

2 New placement process. The original Comprehension Placement Test battery required individual testing of each student. For middle schools and upper elementary classes in which all students are tested, the process was time consuming and presented problems, such as how to occupy students who weren't being tested while the teacher tested one student.

The solution is a testing process that starts with a screening test administered to the entire group. Depending on students' performance, they receive either a shortened version of the original individually administered test or a second group test. All students take two tests, but for some students both tests are group administered and fairly easy to score. For more details, see Appendix A in any of the Comprehension Teacher's Guides or page 58 of this guide.

3 A stronger emphasis on writing in Comprehension B1 and B2. Every lesson has a writing assignment. The assignments are more structured than in earlier editions. Accompanying each assignment are sample words students may use when writing their stories.

There are two main types of writing activities. For the first, students write a story about a picture. They indicate what happened before the picture, what happened in the picture, and what happened after the picture. For the second type of writing activity, students work in teams to revise their stories. Team members make suggestions for improving each story. Then students rewrite their stories based on the team's suggestions.

4 Reformatted Teacher Presentation Books. The main changes address the readability of the exercises. The new presentation books have cleaner line breaks and bullets that help teachers keep track of where they are in the script.

5 Regularly scheduled Mastery Tests. These appear as part of every tenth lesson in all Comprehension levels. The directions for administration, scoring procedures, and test remedies are specified in each Teacher Presentation Book. The test forms are in the back of each Workbook.

Because of the increased number of Mastery Test items, the tests now provide a more detailed account of what students learn and the specific problems individual students experience.

6 **Redesigned Comprehension B2 Workbook.** New headings identify the skill taught in each exercise. Instructions are boxed and clearly separated from the Workbook items.

7 Preceding every five lessons in the Teacher Presentation Books, a one-page summary of Lesson Objectives lists the skills and objectives for those five lessons.

The Comprehension Programs and the Problem Reader

The Comprehension programs are designed to change the behavior of the problem reader. The specific tendencies of this student suggest what a program must do to be effective in changing the student's behavior.

- Because students who are low in comprehension skills do not often accurately decode, they typically do not follow instructions precisely. They have often been reinforced for raising their hand and asking the teacher questions. This strategy has served them in content areas, such as science and social studies, as well as "reading." As a result, they have not developed precision in following instructions presented orally or in writing.

- Because of the way material they have studied has been sequenced, problem readers also have a poor memory for information. Typically, they have never been required to learn information one day and then use it that day and from then on. The usual pattern has been for them to work with vocabulary or facts for only a lesson or two, after which the material disappears. The result is a poorly developed strategy for remembering information, particularly systems of information that contain related facts and rules.

- Problem readers also have poor statement-repetition skills (primarily because they have never practiced these skills). For instance, if told to repeat the statement, "Some of the people who live in America are illiterate," the students may say, "Some people who live in America are ill," or some other inaccurate restatement. The lack of statement-repetition skills places these students at a great disadvantage when they try to read and retain information, even if they decode it correctly.

- Problem readers lack the analytical skills required to process arguments. Often they vacillate from being guarded in believing what others tell them, to being gullible. They often have strong feelings and prejudices, but they are unable to articulate the evidence that supports their beliefs or the conclusions that derive from the evidence. They are not practiced with flaws in arguments that present false analogies, improper deductions, or appeals that are inappropriate (such as arguing about a whole group from information about an individual).

■ Problem readers have a deficiency in vocabulary and common information. This deficiency prevents them from constructing the appropriate *schemata* when reading about situations that assume basic information or vocabulary. They may understand the meaning of the word **colonial,** for instance, but not know the relationship of that word to **colony.**

■ Finally, problem readers are not highly motivated students. For these students, reading has been punishing. The students often profess indifference: "I don't care if I learn that or not." But the students' behavior strongly suggests that they care a great deal. When they learn to use new words like **regulate** and **participate,** they feel proud.

The students' ineffective reading strategies and negative attitudes about reading become more ingrained as the readers get older. To overcome them requires a careful program, one that systematically replaces the strategies with new ones and that provides lots and lots of practice.

In summary, the knowledge and skills of problem readers are spotty. While often exhibiting intelligent behaviors in dealing with their peers, they are remarkably naive in dealing with academic content because they don't know exactly what to attend to, precisely what it means, how to organize it, how to relate it to other known facts and remember it, how to apply it to unique situations, and how to evaluate it in terms of consistency with other facts and rules.

The Solutions

SRA's ***Corrective Reading*** Comprehension programs provide these solutions for the problem reader.

■ **The Comprehension programs are designed to provide extensive practice in following directions.** The various activities presented in the programs are designed so that students must attend to the instructions. On one lesson, for instance, the directions for an activity may be "Circle the verbs." On the next lesson, instructions for the same activity may be "Make a box around the verbs." The direct-instruction activities that address following instructions present directions the students cannot figure out from either the format of the activity or the context. Students, therefore, learn the strategy of reading carefully and attending to the **details** of the instructions. Also, students practice writing instructions so they develop an appreciation of what information is needed to clearly convey the operation.

■ **The Comprehension programs provide practice in statement repetition.** This practice is presented in Level A and Level A Fast Cycle through tasks that don't involve reading. In later levels, the statement-repetition activities are related increasingly to statements the students read. The emphasis on statement repetition both makes students more facile in repeating statements (requiring only one or two attempts, compared to the many attempts that would be required early in the program) and helps reinforce the general strategy that one must be precise when dealing with statements in what is read as well as in what is heard.

■ **The Comprehension programs are designed so that whatever is taught is used.** In the programs, nothing goes away. The vocabulary that is introduced is integrated so the students use the vocabulary in following instructions, making analogies and deductions, identifying flaws in arguments, and in various other activities. Similarly, facts that are learned are integrated and applied to a wide range of applications. This nonspiral approach to instruction demonstrates to students that they must develop strategies for retaining the information that is taught and relating it to other information. The format ensures that students will learn how to learn, organize, and process what is taught. Fact Games and Mastery Tests within the programs document to both teacher and students that the skills and information presented in the program are mastered.

■ **The Comprehension programs present various analytical skills that can be applied to "higher-order" thinking tasks.** The *Corrective Reading* Comprehension strand teaches students how analogies work, how logical reasoning is applied to arguments, how conclusions depend on evidence, and how to evaluate the adequacy of the evidence. Deductions are emphasized because basic arguments that affect everyday life are usually presented as deductions. The Comprehension strand presents specific common fallacies (arguing from part to whole, arguing from whole to part, arguing from a false cause, arguing from limited choices). Students also learn to identify contradictions, at first simple ones, and later ones that are inferred from facts the students have learned. The focus of the programs, in other words, is not simply on narrowly defined logical-reasoning skills but on logical-reasoning skills as they apply to all aspects of reading.

■ **To compensate for the deficiencies in vocabulary and common information, the Comprehension programs introduce both "fact systems" and vocabulary words.** The fact systems that have been selected include body systems (skeletal, muscular, circulatory, etc.), calendar information, animal information (classifications such as fish, amphibian, reptile, mammal, bird), economic rules (supply-demand), and plants. These systems provide a vehicle for teaching vocabulary. Additional vocabulary is introduced in all levels. In Levels B1 and B2, for example, vocabulary is introduced in connection with parts of speech. Some of these words were selected because they have a verb, noun, and adjective form (for example, **protect, protection,** and **protective**). In Level C, students are taught how to infer the meaning of words from context. Note that all words, once introduced, appear in various activities—from following instructions to identifying contradictions.

■ **Finally, the Comprehension programs address the issue of the problem reader's low self-image.** The programs are designed so the students can succeed in learning sophisticated skills (such as identifying the missing premise in an argument). Furthermore, a point system that is based on realistic performance goals ensures that the student who tries will succeed and will receive reinforcement for improved performance.

In summary, the programs use a two-pronged approach. Each level teaches specific skills to replace the student's ineffective approach to comprehension. Each level also contains an effective management system that turns students on to reading. The approach **works.**

Progress Through the Comprehension Programs

The programs are designed with a careful progression of skill development from level to level. There are **five** entry points.

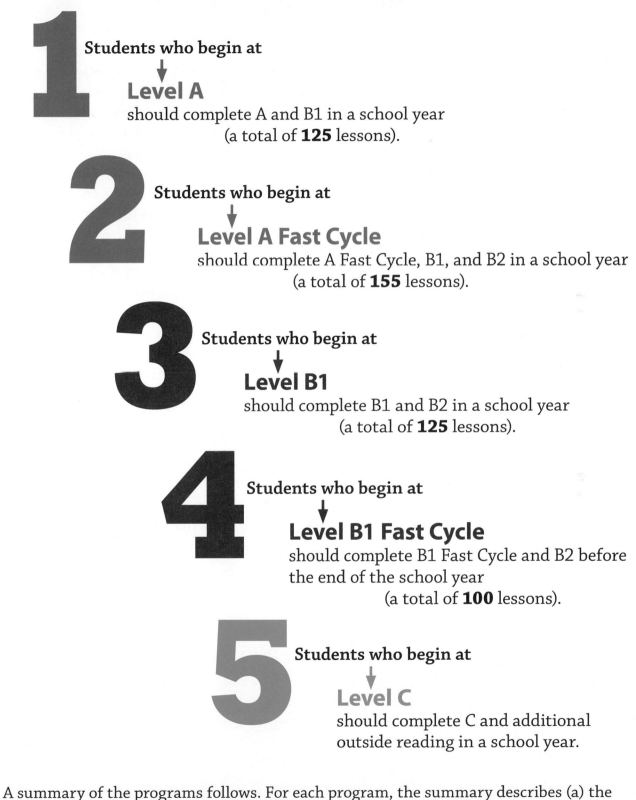

1 Students who begin at

Level A

should complete A and B1 in a school year
(a total of **125** lessons).

2 Students who begin at

Level A Fast Cycle

should complete A Fast Cycle, B1, and B2 in a school year
(a total of **155** lessons).

3 Students who begin at

Level B1

should complete B1 and B2 in a school year
(a total of **125** lessons).

4 Students who begin at

Level B1 Fast Cycle

should complete B1 Fast Cycle and B2 before
the end of the school year
(a total of **100** lessons).

5 Students who begin at

Level C

should complete C and additional
outside reading in a school year.

A summary of the programs follows. For each program, the summary describes (a) the reading behavior of students typically placed in that program, (b) what is taught, and (c) what students should be able to do at the end of the program.

Comprehension A, Comprehension A Fast Cycle— Thinking Basics

Who They're For

Comprehension A and **Comprehension A Fast Cycle** are designed for problem readers in grades 3 through 12 who speak and understand basic English and whose scores on the *Corrective Reading* Comprehension Placement Test indicate that they belong in one of the programs. The programs are not appropriate for students who speak no English or for students whose grasp of English is weak.

Tryouts of **Comprehension A** with average students in grades 1 through 3 demonstrated that the program provides solid reinforcement in comprehension skills for whatever reading system is being taught.

Students who place in **Comprehension A** or **Comprehension A Fast Cycle** do not understand the concepts underlying much of the material being taught in classrooms. They do not have well-developed recitation skills. They cannot repeat sentences they hear, so they have trouble retaining and answering questions about information that is presented. These students are often prevented from comprehending what they read because they don't even understand the material when it is presented orally.

What Is Taught

The skills taught in **Comprehension A** and **Fast Cycle A** fall into three broad categories: Thinking Operations, Workbook Exercises, and Information.

Thinking Operations concentrate on those general operations useful to students in solving a wide range of problems. These operations apply to virtually any content area. Here are the specific skill areas (tracks) taught in Thinking Operations:

- Analogies

- And/Or

- Basic Evidence

- Classification

- Deductions

- Definitions

- Description

- Inductions

- Opposites

- Same

- Some, All, None

- Statement Inference

- True–False

Workbook Exercises provide students with practice in applying the skills taught in Thinking Operations and the facts taught in Information. Workbook practice serves as a bridge between teacher-directed activities and those in which the student uses the skills independently. Here are the skills practiced in the Workbooks:

- Analogies

- Classification

- Deductions

- Description

- Inductions

- Same

- Some, All, None

- True–False

Information Exercises are designed (1) to teach information that should be useful to students, and (2) to give students practice in organizing groups of related facts. Probably more important than the actual information taught is the practice students get in learning groups of related facts. Facility in learning new names comes with practice, and any body of related information will help to meet the need for practice. Of course, it is best if the information is also useful. Here are the tracks taught in Information:

- Calendar (months, seasons, holidays)

- Poems

- Animals (mammals, reptiles, etc.; felines, canines; herbivorous, carnivorous)

Outcome Behavior

At the end of **Comprehension A,** students are able to handle items such as the following:

━━━━━━ EXERCISE 7 ━━━━━━

ANALOGIES: Synonyms

1. Here's an analogy about words: **Ask** is to **inquire** as **weep** is to...(Pause 2 seconds.) Get ready. (Signal.) *Cry.*
- Everybody, say that analogy. (Signal.) *Ask is to inquire as weep is to cry.* (Repeat until firm.)

Lesson 59, Exercise 7, Comprehension A TPB-2

---

4. Listen. The buffalo ambled to the pond. Say that. (Signal.) *The buffalo ambled to the pond.* (Repeat until firm.)
- Now you're going to say that sentence with different words for **ambled.** (Pause.) Get ready. (Signal.) *The buffalo walked slowly to the pond.* (Repeat until firm.)
- (Repeat step 4 until firm.)

Lesson 59, Exercise 10, Comprehension A TPB-2

B				
1. lizard, bat, trunk	(objects)	actions	tell what kind
2. bathe, tell, modify	objects	(actions)	tell what kind
3. healthy, sick, dry	objects	actions	(tell what kind)
4. exhibit, bush, tiger	(objects)	actions	tell what kind
5. deduce, decrease, dig	objects	(actions)	tell what kind

Lesson 59, part B, Comprehension A Workbook

BASIC EVIDENCE: Using Facts

The next Thinking Operation is **Basic Evidence.**

1. You're going to use two facts to explain things that happened. (Hold up one finger.) First fact. Louis owned an expensive diamond. Say it. (Signal.) *Louis owned an expensive diamond.* (Repeat until firm.)

- (Hold up two fingers.) Second fact. The diamond was very well hidden. Say it. (Signal.) *The diamond was very well hidden.* (Repeat until firm.)

2. Everybody, say those facts again. (Hold up one finger.) First fact. *Louis owned an expensive diamond.*

- (Hold up two fingers.) Second fact. *The diamond was very well hidden.*

- (Repeat until the students say the facts in order.)

> **Individual test**
> (Call on individual students to say the facts.)

3. Here's what happened: He didn't bother to get a burglar alarm. You're going to tell me the fact that explains **why** that happened. (Pause.) Get ready. (Signal.) *The diamond was very well hidden.*

4. Listen. First fact. Louis owned an expensive diamond. Second fact. The diamond was very well hidden.

5. Here's what happened: He bought insurance. You're going to tell me the fact that explains **why** that happened. (Pause.) Get ready. (Signal.) *Louis owned an expensive diamond.*

6. Here's what happened: Some robbers broke into his apartment. You're going to tell me the fact that explains **why** that happened. (Pause.) Get ready. (Signal.) *Louis owned an expensive diamond.*

7. Here's what happened: The robbers were still looking for the diamond when the police showed up. You're going to tell me the fact that explains **why** that happened. (Pause.) Get ready. (Signal.) *The diamond was very well hidden.*

8. (Repeat steps 5–7 until firm.)

The students are able to recite poems, give functional definitions for approximately 50 words—including **indolent, herbivorous,** and **majority**—and perform a variety of tasks in following instructions. Although students will still have an enormous number of comprehension skills to learn, they now have a foundation on which to build.

Comprehension B1, Comprehension B1 Fast Cycle, Comprehension B2—Comprehension Skills

Who They're For

Comprehension B1, B1 Fast Cycle, and **Comprehension B2** are designed for problem readers in grades 4 through 12 who understand English. **Comprehension B1** and **B1 Fast Cycle** are appropriate for students whose scores on the *Corrective Reading* Comprehension Placement Test indicate that they belong in the program. **Comprehension B2** is appropriate for students who have completed **Comprehension B1** or **B1 Fast Cycle. Comprehension B2** is not an entry point for the Comprehension series. The programs are not appropriate for students who speak no English or for students whose grasp of English is weak.

Students who place in **Comprehension B1** or **B1 Fast Cycle** exhibit many of the deficiencies observed in students who place in **Comprehension A.** They lack some common basic information, such as how many months are in a year. They are deficient in thinking operations, but usually they are more advanced in thinking operations than Level A students. They tend to have trouble with difficult statement-repetition tasks, deductions that involve *maybe,* relating conclusions to evidence, identifying contradictions, following written directions, and writing. Their deficiencies in vocabulary and information make it difficult for them to perform many reading comprehension activities.

What Is Taught

Reading comprehension is a complex process that requires a number of separate skills. For example, when students are asked to write answers to questions about a written passage, they may have to use the following skills:

■ Formulate a deduction (reasoning skill)

■ Understand basic classes (information skill)

■ Identify the precise meaning of a word (vocabulary skill)

■ Understand the structure of complicated sentences (sentence skill)

■ Answer a question or follow a direction (basic comprehension skill)

■ Write their answers correctly (writing skill)

Students who have mastered these skills are more likely to understand what they read. Therefore, **Comprehension B1** and **B2** teach all these skills, many of which are developed from skills taught earlier. The teaching is done so that what is introduced is used, applied, reinforced, and repeated with sufficient frequency to assure mastery.

The skills that are taught can be grouped into several skill areas.

- Reasoning skills

- Information skills

- Vocabulary skills

- Sentence skills

- Basic comprehension skills

- Writing skills

Reasoning Skills. Textbook material that students are expected to read usually proceeds on an implicitly logical basis. Students who don't grasp the logic underlying a passage probably won't be able to answer questions about the passage that involve any sort of analogy, deduction, or rule application. They will experience difficulty when they try to defend an interpretation of the passage or identify contradictory elements in the passage.

The following tracks teach reasoning skills: Deductions, Basic Evidence, Analogies, Contradictions, and Similes.

- The **Deductions** track introduces basic reasoning strategies. The students learn how to draw conclusions and how to apply rules to diverse situations.

- The **Basic Evidence** track teaches the students to distinguish between what does and what does not follow from a given fact or rule.

- The **Analogies** track introduces another basic reasoning strategy. The students learn how to formulate analogies and how to understand what analogies imply.

- The **Contradictions** track teaches the students to recognize contradictions and shows them how to analyze flaws in passages.

- The **Similes** track teaches the students to understand figurative language and the relationships implied by such language. Students learn to analyze and to create similes.

Information Skills. Students who do not have an adequate store of common information are at a disadvantage when they read selections that assume possession of such common information. Typically, such students will not know basic classifications, the names of such things as body systems and body organs, or basic rules about how things work. Moreover, they frequently lack a systematic method of retaining new information because they are unpracticed in organizing groups of related facts.

The following tracks teach information skills: Classification, Body Systems, Body Rules, and Economics Rules.

- The **Classification** track teaches the students various conventional categories and rules for determining how to put objects into categories.

- The **Body Systems** track teaches the names and parts of the major body systems. The track also provides the students with a successful experience in mastering a group of related facts.

- The **Body Rules** track teaches rules that explain how the various body systems work. The students use the skills taught in the Deductions track to apply those rules.

- The **Economics Rules** track introduces rules that help the students become more knowledgeable consumers. The track also extends the students' experience in applying rules to diverse situations.

Vocabulary Skills. Students with a limited vocabulary encounter many unfamiliar words when they read material designed for their grade level. They may not know how to look up words in a dictionary or how to interpret a definition if they find it. They also may not understand such things as how different affixes affect the meaning of a word.

All vocabulary skills are taught in the Definitions track. This track teaches many new words and general procedures that help the students understand new words. All words taught in the Definitions track are carefully integrated into other tracks in the program.

Sentence Skills. Students with a faulty understanding of basic sentence structure will have difficulty comprehending complicated sentences. Those students may be unfamiliar with the classification of sentence parts. Because of their lack of understanding of sentence structure, it is often difficult to discuss written materials with them.

The following tracks teach sentence skills: Parts of Speech, Subject/Predicate, Sentence Combinations, and Sentence Analysis.

- The **Parts of Speech** track teaches the students to identify nouns, verbs, and adjectives in sentences. The students learn to look at sentences in terms of their structure.

- The **Subject/Predicate** track teaches the students to identify subjects and predicates. They also learn that parts of certain predicates can be placed in front of the subject.

- The **Sentence Combinations** track teaches the students how to combine sentences by using such words as **however** and **especially.** The students also learn how those words relate one sentence part to another.

- The **Sentence Analysis** track gives the students practice in breaking down complex sentences into their simple-sentence components. After the students have mastered sentence-combination techniques, they are given complex sentences to rewrite in simple-sentence form.

Basic Comprehension Skills. Students who have difficulty answering questions or following directions seldom are able to show that they comprehend what they read, even though their comprehension might be adequate.

The following tracks teach two basic comprehension skills: Inference and Following Directions.

- The **Inference** track teaches the students to answer questions based on simple sentences at first and, later, on extended passages. Often, the students are required to explain how they arrived at the answer to a particular question. The sentences and passages the students read incorporate the vocabulary, rules, and information presented in other tracks. Many passages elaborate upon the Body Systems and Economics Rules tracks.

- The **Following Directions** track teaches the students to draw a picture by following a set of directions. The directions emphasize the function of prepositions and also make extensive use of vocabulary, rules, and information.

Writing Skills. Students who do not have adequate writing skills are likely to be misunderstood. They tend to make errors in punctuation and grammar and also tend to repeat themselves. They are particularly weak in the use of descriptive prose.

The following tracks teach writing skills: Writing Directions, Writing Paragraphs, Editing, and Writing Stories.

- The **Writing Directions** track is the reverse of the Following Directions track. In Following Directions, students follow written directions to draw a picture. In Writing Directions, students are given a picture and then write a set of directions for creating that picture.

- The **Writing Paragraphs** track requires students to rewrite carefully controlled paragraphs by combining sentences and correcting mistakes. The track helps students become more facile with the paragraph form and more practiced in the writing of extended passages.

- The **Editing** track teaches students to correct many different kinds of writing mistakes, such as redundancy, faulty subject-verb agreement, and incorrect punctuation.

- The **Writing Stories** track allows the students to apply their newly acquired writing skills in a creative manner. In every lesson, students write or revise a story about a picture that appears in the Workbook. The stories provide the teacher with tangible evidence of the students' writing ability.

After a new skill is taught in a particular track, that skill is applied in many other tracks. For example, the word **artery** is introduced in the Body Systems track. It is then used in Analogies, Deductions, Writing, Following Directions, Sentence Combinations, and Body Rules.

The overall sequencing in **Comprehension B1** and **B2** places increasing demands on writing performance as students progress through the program.

Outcome Behavior

After completing **Comprehension B2,** students have learned many of the skills associated with reading carefully, operating on information that they read, and following specific instructions. Although students may lack specific information—particularly information about vocabulary—they have the important skills necessary to perform reading-comprehension exercises. For example, they may not know the definition of all words, but they can decode a statement with a definition, determining which word is being defined and which words define it. They also understand the definitions of some words and are able to place those words in sentences. The exercise to the right shows some of the definitions that students in **Comprehension B1** and **B2** have learned.

D DEFINITIONS

Fill in each blank with the word that has the same meaning as the word or words under the blank.

1. We stayed until the __conclusion__ of the concert.
   (end)

2. Dentists __examine__ many teeth every day.
   (look at)

3. Some things are very easy to __criticize__.
   (find fault with)

4. People cannot __produce__ storms.
   (make)

5. To save gas, this car must be __modified__.
   (changed)

Lesson 28, part D, Comprehension B2 Workbook

E BODY RULES

Draw in the arrows. Write **vein** or **artery** in each blank. Also write **oxygen** or **carbon dioxide** in each blank.

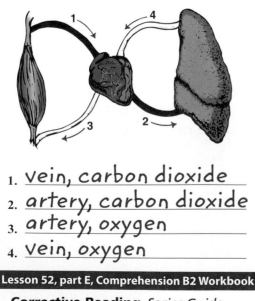

1. vein, carbon dioxide
2. artery, carbon dioxide
3. artery, oxygen
4. vein, oxygen

Lesson 52, part E, Comprehension B2 Workbook

Students who finish **Comprehension B2** don't know the details of every system (such as solar systems, plant classification systems, etc.), but they do understand what systems are and how they work. They know that a system is made up of parts that have names and that a system is governed by rules. They can handle systems-related information and can complete exercises like the one to the left. The exercise is from **Comprehension B2,** Lesson 52.

The students do not know all parts of speech when they complete the program; however, they understand that when words function in the same way, they are the same part of speech. For example, a word representing the action in a sentence will always be the verb. Students also understand that the construction of a word often indicates its part of speech. For example, the endings of words like **selective, consumable,** and **explanatory** indicate that the words are adjectives. The students show their ability to work with parts of speech in exercises like the one shown to the right, which is from **Comprehension B2,** Lesson 63.

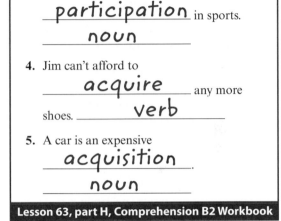

H **DEFINITIONS**

Write a word that comes from **acquire** or **participate** in each blank. Then write **verb, noun,** or **adjective** after each item.

1. Soccer is a ___*participatory*___ sport. ___*adjective*___

2. Mary was selected to ___*participate*___ in the school play. ___*verb*___

3. Some people choose to limit their ___*participation*___ in sports. ___*noun*___

4. Jim can't afford to ___*acquire*___ any more shoes. ___*verb*___

5. A car is an expensive ___*acquisition*___. ___*noun*___

Lesson 63, part H, Comprehension B2 Workbook

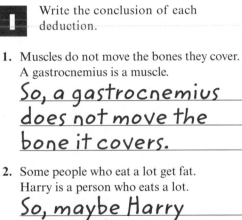

I Write the conclusion of each deduction.

1. Muscles do not move the bones they cover. A gastrocnemius is a muscle.
   So, a gastrocnemius does not move the bone it covers.

2. Some people who eat a lot get fat. Harry is a person who eats a lot.
   So, maybe Harry will get fat.

3. Every fish can swim. A snake is not a fish.
   So, nothing

Lesson 46, part I, Comprehension B1 Workbook

Upon completing the program, students do not understand every type of fallacy contained within faulty arguments; but they do understand the basic procedures for drawing conclusions from facts, which is the first step in recognizing faulty arguments. In exercises like the one to the left, students develop the ability to draw conclusions from facts. The exercise is from **Comprehension B1,** Lesson 46.

Another step in understanding faulty arguments is to determine which evidence in the argument is relevant to the argument and which evidence is irrelevant. At the end of **Comprehension B2,** students have developed this skill and can do tasks like the one to the right. The task is from **Comprehension B2,** Lesson 4.

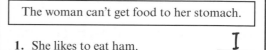

E **EVIDENCE**

Write **R** for each fact that is **relevant** to what happened. Write **I** for each fact that is **irrelevant** to what happened.

The woman can't get food to her stomach.

1. She likes to eat ham. I
2. Her esophagus is blocked. R
3. She can't open her mouth. R
4. She liked her doctor. I

Lesson 4, part E, Comprehension B2 Workbook

H **CONTRADICTIONS**

Underline the contradiction and circle the statement it contradicts. Then tell **why** the underlined statement contradicts the circled statement.

From the outside, your upper arm looks pretty simple. But inside, many complex things are happening. (Arteries are carrying blood to your biceps.) Sensory nerves are sending feelings to the brain.* The nerves carry little bits of electricity. The arteries carry carbon dioxide. All this is going on, but you never have to think about it.

Idea: because arteries carry oxygen to the biceps

Lesson 31, part H, Comprehension B2 Workbook

The first step in critiquing an argument is to determine whether it is internally consistent. In order to determine internal consistency, one must be able to identify possible inconsistencies. **Comprehension B1** and **B2** teach students how to do this. By the end of **Comprehension B2,** students can handle exercises like the one shown to the left. The exercise is from **Comprehension B2,** Lesson 31.

At the end of **Comprehension B2,** students can follow specific instructions of the sort found in work applications, tax returns, and other similar forms. The exercise to the right, from Lesson 44 of **Comprehension B2,** is an example of what they can do.

Students who have completed **Comprehension B2** do not know all the rules of correct writing; however, they have had practice in reading material while attending to its form. They have edited material to eliminate incorrect grammar, redundancies, and punctuation errors. Performance on passages like the one below demonstrates their basic understanding of writing form. The passage is from **Comprehension B2,** Lesson 65.

H   EDITING

Underline the redundant sentences.
Circle and correct the punctuation errors.
Cross out and correct the wording errors.

  Duke Ellington was the greatest jazz band
leader ~~what~~ *that* ever lived. He formed his first band
in the 1920ⓢ which was when jazz first became
popular. Although many of the players
changed⟳the band stayed together for almost
fifty ~~year~~ *years*. No band leader was better than
Ellington. Everybody wanted to play with
Ellington, so he had no trouble finding the best
players. The Ellington band could really swingⓞ
All kinds of players wanted to belong to it.

Lesson 65, part H, Comprehension B2 Workbook

J   INFERENCE

Use the facts to fill out the form.

Facts: Your name is Brian Ozaki. You have just graduated from State University in Rushville with a B.A. degree in journalism. You are applying for a job with a newspaper. You were editor of your high school and college newspapers. You are 22 years old. You are single and unemployed. Your address is 22 W. Main, Farmington, NM. You want to write for the sports page.

1. Name, last name first (please print)
   Ozaki, Brian

2. Colleges or universities attended
   State University in Rushville

3. Degrees, if any
   B.A.

4. Journalism experience, if any
   Idea: editor of high school and college newspapers

5. Current employer
   Idea: none

6. Are you married? *no*

7. Address
   22 W Main Farmington, NM

8. What section do you prefer to write for?
   sports

Lesson 44, part J, Comprehension B2 Workbook

Comprehension B1 and **B2** teach basic skills that set the stage for more sophisticated skill applications. The students are provided with the basic skills needed to understand what is read and to understand some of the conventions associated with the written word. With these basic abilities, they can readily learn how to identify fallacies in arguments, how to read critically, and how to resolve possible inconsistencies encountered in reading.

Comprehension C—Concept Applications

Who It's For

Comprehension C is designed for students who have completed **Comprehension B2** in the *Corrective Reading* series and for students whose scores on the Comprehension Placement Test qualify them for entry into the program. These students are probably in grades 6 through 12 and may even be found in community colleges. The program may also be used developmentally for students of average or above-average ability, beginning in grade 5.

Students who place in **Comprehension C** have already learned many skills. Specifically, they understand basic logical operations, they can draw conclusions from evidence, their basic vocabularies are reasonably broad, and their recitation and statement-repetition skills are fairly good.

These students, however, have several common skill deficiencies.

- Although they are fairly proficient in logical reasoning, they have not mastered reasoning skills to the point where applying them is nearly automatic.

- They have trouble learning a new concept or discrimination from written instructions, although the same concept or discrimination would not be difficult to learn if it were presented orally by the teacher.

- They are deficient in advanced vocabulary.

- They are weak in the mechanics of writing and editing.

- They lack facility in extracting information from sources—such as from a written passage or a graph.

- They do not have a facility for working independently.

What Is Taught

The objectives for **Comprehension C** are the same as those in **Comprehension B1** and **B2:** namely, to teach and reinforce a substantial amount of information and many reasoning operations. However, the emphasis in **Comprehension C** is on independent application of learned skills. Eventually, the students use the skills to analyze arguments and to respond to propaganda.

The skills that are taught in **Comprehension C** fall into five categories. Three categories teach component skills and are classified as "basic tools." The two remaining categories teach the application of the component skills to higher-order operations and are classified as "higher-order skills." The diagram below shows that the basic tools skills are cycled into the higher-order, or application, categories.

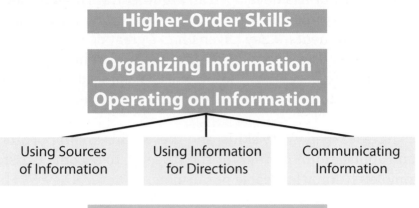

Following is a list of the specific skills taught in each category:

- **Organizing Information** includes main idea, outlining, specific-general, morals, and visual-spatial organization.

- **Operating on Information** includes deductions, basic evidence, argument rules, *ought* statements, and contradictions.

- **Using Sources of Information** includes basic comprehension passages, words or deductions, maps, pictures and graphs, and supporting evidence.

- **Using Information for Directions** includes writing directions, filling out forms, and identifying contradictory directions.

- **Communicating Information** includes definitions, combining sentences, editing, and meaning from context.

Because a primary objective of **Comprehension C** is independence, the procedures for presenting new skills (or for reinforcing skills) are different from those of **Comprehension B1** and **B2.** In **Comprehension C,** new skills are presented in the student material. Instead of the teacher reading a script that explains a concept or application, the students read the script and then apply the concept to specific examples in an exercise. The teacher's role is to monitor this process and ask questions to ensure that the students understand what they read.

Outcome Behavior

Students completing **Comprehension C** have some fairly well-developed skills. They are proficient at analyzing arguments. They have a good understanding of the intent of arguments (which is to convince the reader), and they have the skills necessary to be skeptical about how an author has developed an argument. Although they still may have vocabulary deficiencies, they are able to infer the meaning of a word from its context and to decode definitional statements. They haven't had a great deal of practice in the use of reference material; however, they understand the purpose of the "expert testimony" provided by appropriate references. They know the basic procedures for editing and understand how to correct some of the more common writing errors.

In short, students have learned many skills, and these skills are important facilitators of future learning and application. In order for the students to become experienced, proficient, and completely knowledgeable performers, however, they will have to continue developing these skills. **Comprehension C** provides a solid framework of skills for such development.

PLACEMENT TESTING

The **Corrective Reading** Decoding Placement Test and the Comprehension Placement Test provide detailed information for the accurate placement of students in SRA's **Corrective Reading** Decoding and Comprehension programs.

> Administer the Placement Test to all students before placing them in any of the programs.

If you plan to place students in a single strand, administer the placement test for only that strand (Decoding or Comprehension). If you plan to place students in a double-strand sequence, administer both placement tests. After the Decoding placement is determined, place the students at the same level or a lower level in the Comprehension strand. The best double-strand placement is for the students to begin the Comprehension strand one level lower than their Decoding placement.

Decoding Placement

The Decoding Placement Test is individually administered and measures each student's reading accuracy and oral-reading rate. Placement takes into account the student's ability to decode words in sentences and stories.

The test has four parts. Students with serious decoding problems are first tested with part I, which is a timed reading passage. Students who perform below specified accuracy and rate criteria are given part II of the test, a series of sentences the students read aloud. Students who perform above the specified rate and accuracy criteria on part I are given parts III and IV of the test, both of which are timed reading passages.

If a student's performance level is known to be relatively high, you may begin testing with part III of the test. If you don't have accurate information about a student's performance level, which frequently occurs when students have been in reading programs that do not require oral responding, begin testing with part I.

A reproducible copy of the Decoding Placement Test and details on how to administer it appear in Appendix A at the end of this guide.

Comprehension Placement

The Comprehension placement procedure is designed so that each student takes two tests. The first is a screening test (Test 1) that requires written responses and is administered to a whole class or group. Test 1 provides an evaluation of the following skills and content:

- Deductions (drawing conclusions)

- Classification of common objects

- General information (holidays, seasons)

- Vocabulary and equivalent meanings

Students who make more than 7 errors on the screening test take a second test (Test 2) that places them in **Comprehension A, Comprehension A Fast Cycle,** or **Comprehension B1.** This test is individually administered. Test 2 provides an evaluation of the following skills:

- Recitation behavior (repeating orally presented sentences)

- Deductions (drawing one conclusion)

- Analogies

- Basic information (common facts that students should know)

- Divergent reasoning skills (stating how things are the same and how they are different)

Students who make 7 or fewer errors on the screening test take Test 3, which places them in **Comprehension B1, Comprehension B1 Fast Cycle,** or **Comprehension C.** This test requires written responses and is presented to a whole class or group. Test 3 provides an evaluation of the following skills:

- Statement-inference skills (determining which word in a sentence is being defined and which words define it)

- Rule-application skills

- Vocabulary skills

A reproducible copy of the Comprehension Placement Test and details on how to administer it appear in Appendix B at the end of this guide.

The battery of placement tests is also designed to identify students who perform either too low or too high for the *Corrective Reading* sequence.

MASTERY TESTS

The purpose of the Mastery Tests is to provide you with detailed information about student performance and to indicate remedies for groups of students who have not mastered specific reading skills. In all programs, Mastery Tests are scheduled regularly after a specified number of lessons. In most programs, the Mastery Tests appear every tenth lesson. Directions for administering the tests appear as part of each test lesson in the Teacher Presentation Books. The student materials for the tests are in the back of the student Workbook. Most tests are administered to the entire group; however, parts of some Decoding tests are administered to individual students. Remedies for tests can be found in the Teacher Presentation Books. For all programs, remedies involve reteaching specified exercises or lessons.

On pages 60 through 70 are sample tests and summary forms for the Decoding and Comprehension programs.

MASTERY TEST 1

— AFTER LESSON 10, BEFORE LESSON 11 —

- (Mastery Test 1 is located at the back of each student's Workbook.)

> **Note:** Mastery Test 1 is a group test.

Part 1 Identifying words without endings

1. Turn to Mastery Test 1 on page 66 of your Workbook. ✓
- Find part 1. ✓
2. The list in part 1 shows words in alphabetical order. None of these words has endings like **S** or **E–R**.
- For each item, you will write the number of one of these words.
- For the test items, I'll say a word with an ending. You'll find the same word without an ending.
3. Here's a practice item. Don't write anything. **Stepping.** What word? (Signal.) *Stepping.*
- Say that word without an ending. (Signal.) *Step.* Yes, **step.**
- Find **step** in the list. Raise your hand when you know the number. ✓
- Everybody, what number? (Signal.) *22.* Yes, 22. That's the number for **step.**
4. Here's another practice item: **soiled.** What word? (Signal.) *Soiled.*
- Raise your hand when you know the number that you would write in the blank. ✓
- Everybody, what number? (Signal.) *18.* Yes, the word without an ending is **soil.** That's number 18.
5. Here's the first test item. Item A: **hoped.** What word? (Signal.) *Hoped.*
- He **hoped** it would rain. Write the number for **hoped** without an ending in blank A.
  (Observe, but do not give feedback.)

6. Item B: **fates.** What word? (Signal.) *Fates.*
- Their **fates** were not certain. Write the number for **fates** without an ending in blank B.
  (Observe, but do not give feedback.)
7. (Repeat step 6 for the remaining words:)
- Item C: **strained.** What word? (Signal.) *Strained.*
  The horses pulled and **strained.**
- Item D: **timed.** What word? (Signal.) *Timed.*
  The event was **timed.**
- Item E: **files.** What word? (Signal.) *Files.*
  There was a stack of **files** on his desk.
- Item F: **filled.** What word? (Signal.) *Filled.*
  She **filled** the cup with butter.
- Item G: **slides.** What word? (Signal.) *Slides.*
  There were five **slides** in the park.
- Item H: **steeper.** What word? (Signal.) *Steeper.*
  The hills were **steeper** than he thought.
- Item I: **sailed.** What word? (Signal.) *Sailed.*
  The ball **sailed** over their heads.
- Item J: **stripes.** What word? (Signal.) *Stripes.*
  She painted red **stripes** on her bike.

Part 2 Identifying words

1. Find part 2. ✓
- I'll say a word. You circle the word I say.
2. Item 1: **streak.** What word? (Signal.) *Streak.*
- There was a **streak** of dirt on the car. Circle the word **streak.**
  (Observe, but do not give feedback.)
3. (Repeat step 2 for the remaining words:)
- Item 2: **batter.** What word? (Signal.) *Batter.*
  She was the best **batter** on the team.
- Item 3: **led.** What word? (Signal.) *Led.*
  She **led** the team out onto the field.
- Item 4: **burn.** What word? (Signal.) *Burn.*
  The grass started to **burn.**
- Item 5: **pouch.** What word? (Signal.) *Pouch.*
  He carried his money in a **pouch.**
- Item 6: **bait.** What word? (Signal.) *Bait.*
  They put **bait** on their hooks.

- Item 7: **cheeks.** What word? (Signal.)
  Cheeks. I had sunburned **cheeks.**
- Item 8: **stacks.** What word? (Signal.)
  Stacks.
  They ordered **stacks** of pancakes.
- Item 9: **stinks.** What word? (Signal.)
  Stinks.
  Watch out because that weed **stinks.**
- Item 10: **loan.** What word? (Signal.) *Loan.*
  She asked her mom for a **loan.**

Scoring the test

1. (Count the number of errors in the whole test. Write that number in the box at the top of the page.)
2. (Pass criterion: 0, 1, or 2 errors. Circle **P.**)
- (Fail criterion: 3 or more errors. Circle **F.**)
3. (Record each student's **P** or **F** score on the Mastery Test Group Summary form under Test 1.)

Remedies

1. (If **30 percent or more** of the students fail the test by making **3 or more errors** in the 20-item test, present the following firm-up procedure.
   a. Give feedback on answers.
   - Read each item.
   - Tell the number or letter of the word.
   - Direct the students to spell the word.
   b. Repeat parts of Lessons 8 through 10:
   - Repeat Word-Attack exercises.
   - Repeat Story reading exercises and Fluency Assessment—Individual timed reading checkouts.
   - Present no Workbook tasks except Writing letters for sounds exercises. Direct students to write their responses on lined paper.
   c. After students have successfully completed the remedies, retest them on Mastery Test 1. Reproduce the Mastery Test as needed.)
2. (If **fewer than 30 percent** of students fail Mastery Test 1, give these students information on the items they missed.)
- (During Lessons 11 through 20, monitor these students closely during Fluency Assessment—Individual timed reading checkouts.)

Total errors - Test 1

P F

20 items

Name: _____ Date: _____

1

1. fat	6. fill	11. pal	16. slid	21. steep	26. strip
2. fate	7. hop	12. pale	17. slide	22. step	27. stripe
3. fail	8. hope	13. sail	18. soil	23. stick	28. tim
4. fell	9. male	14. slack	19. spring	24. strain	29. time
5. file	10. mall	15. slick	20. stack	25. string	

a. _8_ c. _24_ e. _5_ g. _17_ i. _13_

b. _2_ d. _29_ f. _6_ h. _21_ j. _27_

2

1. strike	strip	(streak)	struck
2. better	bitter	butter	(batter)
3. lad	load	(led)	loud
4. born	(burn)	barn	turn
5. punch	pinch	poach	(pouch)
6. (bait)	bet	beat	boat
7. checks	cheers	(cheeks)	chests
8. sticks	stops	stocks	(stacks)
9. stings	(stinks)	springs	strings
10. lean	line	(loan)	lane

Total errors - Test 1

☐ **P F**

20 items

Name: _____ Date: _____

1

1. fat	**6.** fill	**11.** pal	**16.** slid	**21.** steep	**26.** strip
2. fate	**7.** hop	**12.** pale	**17.** slide	**22.** step	**27.** stripe
3. feel	**8.** hope	**13.** sail	**18.** soil	**23.** stick	**28.** tim
4. fell	**9.** male	**14.** slack	**19.** spring	**24.** strain	**29.** time
5. file	**10.** mall	**15.** slick	**20.** stack	**25.** string	

a. _____   c. _____   e. _____   g. _____   i. _____

b. _____   d. _____   f. _____   h. _____   j. _____

2

1. strike	strip	streak	struck
2. better	bitter	butter	batter
3. lad	load	led	loud
4. born	burn	barn	turn
5. punch	pinch	poach	pouch
6. bait	bet	beat	boat
7. checks	cheers	cheeks	chests
8. sticks	stops	stocks	stacks
9. stings	stinks	springs	strings
10. lean	line	loan	lane

Mastery Test 1, Decoding B2 Workbook

Decoding B2 Mastery Test Group Summary

Test number	1	1-R	2	2-R	3 Fluency Assessment Part 6	3 Parts 1–5 and Part 7	3-R	4	4-R	5	5-R	6 Fluency Assessment Part 6	6 Parts 1–5 and Part 7	6-R
Name:														
Date:														
1.	P F	P F	P F	P F		P F	P F	P F	P F	P F	P F	P F	P F	P F
2.	P F	P F	P F	P F		P F	P F	P F	P F	P F	P F	P F	P F	P F
3.	P F	P F	P F	P F		P F	P F	P F	P F	P F	P F	P F	P F	P F
4.	P F	P F	P F	P F		P F	P F	P F	P F	P F	P F	P F	P F	P F
5.	P F	P F	P F	P F		P F	P F	P F	P F	P F	P F	P F	P F	P F
6.	P F	P F	P F	P F		P F	P F	P F	P F	P F	P F	P F	P F	P F
7.	P F	P F	P F	P F		P F	P F	P F	P F	P F	P F	P F	P F	P F
8.	P F	P F	P F	P F	P F	P F	P F	P F	P F	P F	P F	P F	P F	P F
9.	P F	P F	P F	P F	P F	P F	P F	P F	P F	P F	P F	P F	P F	P F
10.	P F	P F	P F	P F	P F	P F	P F	P F	P F	P F	P F	P F	P F	P F
11.	P F	P F	P F	P F	P F	P F	P F	P F	P F	P F	P F	P F	P F	P F
12.	P F	P F	P F	P F	P F	P F	P F	P F	P F	P F	P F	P F	P F	P F
13.	P F	P F	P F	P F	P F	P F	P F	P F	P F	P F	P F	P F	P F	P F
14.	P F	P F	P F	P F	P F	P F	P F	P F	P F	P F	P F	P F	P F	P F
15.	P F	P F	P F	P F	P F	P F	P F	P F	P F	P F	P F	P F	P F	P F
16.	P F	P F	P F	P F	P F	P F	P F	P F	P F	P F	P F	P F	P F	P F
17.	P F	P F	P F	P F	P F	P F	P F	P F	P F	P F	P F	P F	P F	P F
18.	P F	P F	P F	P F	P F	P F	P F	P F	P F	P F	P F	P F	P F	P F
19.	P F	P F	P F	P F	P F	P F	P F	P F	P F	P F	P F	P F	P F	P F
20.	P F	P F	P F	P F	P F	P F	P F	P F	P F	P F	P F	P F	P F	P F
21.	P F	P F	P F	P F	P F	P F	P F	P F	P F	P F	P F	P F	P F	P F
22.	P F	P F	P F	P F	P F	P F	P F	P F	P F	P F	P F	P F	P F	P F
23.	P F	P F	P F	P F	P F	P F	P F	P F	P F	P F	P F	P F	P F	P F
24.	P F	P F	P F	P F	P F	P F	P F	P F	P F	P F	P F	P F	P F	P F
25.	P F	P F	P F	P F	P F	P F	P F	P F	P F	P F	P F	P F	P F	P F
Number failed:														
Percent failed:														

Note: Record retest in **R** columns.

━━━ MASTERY TEST 3 ━━━

1. Open your Workbook to page 343. ✓
- This is a test on what you have learned in Lessons 21 to 30. You'll write your answers on the test.
2. There's no time limit, so check your answers to make sure you got them right. Raise your hand when you're done.
- (Wait for all students to finish the test.)
3. (Gather Workbooks and grade tests using the Answer Key below. Write the number of errors in the **error** box.)
4. (Return Workbooks and award points.)
5. (Direct students to record their points for Mastery Test 3 on the Point Summary Chart.)

12-Lesson Point Summary
(Tell students to add the point totals for Lessons 21 to 30 on the Point Summary Chart and to write the totals for Block 3.)

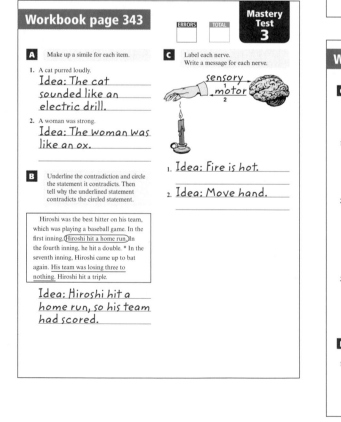

Workbook page 343

Mastery Test 3

ERRORS   TOTAL

A Make up a simile for each item.

1. A cat purred loudly.
   Idea: The cat sounded like an electric drill.

2. A woman was strong.
   Idea: The woman was like an ox.

B Underline the contradiction and circle the statement it contradicts. Then tell why the underlined statement contradicts the circled statement.

Hiroshi was the best hitter on his team, which was playing a baseball game. In the first inning, Hiroshi hit a home run. In the fourth inning, he hit a double. * In the seventh inning, Hiroshi came up to bat again. His team was losing three to nothing. Hiroshi hit a triple.

Idea: Hiroshi hit a home run, so his team had scored.

C Label each nerve. Write a message for each nerve.

sensory 1
motor 2

1. Idea: Fire is hot.

2. Idea: Move hand.

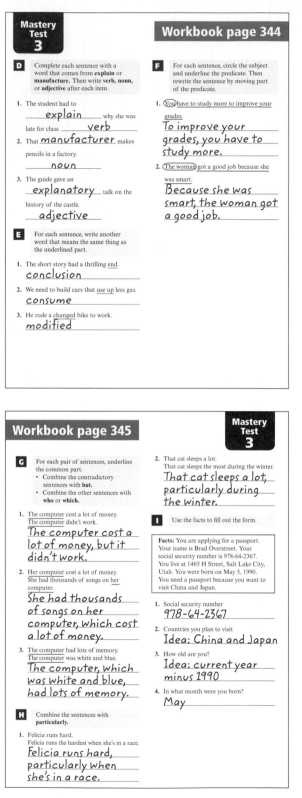

Workbook page 344

Mastery Test 3

D Complete each sentence with a word that comes from **explain** or **manufacture**. Then write **verb, noun,** or **adjective** after each item.

1. The student had to ___explain___ why she was late for class. ___verb___

2. That ___manufacturer___ makes pencils in a factory. ___noun___

3. The guide gave an ___explanatory___ talk on the history of the castle. ___adjective___

E For each sentence, write another word that means the same thing as the underlined part.

1. The short story had a thrilling end.
   conclusion

2. We need to build cars that use up less gas.
   consume

3. He rode a changed bike to work.
   modified

F For each sentence, circle the subject and underline the predicate. Then rewrite the sentence by moving part of the predicate.

1. (You) have to study more to improve your grades.
   To improve your grades, you have to study more.

2. (The woman) got a good job because she was smart.
   Because she was smart, the woman got a good job.

Workbook page 345

Mastery Test 3

G For each pair of sentences, underline the common part.
- Combine the contradictory sentences with **but**.
- Combine the other sentences with **who** or **which.**

1. The computer cost a lot of money.
   The computer didn't work.
   The computer cost a lot of money, but it didn't work.

2. Her computer cost a lot of money.
   She had thousands of songs on her computer.
   She had thousands of songs on her computer, which cost a lot of money.

3. The computer had lots of memory.
   The computer was white and blue.
   The computer, which was white and blue, had lots of memory.

H Combine the sentences with **particularly.**

1. Felicia runs hard.
   Felicia runs the hardest when she's in a race.
   Felicia runs hard, particularly when she's in a race.

2. That cat sleeps a lot.
   That cat sleeps the most during the winter.
   That cat sleeps a lot, particularly during the winter.

I Use the facts to fill out the form.

Facts: You are applying for a passport. Your name is Brad Overstreet. Your social security number is 978-64-2367. You live at 1465 H Street, Salt Lake City, Utah. You were born on May 5, 1990. You need a passport because you want to visit China and Japan.

1. Social security number
   978-64-2367

2. Countries you plan to visit
   Idea: China and Japan

3. How old are you?
   Idea: current year minus 1990

4. In what month were you born?
   May

Mastery Test 3, Comprehension B2 TPB

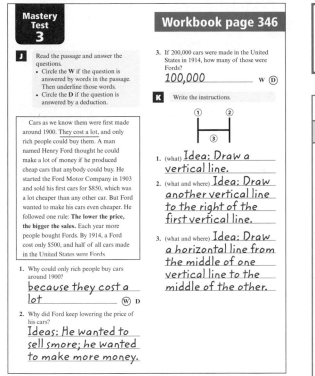

REMEDIAL EXERCISES

The Mastery Tests are divided into lettered parts, with two to five questions per part. Students who miss more than 25% of the questions in a particular part are considered to have failed that part.

- If a part has two or three questions, students who miss one or more questions fail the part.
- If a part has four or five questions, students who miss two or more questions fail the part.

The following remedial exercises can be used with students who fail one or more parts of the Mastery Test. If more than 25% of your students fail a particular part of the test, present the remedial exercises **for that part** to those students. All the exercises appear in the Teacher Presentation Book. For exercises that involve the Workbook, make copies of unused Workbook pages. Permission is granted to reproduce the Workbook pages from these lessons for classroom use.

Remedy Table		
Part	**Lesson**	**Exercise**
A	25	2
	28	3
B	24	4
	26	5
C	24	6
	28	4
D	29	4
	24	5
E	23	2
	26	3
F	21	4
	22	4
G	22	5
	25	4
H	29	2
	30	2
I	26	4
	27	4
J	29	5
	23	5
K	26	6
	27	2

End of Mastery Test 3

ERRORS

TOTAL

A Make up a simile for each item.

1. A cat purred loudly.

_____

_____

_____

2. A woman was strong.

_____

_____

_____

B Underline the contradiction and circle the statement it contradicts. Then tell why the underlined statement contradicts the circled statement.

Hiroshi was the best hitter on his team, which was playing a baseball game. In the first inning, Hiroshi hit a home run. In the fourth inning, he hit a double. * In the seventh inning, Hiroshi came up to bat again. His team was losing three to nothing. Hiroshi hit a triple.

_____

_____

_____

C Label each nerve.
Write a message for each nerve.

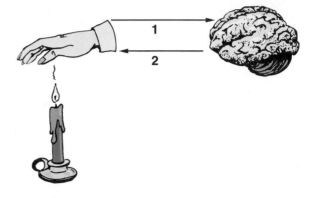

1. _____

_____

2. _____

_____

D Complete each sentence with a word that comes from **explain** or **manufacture.** Then write **verb, noun,** or **adjective** after each item.

1. The student had to

_____ why she was

late for class. _____

2. That _____ makes

pencils in a factory.

_____

3. The guide gave an

_____ talk on the

history of the castle.

_____

E For each sentence, write another word that means the same thing as the underlined part.

1. The short story had a thrilling <u>end</u>.

_____

2. We need to build cars that <u>use up</u> less gas.

_____

3. He rode a <u>changed</u> bike to work.

_____

F For each sentence, circle the subject and underline the predicate. Then rewrite the sentence by moving part of the predicate.

1. You have to study more to improve your grades.

_____

_____

_____

2. The woman got a good job because she was smart.

_____

_____

G For each pair of sentences, underline the common part.
- Combine the contradictory sentences with **but.**
- Combine the other sentences with **who** or **which.**

1. The computer cost a lot of money.
The computer didn't work.

_____

_____

_____

2. Her computer cost a lot of money.
She had thousands of songs on her computer.

_____

_____

_____

3. The computer had lots of memory.
The computer was white and blue.

_____

_____

_____

H Combine the sentences with **particularly.**

1. Felicia runs hard.
Felicia runs the hardest when she's in a race.

_____

_____

_____

2. That cat sleeps a lot.
That cat sleeps the most during the winter.

_____

_____

_____

I Use the facts to fill out the form.

Facts: You are applying for a passport. Your name is Brad Overstreet. Your social security number is 978-64-2367. You live at 1465 H Street, Salt Lake City, Utah. You were born on May 5, 1990. You need a passport because you want to visit China and Japan.

1. Social security number

_____

2. Countries you plan to visit

_____

3. How old are you?

_____

4. In what month were you born?

_____

J Read the passage and answer the questions.
- Circle the **W** if the question is answered by words in the passage. Then underline those words.
- Circle the **D** if the question is answered by a deduction.

Cars as we know them were first made around 1900. They cost a lot, and only rich people could buy them. A man named Henry Ford thought he could make a lot of money if he produced cheap cars that anybody could buy. He started the Ford Motor Company in 1903 and sold his first cars for $850, which was a lot cheaper than any other car. But Ford wanted to make his cars even cheaper. He followed one rule: **The lower the price, the bigger the sales.** Each year more people bought Fords. By 1914, a Ford cost only $500, and half of all cars made in the United States were Fords.

1. Why could only rich people buy cars around 1900?

_____ **W** **D**

2. Why did Ford keep lowering the price of his cars?

_____

_____

_____

3. If 200,000 cars were made in the United States in 1914, how many of those were Fords?

_____ **W** **D**

K Write the instructions.

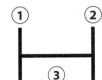

1. (what) _____

_____

2. (what and where) _____

_____

_____

_____

3. (what and where) _____

_____

_____

_____

_____

Mastery Test 3 Group Summary Sheet

Teacher _____ Group _____ Date _____

INDIVIDUAL PERFORMANCE

Student	Percentage of Skills Passed by Student	Test Part										
		A	B	C	D	E	F	G	H	I	J	K

GROUP PERFORMANCE

Number of students failing each skill												
Percentage of students failing each skill												

TEACHING TECHNIQUES

The ***Corrective Reading*** teacher must do two things effectively: teach the exercises and manage the students. The following section summarizes the Direct Instruction teaching techniques used in SRA's ***Corrective Reading*** series.

Setup for the Lesson

Assign permanent seats if possible. The lower-performing students, or those whose responses and behavior require more monitoring, should be seated directly in front of the teacher. Students in **Decoding A** must be able to see the display in the Teacher Presentation Books. In **Decoding B1, B2,** and **C,** the teacher sometimes presents a short exercise on the board or on an overhead projector. It is also important for the teacher to move around the room to monitor student performance.

To the right is one room arrangement with higher-performing students seated on the sides and back row and lower-performing students in the front rows.

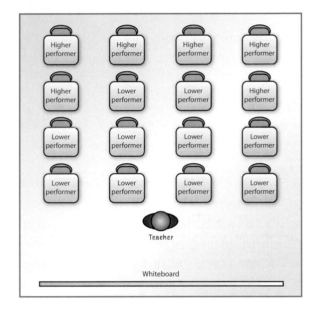

In the room arrangement for a small group, to the left, higher-performing students are on the ends, and lower-performing students are in the middle or next to the teacher.

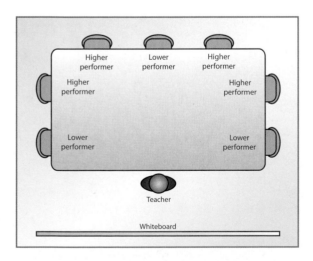

In the room arrangement to the right, higher-performing students are in the back row, and lower-performing students are in the front row and near the middle of the back row.

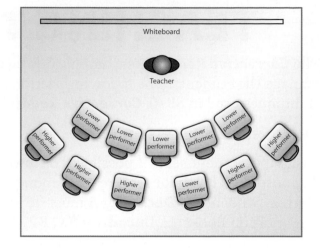

Introducing the Program

At the beginning of the first three or four lessons, go over the STAR rules with students.

1. (Print on the board:)

> S
> T
> A
> R

2. Everybody in this group will follow the STAR rules. **STAR** is spelled **S-T-A-R.**
- **S** is for **sit tall.** That means look at me when I am telling you things.
- **T** is for **track.** When you are reading aloud or other students are reading aloud, you touch under the words as they are read.
- **A** is for **answer on signal.** We'll practice later.
- **R** is for **respect others.** Nobody makes fun of anybody else. We are all on the same team, and we work together when we're in this class.
3. Once more:
   S is for **sit tall.**
   T is for **track.**
   A is for **answer on signal.**
   R is for **respect others.**
4. (Tell students that they also earn points for each part of the lesson. See page 78.)

Scripted Presentations

An important feature of the series is that it controls a wide range of details that are essential to successful teaching—the sequence of tasks that constitute a lesson, the instructions given to students, the number and type of examples that are practiced, and the precise steps in the development of each skill. Typically, a skill is first presented in isolation in a tightly structured format, and it is developed until the students are asked to apply the skill, along with others, in a variety of contexts.

To control these details, the daily lessons are scripted. What the teacher says for each activity and how the teacher corrects mistakes are specified. The scripts have been designed to ensure a smooth and precise presentation.

These are the typefaces used in the Teacher Presentation Book in the Decoding and Comprehension programs:

■ This blue type indicates what the teacher says.

■ (This type indicates what the teacher does.)

■ *This italic type shows the students' response.*

The following exercises from **Comprehension A,** Lesson 35, and from **Decoding B2,** Lesson 4, show how the type is used.

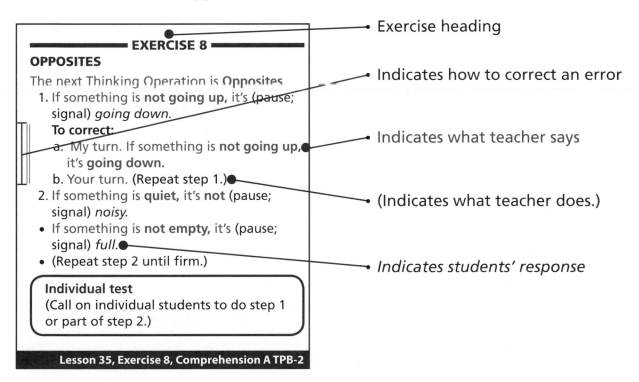

EXERCISE 8

OPPOSITES

The next Thinking Operation is **Opposites**
1. If something is **not going up,** it's (pause; signal) *going down.*
   To correct:
   a. My turn. If something is **not going up,** it's **going down.**
   b. Your turn. (Repeat step 1.)
2. If something is **quiet,** it's **not** (pause; signal) *noisy.*
• If something is **not empty,** it's (pause; signal) *full.*
• (Repeat step 2 until firm.)

Individual test
(Call on individual students to do step 1 or part of step 2.)

Lesson 35, Exercise 8, Comprehension A TPB-2

- Exercise heading
- Indicates how to correct an error
- Indicates what teacher says
- (Indicates what teacher does.)
- *Indicates students' response*

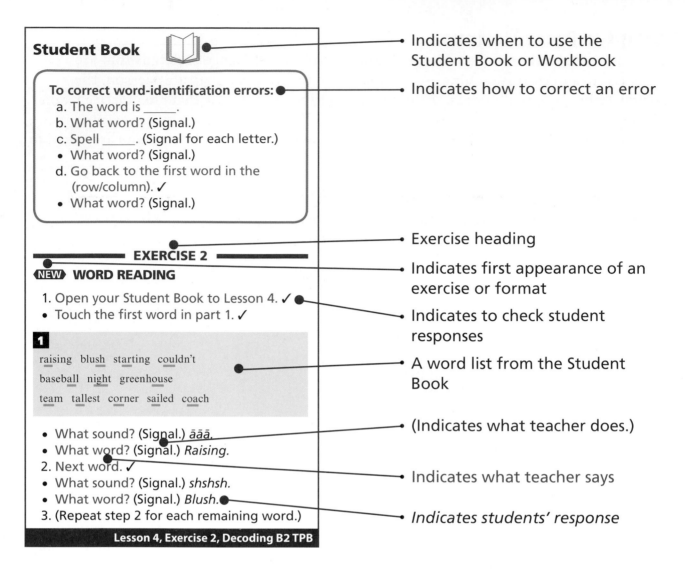

Student Book — Indicates when to use the Student Book or Workbook

To correct word-identification errors: — Indicates how to correct an error
a. The word is _____.
b. What word? (Signal.)
c. Spell _____. (Signal for each letter.)
• What word? (Signal.)
d. Go back to the first word in the (row/column). ✓
• What word? (Signal.)

━━━━━━ **EXERCISE 2** ━━━━━━ — Exercise heading

NEW **WORD READING** — Indicates first appearance of an exercise or format

1. Open your Student Book to Lesson 4. ✓ — Indicates to check student responses
• Touch the first word in part 1. ✓

1

raising blush starting couldn't

baseball night greenhouse

team tallest corner sailed coach

— A word list from the Student Book

• What sound? (Signal.) *āāā.* — (Indicates what teacher does.)
• What word? (Signal.) *Raising.*
2. Next word. ✓
• What sound? (Signal.) *shshsh.* — Indicates what teacher says
• What word? (Signal.) *Blush.*
3. (Repeat step 2 for each remaining word.) — *Indicates students' response*

Lesson 4, Exercise 2, Decoding B2 TPB

In addition to controlling program sequences, scripted presentations have other advantages:

■ Scripted directions allow teachers to present a number of examples quickly. Without scripted directions, some teachers might present wordy explanations that do not permit the time to present many examples.

■ Scripted directions standardize the wording from example to example so that students will not be confused by varying instructions.

■ Teacher training is simplified because trainers can work on common presentation problems.

■ Scripts provide efficient correction procedures that contain few words and build on what the students have already been taught.

■ The time spent on each activity is controlled; therefore, a more effective development of a range of skills is guaranteed.

Formats

Formats are used throughout the programs to make the presentation of similar activities easier for the teacher and the students. A format is an exercise structured so that the same form can be used to accommodate similar tasks. By changing some details of an exercise that is formatted, another exercise can be created. Formats simplify the presentation of similar activities because the teacher's behavior remains basically the same for all examples of a given format. Once the teacher learns the format, handling various examples is relatively easy. Formatted exercises help students understand what is being presented, because the directions and wording are the same for all examples of a particular format. The format, therefore, functions as a prompt for applying a skill to new examples.

Some formats are presented for twenty or more lessons; other formats, only two or three lessons. The word **NEW** next to the exercise heading in the Teacher Presentation Book indicates a format with a new skill or a new procedure, such as a modification in the teacher wording or a change in the number of words that must be read in 1 minute to earn points.

The following example is the same format as the one shown in the preceding section, *Scripted Presentations*. A different exercise has been created by changing the examples given in the format.

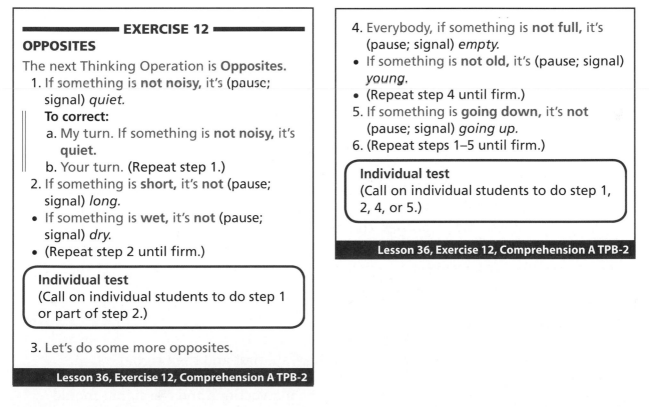

EXERCISE 12

OPPOSITES

The next Thinking Operation is **Opposites**.
1. If something is **not noisy,** it's (pause; signal) *quiet.*
   To correct:
   a. My turn. If something is **not noisy,** it's **quiet.**
   b. Your turn. (Repeat step 1.)
2. If something is **short,** it's **not** (pause; signal) *long.*
   • If something is **wet,** it's **not** (pause; signal) *dry.*
   • (Repeat step 2 until firm.)

   Individual test
   (Call on individual students to do step 1 or part of step 2.)

3. Let's do some more opposites.

Lesson 36, Exercise 12, Comprehension A TPB-2

4. Everybody, if something is **not full,** it's (pause; signal) *empty.*
   • If something is **not old,** it's (pause; signal) *young.*
   • (Repeat step 4 until firm.)
5. If something is **going down,** it's **not** (pause; signal) *going up.*
6. (Repeat steps 1–5 until firm.)

   Individual test
   (Call on individual students to do step 1, 2, 4, or 5.)

Lesson 36, Exercise 12, Comprehension A TPB-2

Included in the format is the specification of a correction procedure for the mistakes that students most likely will make when introduced to that format. Correction procedures are usually specified the first two or three times a format appears; then the correction is dropped from the format, but it should still be followed by the teacher when necessary.

Corrections

All students make mistakes. Mistakes provide valuable information about what kinds of difficulties students are having. Knowing how to correct effectively is essential to good teaching. Two kinds of correction procedures are used in **Corrective Reading**—general correction procedures and specified correction procedures. (See pages 87–92.)

Pacing the Exercises

Because a great deal of information must be taught during the daily presentation, it is important for the teacher to move quickly but not to rush the students so much that they make mistakes. To ensure a smoothly paced lesson, the teacher should become familiar with the exercises before presenting them. The teacher must be able to present them without having to refer to the page for every word. Lines should be said quickly, and instructions should be concise.

Fast pacing is important for the following reasons:

■ It reduces problems of managing students and maintaining on-task behavior. This has been demonstrated through studies of the relationship between student engagement in tasks and the rate at which the tasks are paced. Faster pacing secures more student interest for a longer period of time, which means that management problems are reduced.

■ It results in greater student achievement. With faster pacing, a teacher can cover more material in a fixed amount of time and provide more student practice in that time.

■ Many tasks become more difficult if they are presented slowly. Slower pacing places greater memory demands on students. Faster pacing, on the other hand, reduces the memory load by giving students less time to forget and allows students to learn by doing the tasks.

Signals

When tasks calling for a group answer are presented, the entire group should respond on signal. This means that all the students respond in unison when the teacher signals them. By listening carefully to the responses, the teacher can tell both which students make mistakes and which ones respond late, copying those who responded first. As a result, the teacher will be able to correct specific mistakes, maximize the amount of practice, and evaluate the performance of each student.

Here are the rules for effective signaling:

■ The teacher should never signal while talking. Talk first and then signal.

■ The time interval between the last word of the instructions and the signal should always be about 1 second. Signals should be consistently timed so that students can respond together.

If a student fails to answer when the signal is given, the teacher corrects by saying I have to hear everybody and then returns to the beginning of the task.

If a student responds either before or too long after the signal, the teacher calls attention to the signal and returns to the beginning of the task. For example, if students respond before the signal, say You've got to wait until I signal. Let's try it again.

Teaching to Lower-Performing Students

Often the teacher will have to repeat tasks to make sure that students are firm (that they can do the task). The teacher must judge whether the group is firm on the basis of the lower performers, not the higher performers. When the lower performers are firm, chances are that all students in the group are firm. Rapidly paced repetitions take very little time; therefore, teaching to the lower performers does not substantially slow the progress of the higher performers. The procedure assumes that the performances of students in a particular group are not markedly different.

Individual Turns

At the end of some exercises, individual turns are specified. The teacher repeats certain tasks in the exercise, calling on different students to respond individually. The teacher sees that both higher and lower performers get a chance to respond. Individual turns provide more precise information about a student's performance than group turns do. For example, a student may be able to say a poem when supported by the group. That student may be unable, however, to say the poem without the group prompts.

Positive Reinforcement

Poor readers typically conclude that learning to read is futile, that it is a punishing activity, that it is intimidating, and that because they will never read well, they should not bother trying. Changing this attitude involves thoroughly restructuring the reading situation. This can be done through program design and the use of positive reinforcement. The reading program must be designed so that the sequence of tasks is readily learnable. Without achievable tasks, students will continue to make many mistakes and, therefore, their negative attitude will not change. The program must provide students with the evidence that they are improving to counter their tendency to interpret every mistake as proof of failure. The sequence must be planned so that students realize there is indeed a purpose, a direction, a development in their reading performance.

Two essential features of the programs' reinforcement system are that students earn points for their low error rates and that they summarize their progress on a chart. These features help to provide a positive focus to the learning activities. The use of positive reinforcement is an important technique in turning on students, improving their performance, and increasing the likelihood that they will practice the skills taught in the program.

Use of Points

Point schedules are specified for each program. In the Level A and Level B programs, points are awarded for performance on each part of the lesson. In **Comprehension C,** points are awarded for applying skills, not for the process of acquiring the skills. The following chart shows the activities in each program for which points are awarded.

DECODING		COMPREHENSION	
A	Word-Attack Skills Workbook Exercises Individual Reading Checkouts	**A** **&** **A Fast Cycle**	Thinking Operations Workbook Exercises Information Fact Games Mastery Tests
B1 **&** **B2**	Word-Attack Skills Group Reading Individual Reading Checkouts Workbook Exercises	**B1,** **B1 Fast Cycle** **&** **B2**	Oral Exercises Workbook Exercises Fact Games Mastery Tests
C	Word-Attack Skills Group Reading Individual Reading Checkouts Workbook Exercises	**C**	Workbook Exercises Student Book Exercises Fact Games Mastery Tests

The rules for earning points are specified in the lessons. Following are the directions for earning points in Lesson 1 of **Decoding A.**

- We're going to do things together. If you all do a good job, everybody in this group will get 6 points.
- You must respond on signal, answer when I give individual turns, follow along when somebody else is reading, and try hard. The group will earn points even if you make mistakes—but everybody must try.
- If the group does not do a good job, nobody will get any points.

Lesson 1, Decoding A TPB-1

The point system requires students to record their daily points. Point Charts appear on the inside front cover of the **Decoding A** Workbook and at the back of every other **Corrective Reading** Workbook. During different parts of the lesson, students record points in the appropriate boxes of their point charts. Below is a sample Point Chart from **Decoding B1.**

Lesson	Group Points A	B	Individual Points C-1	C-2	D	Bonus		TOTAL
41							=	
42							=	
43							=	
44		.					=	
45							=	

In **Decoding B1,** students earn points for Word-Attack Skills (Box A), Group Reading (Box B), Individual Reading Checkout (Box C-1), Timed Reading Checkout (Box C-2), and Workbook Exercises (Box D).

The maximum possible points students can earn for each **Decoding B1** lesson, not counting bonus points, is 20 points. The Point Charts are designed to show total points for five-lesson periods. At the end of every five lessons, students total points in their Point Charts. For **letter grades** based on points for a five-lesson block, tell students to compute the total for the blue boxes (C, D, and Bonus in Lessons 1 through 15; C-1, C-2, D, and Bonus in Lessons 16 through 65) and write the number in the Total box at the end of each row in their Point Chart. Students then add the totals and write the sum in the green box. In the following example from Lessons 11 through 15, the maximum number of points a student can earn is 60. In this example, the student earned 48 points, the total for the blue boxes (C, D, and Bonus).

Lesson	Group Points A	B	Individual Points C	D	Bonus		TOTAL
11	5	3	6	6		=	12
12	0	2	6	6		=	12
13	5	1	0	6		=	6
14	0	3	6	6		=	12
15	5	3	6	0		=	6
							48

The teacher can use the performance on the daily lessons as data for awarding letter grades. Simply make a fraction based on the number of points earned and total possible points. For the example above, the fraction would be $\frac{48}{60}$, which is 80 percent.

The system is objective and may represent the students' first opportunity to earn a grade that requires good performance. The grade is a strong reinforcer for many students (although they often try to act as if it is not important to them).

For **rewards** based on points, tell students to compute the total for all boxes (A, B, C, D, and Bonus for Lessons 1 through 15; A, B, C-1, C-2, D, and Bonus for Lessons 16 through 65) and write the number in the Total box at the end of each row. Students then add the totals and write the sum in the green box. In the following example from Lessons 16 through 20, the maximum number of points a student can earn is 100.

Lesson	Group Points		Individual Points					TOTAL
	A	B	C-1	C-2	D	Bonus		
16	5	3	0	3	6		=	17
17	4	4	3	0	0		=	11
18	3	2	3	3	6		=	17
19	4	4	0	3	6		=	17
20	3	4	3	3	6		=	19
								81

One example of a reward would be to arrange special activities for all students who earn more than 80 points during a week. Possibly, younger students can earn tangible reinforcers (especially things like decals and stickers).

The point system also contains provisions for awarding bonus points. This bonus-point provision permits you to deal with special problems. Early in the program, you may award bonus points to students who get to their seats on time, have their material ready for the lesson, or exhibit other behavior that shows their readiness to learn. You may also use bonus points for success on any activity that is especially difficult for the students.

Adjusting Teaching Techniques

It is more important to follow the techniques described in the previous section with lower-performing students than with higher-performing students. If higher-performing students are not brought to a 100 percent accuracy criterion on every task, their overall performance probably will not suffer appreciably. Neither will their performance suffer if the teacher does not return to the beginning of a list following a mistake or if the teacher does not use elaborate reinforcement procedures.

This does not mean that a teacher working with students who are placed in a Level C program should drop the techniques of signaling, pacing, correcting errors, and reinforcing. The teacher should move as fast as students are capable of learning. The teacher should use signals but should not be overly concerned if students do not respond exactly on signal. The teacher should pay close attention to students' Workbook and oral reading performance, using these as guides.

When working with lower-performing students, especially in Levels A and B, the teacher should follow the specified teaching techniques very closely.

PRACTICING SIGNALS and CORRECTION PROCEDURES

This section is designed for practice in executing signals and correcting different kinds of mistakes.

Signal Practice

The hand-drop, audible, and **point-touch signals** are used in both the Decoding and the Comprehension programs. The **sound-out signal** is used only in **Decoding A.** The **sequential-response signal** is used primarily in the Comprehension programs.

The Hand-Drop Signal

This signal is used for tasks that are presented orally. The following exercise is from **Comprehension B1,** Lesson 51.

═══ EXERCISE 2 ═══

BODY SYSTEMS

1. Everybody, name the body system that moves blood around the body. (Signal.) *The circulatory system.*
- Name the body system of muscles. (Signal.) *The muscular system.*
- Name the body system of bones. (Signal.) *The skeletal system.*
- Name the body system that changes food into fuel. (Signal.) *The digestive system.*
- (Repeat step 1 until firm.)
2. You're going to name the tubes that carry blood back to the heart. (Pause.) Get ready. (Signal.) *The veins.*
- You're going to name the tubes that carry blood away from the heart. (Pause.) Get ready. (Signal.) *The arteries.*
- You're going to name the pump that moves the blood. (Pause.) Get ready. (Signal.) *The heart.*
- You're going to name the very small tubes that connect the veins and arteries. (Pause.) Get ready. (Signal.) *The capillaries.*
- (Repeat step 2 until firm.)

> **Individual test**
> (Repeat steps 1 and 2 with individual students.)

Lesson 51, Exercise 2, Comprehension B1 TPB

To execute the hand-drop signal in steps 1 and 2:

1 Hold your hand out (as if you're stopping traffic) while you are saying the instructions or presenting the question.

2 Continue to hold your hand still for 1 second after you have completed the instructions or the question.

3 Then quickly drop your hand. The students should respond the instant your hand drops.

The Audible Signal

This signal is used primarily when students are attending to material in the Workbook and not looking at the teacher. The teacher can use any audible method to produce this signal—finger snapping, clapping, or foot tapping. The following exercise is from **Comprehension A,** Lesson 31.

━━━━ **EXERCISE 12** ━━━━
(NEW) **INDUCTIONS**

1. Everybody, touch part B in your Workbook. ✓
2. Let's find out the rule for these triangles. Everybody, touch triangle 1. ✓
• Move to triangle 2. Triangle 2 is different from triangle 1.
Everybody, how is it different? (Signal.) *It's smaller.*
• Yes, it's smaller.
3. Move to triangle 3. ✓
Everybody, how is triangle 3 different from triangle 2? (Signal.) *It's smaller.*
• Yes, it's smaller.

Lesson 31, Exercise 12, Comprehension A TPB-2

4. What happens to the triangles as you go from triangle 1 to triangle 3? (Signal.) *They get smaller.*
• Yes, they get smaller. So, what's the rule for the triangles? (Signal.) *The triangles get smaller.* (Repeat until firm.)
• Yes, the triangles get smaller.
5. You're going to draw two more triangles that follow the same rule. What's the rule? (Signal.) *The triangles get smaller.*
• Draw triangles 4 and 5 so that they follow the rule.
(Observe students and give feedback.)

Lesson 31, Exercise 12, Comprehension A TPB-2

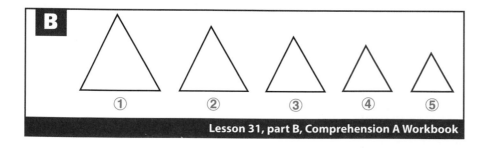

Lesson 31, part B, Comprehension A Workbook

To execute the audible signal in steps 2, 3, and 4:

1 Say the instructions quickly.

2 Pause 1 second.

3 Clap. Students should respond the instant that you clap. (Note that in place of the clap, any audible signal is acceptable.)

Following is a word-reading exercise from **Decoding B1,** Lesson 58. In this exercise, students read a random list of words, each with an underlined part. This activity serves as an ongoing review of the sounds of the letters and letter combinations. For each word, students first say the sound for the underlined part and then read the word.

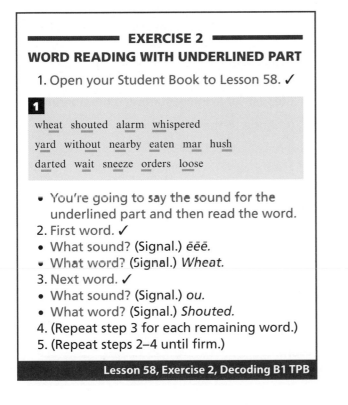

Students are looking at the words in their Student Book. Use an audible signal (a snap, clap, or tap) to indicate when they should respond. The pattern is the same for all words.

To execute the signal in step 3:

1 Next word. Check (✓) that students are touching the word.

2 What sound? Pause 1 second. Signal. Students should respond the instant you signal.

3 What word? Pause 1 second. Signal.

Maintain a rapid pace. The steps for each word should take no more than about 3 seconds.

The Point-Touch Signal

This signal is used when pointing to words or symbols in the presentation book or on the board. The following exercise is from **Decoding B2,** Lesson 7. In this exercise, the teacher writes a list of words on the board (or on an overhead transparency). After the students read each word in the list, the teacher then changes each word by adding specified endings.

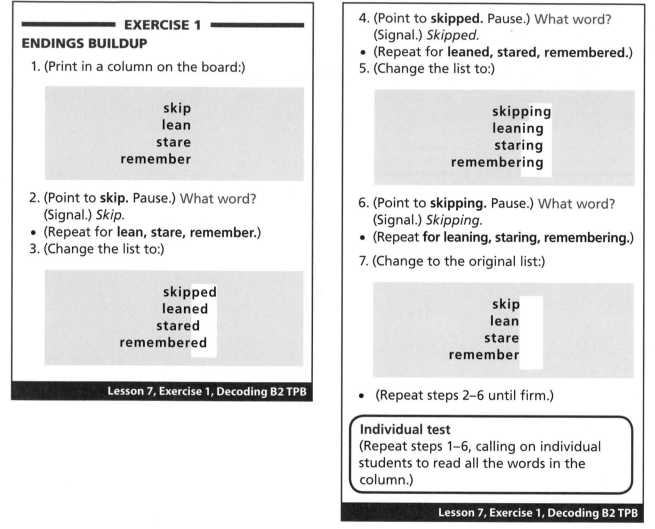

To execute the point-touch signal in step 2:

1 Hold your finger in front of the word, about an inch away from the board. Be careful not to cover any part of the word or obscure it from any student's view.

2 As you point, say What word?

3 Pause 1 second.

4 Signal by tapping in front of the word. Students should respond the instant you signal.

The Sound-Out Signal

This signal provides timing for students as they sound out the parts of a word. It is used in **Decoding A** and in early lessons in **Decoding B1** to teach new words. The following sample is from **Decoding A,** Lesson 3.

Task G Me

1. (Point to **m:**) What sound? (Touch under **m:**) *mmm.*
2. (Point to **e:**) What sound? (Touch under **e:**) *ēēē.*
3. (Touch the ball of the arrow:) My turn to sound out this word.
   - (Touch under **m, e** as you say:) **mmmēēē.** (Do not pause between the sounds.)
4. (Touch the ball of the arrow:) Your turn. Sound it out. Get ready. (Touch under **m, e:**) *mmmēēē.* (Repeat until the students say the sounds without pausing.)
5. (Touch the ball of the arrow:) Say it fast. (Slash right, along the arrow:) *Me.* Yes, **me.**

me

Lesson 3, Exercise 5, Task G, Decoding A TPB-1

To execute the signal:

1 Touch the ball of the arrow as you say Sound it out. Get ready.

2 Pause 1 second.

3 Quickly loop your finger to a point just under the first sound of the word.

4 Hold your finger there for 2 seconds (if the sound is continuous). Students should respond as soon as you touch under the sound, and they continue saying the sound as long as you touch under it.

5 Quickly loop to the next sound and hold for 2 seconds (if the sound is continuous). As soon as you touch under it, students should say this sound without pausing between the sounds.

6 Quickly remove your finger from the page.

The diagram below shows the pointing, looping, and student response. You must loop very quickly from sound to sound. If you loop slowly, students may come in at different times or stop between sounds.

Student response: *mmmmmmeeeeeeee*

The Sequential-Response Signal

This signal is used in orally presented tasks that require students to produce different responses in a specified sequence. The following sample is an exercise from **Comprehension A,** Lesson 15.

━━━━━━ **EXERCISE 1** ━━━━━━
(NEW) **BASIC EVIDENCE: Using Facts**

The first Thinking Operation today is **Basic Evidence.**

1. You're going to use two facts to explain things that happened. These are the only facts you can use. (Hold up one finger.) First fact. The man was very strong. Say it. (Signal.) *The man was very strong.* (Repeat until firm.)
- (Hold up two fingers.) Second fact. The plane had a broken engine. Say it. (Signal.) *The plane had a broken engine.* (Repeat until firm.)

Lesson 15, Exercise 1, Comprehension A TPB-1

2. Everybody, say those facts again. (Hold up one finger.) First fact. *The man was very strong.*
- (Hold up two fingers.) Second fact. *The plane had a broken engine.*
- (Repeat until the students say the facts in order.)

Lesson 15, Exercise 1, Comprehension A TPB-1

To execute the signal in step 1:

1 Hold up one finger while you are presenting the statement. First fact. The man was very strong.

2 Pause for 1 second after you say Say it. Don't move your finger or your hand during the pause.

3 Quickly move your finger (or your hand). Students should respond the instant your finger (hand) moves.

4 Then follow the same procedure with two fingers.

The sequential-response signal is also used in step 2.

Correction Procedures Practice

A correction procedure should be presented to the entire group of students, not just to those who made the mistake. Since corrections are not meant as punishment, it is important to present them as just another step in the lesson. Although many correction procedures are specified in the **_Corrective Reading_** programs, there is one general procedure for correcting just about any mistake that students make.

The General Correction Procedure

The correction procedure involves five steps.

1 Say the answer.

2 Repeat the task.

3 Back up in the exercise and present the activities in order.

4 Finish the remaining steps in the exercise.

5 Repeat the entire exercise **if** students make more than one or two mistakes.

■ **Step 1: Say the answer.** When you say the answer, do it immediately, the moment you hear an incorrect response. For example, if students omit a word in a verbal rule, do not wait until the students have completed trying to say the rule before correcting the error. Say the correct answer as soon as you hear the word omitted. If a student makes a mistake while orally reading a sentence, do not wait until the student completes reading the sentence to correct the error. Say the correct word as soon as you hear the misidentified word.

■ **Step 2: Repeat the task.** When you repeat the task, repeat the instructions you gave the students. If you said What word? that's the task you repeat. If you said What's the rule about living things? those are the words you present after saying the correct answer. Do not let the students just repeat the correct answer after you say it. Make sure they respond to the specific question or instructions (the task) they missed.

■ **Step 3: Back up in the exercise and present the steps in order.** The purpose of going back in the exercise is to make sure the students can remember the answer to the task you just corrected. If you only say the answer and then go on, you have no idea whether the correction procedure was effective. If you back up in the exercise and present the activities as they are specified in the Teacher Presentation Book, you'll see if the students remember the correct response. When you come to the step where students previously made the error, they will either make a correct response or make an error. If they answer correctly, you know they remembered the information. If they answer incorrectly, you know that they didn't and that they need more practice.

When you back up in an exercise, go back at least three tasks (whenever possible). A simple procedure in the Word-Attack Skills exercises of the Decoding programs is to use the columns or rows of words as markers for going back. If a mistake occurs in the middle of column 3, go back to the beginning of column 3.

Following is a sample exercise from **Comprehension A,** Lesson 17. An error is indicated at step 3.

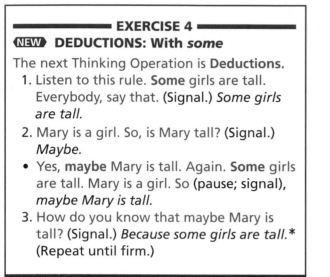

━━━━━━━ **EXERCISE 4** ━━━━━━━
‹NEW› DEDUCTIONS: With *some*

The next Thinking Operation is **Deductions.**
1. Listen to this rule. **Some** girls are tall. Everybody, say that. (Signal.) *Some girls are tall.*
2. Mary is a girl. So, is Mary tall? (Signal.) *Maybe.*
• Yes, **maybe** Mary is tall. Again. **Some** girls are tall. Mary is a girl. So (pause; signal), *maybe Mary is tall.*
3. How do you know that maybe Mary is tall? (Signal.) *Because some girls are tall.** (Repeat until firm.)

Lesson 17, Exercise 4, Comprehension A TPB-1

*Mistake occurs here. Students say *Because Mary is a girl* in response to the task: How do you know that maybe Mary is tall?

Here are steps 1 through 3 of the general correction procedure:

1 (Say the answer.) Because some girls are tall.

2 (Repeat the task.) How do you know that maybe Mary is tall? (Signal.) *Because some girls are tall.*

3 (Return to step 1 of the exercise and present the steps in order.)

If a student makes a decoding mistake in the middle of a sentence, use the same correction procedure. In the following example from **Decoding B2,** an **X** indicates where a student misidentifies a word.

> X
> Hurn's nose, like noses of all wolves, was very keen.

Here are steps 1 through 3 of the general correction procedure:

1 (As soon as you hear the student misidentify the word **noses,** say the correct word.) That word is **noses.**

2 (Repeat the task.) Touch under the word. ✓

- What word? *Noses.*

3 (Direct the student to return to the first word in the sentence and read the sentence again.)

The correction procedure is effective because it ensures that the student is able to respond to the task or specific detail that was missed WITHIN THE CONTEXT IN WHICH THE MISTAKE ORIGINALLY OCCURRED. When you get information that the student is able to perform within this context, you know that you have provided an adequate correction, one that will help shape the student's skills. If you merely say the answer and then go on, you are probably doing little to change the student's reading behavior or skills.

■ **Step 4: Finish the remaining steps in the exercise.** Following a correction (saying the answer, repeating the task, backing up in the exercise), you finish the exercise. If students make another error, use steps 1 through 3 of the correction procedure.

■ **Step 5: Repeat the entire exercise if students made more than one or two mistakes.** At the end of the exercise, you evaluate whether or not to present step 5 of the correction, repeating the entire exercise. The purpose of this step is to make sure the students can do all steps in the exercise without making a mistake. By looking at the presentation from the standpoint of the students, you can appreciate why this step is important. If students make frequent mistakes in an activity, they do not see how the pieces fit together. For them, the activity has not been a series of steps that link together to form a whole. It has been only parts that may have been arbitrarily put together.

The goal is for students to go through an activity at a good pace, making no errors. Therefore, if only one or two errors occur in an exercise, and if these mistakes have been corrected, the students have received a good demonstration of how that activity works. But if there were many mistakes in the activity, you should repeat the entire exercise.

If students continue to have difficulty with an exercise, a good procedure is to go on to the next activity in the lesson and then return to the exercise in which the errors occurred and present the exercise from the beginning. Students will perform better on the repeated exercise if they know you will return to it. Establish a clear expectation: We got through that list, but we're going to come back to it later. Make sure you remember all those words.

Remember, learning is accelerated when students are able to perform perfectly on activities in the program after errors are corrected. Students learn far more slowly if they do not receive clear demonstrations of what perfect performance is.

Specified Correction Procedures

In both the Decoding and Comprehension programs, specified correction procedures are indicated for some of the more troublesome and predictable mistakes students will make. These correction procedures usually include the same steps as the general correction procedure (say the answer, repeat the task, back up in the exercise and start over). The specified correction procedures, however, provide additional steps. These additional steps occur after step 2 in the general procedure.

1 Say the answer.

2 Repeat the task.

* * *

3 Back up in the exercise and present the activities in order.

4 Finish the remaining steps in the exercise.

5 Repeat the entire exercise if students made more than one or two mistakes.

The interpolated step is indicated with **asterisks.** That step varies from program to program; however, it always occurs after you say the answer and repeat the task.

- The interpolated step in **Decoding A** and in early lessons of **Decoding B1** may be to tell the students to sound out the word.

- The interpolated step after Lesson 10 in **Decoding B1** through **Decoding C** may be to tell the students to spell the word.

- The interpolated step in **Comprehension A** may be to say the correct response with the students (lead).

- The interpolated step in **Comprehension B1** and **Comprehension B2** may be to tell the students to say the rule that governs the correct answer.

The rest of the correction procedure remains the same. Following the interpolated step, you back up and present the missed item within the context in which the mistake originally occurred (step 3). You then finish the remaining steps in the exercise (step 4).

The example to the right is from **Decoding B1,** Lesson 11. In this lesson, the specified correction procedure is displayed in a note to the teacher at the beginning of the Student Book Word-Attack Skills exercises.

To correct word-identification errors:
a. The word is _____.
b. What word? (Signal.)
c. Spell _____. (Signal for each letter.)
• What word? (Signal.)
d. Go back to the first word in the (row/column). ✓
• What word? (Signal.)

━━━━━ **EXERCISE 6** ━━━━━

(NEW) WORD READING

Task A **Irregular words**

1. Touch the first word in part 4. ✓

4

know my into question
middle what you they
woman do person

2. That word is **know**. What word? (Signal.) *Know.*
   Yes, I **know** a secret.
3. Spell **know**. (Signal for each letter.) *K–N–O–W.*
• What word? (Signal.) *Know.*
4. Next word. ✓
• That word is **my**. What word? (Signal.) *My.*
5. Spell **my**. (Signal for each letter.) *M–Y.*
• What word? (Signal.) *My.*
6. Next word. ✓
• That word is **into**. What word? (Signal.) *Into.*
7. Spell **into**. (Signal for each letter.) *I–N–T–O.*
• What word? (Signal.) *Into.*
8. Next word. ✓
• That word is **question**. What word? (Signal.) *Question.*
9. Spell **question**. (Signal for each letter.) *Q–U–E–S–T–I–O–N.*
• What word? (Signal.) *Question.*

Task B

1. This time you will just read the words. Go back to the first word. ✓
• What word? (Signal.) *Know.*
2. Next word. ✓
• What word? (Signal.) *My.*
3. (Repeat step 2 for each remaining word.)

Lesson 11, Exercise 6, Decoding B1 TPB

To correct a mistake on the word **question** in step 3 of Task B, follow these steps:

1 (Say the answer:) The word is **question.**

2 (Repeat the task:) What word? (Signal.) *Question.*

* * * Spell **question.** (Signal for each letter.)
  Q-U-E-S-T-I-O-N.
  • What word? (Signal.) *Question.*

3 (Back up in the exercise and present the words in order:)
  Go back to the first word in the row. ✓
  What word? (Signal.) *Know.*
  • Next word. ✓
  What word? (Signal.) *My.*
  • Next word. ✓
  What word? (Signal.) *Into.*
  • Next word. ✓
  What word? (Signal.) *Question.*

In the preceding correction procedure, the spelling step is added to the general correction. The reason for the spelling step is that students may not be attending to the specific arrangement of letters in the word. The spelling step prompts them to attend to the letter details.

Practice using the general correction procedure. If you become facile with this procedure, you will find that the steps in the specified correction procedures are easy to follow. Use this guideline: If you don't remember the specific correction, use the general correction procedure. It will work. The specific correction procedures focus on important details of what and how the students are learning and should be followed when possible, but if in doubt, use the general correction procedure.

LESSON PARTS and FEEDBACK MEASURES

Following is a list of the lesson parts and Mastery Tests in each program. The activities marked with asterisks provide the most critical feedback on students' mastery of skills.

Decoding Lesson Parts

Decoding A

1. Word-Attack Skills
2. Awarding points for Word-Attack Skills
3. Workbook Exercises*
4. Workcheck
5. Awarding points for Workbook
6. Individual Reading Checkouts*
7. Awarding points for Individual Reading Checkouts
8. Totaling points for the lesson

*Mastery Tests**

1. Administer and score the Mastery Test.
2. Record scores on the Mastery Test Group Summary.
3. Provide remedies, retest students, record retest scores.
4. Record scores on the **Decoding A** Mastery Test student profile.

Decoding B1, Decoding B2

1. Word-Attack Skills
2. Awarding points for Word-Attack Skills
3. Group Reading activities*
4. Awarding points for Group Reading
5. Individual Reading Checkouts*
6. Awarding points for Individual Reading Checkouts
7. Workbook Exercises*
8. Workcheck
9. Awarding points for Workbook
10. Totaling points for the lesson

*Fluency Assessment**

- Record each teacher-observed 1-minute timed Individual Reading Checkout on the Fluency Assessment Summary.

*Mastery Tests**

1. Administer and score the Mastery Test.
2. Record scores on the Mastery Test Group Summary.
3. Provide remedies, retest students, record retest scores.

Decoding C

Lessons 1–54 and Regular Lessons 56–124

1. Word-Attack Skills
2. Awarding points for Word-Attack Skills
3. Selection Reading activities*
4. Awarding points for Selection Reading
5. Individual Reading Checkouts*
6. Awarding points for Individual Reading Checkouts
7. Workbook Exercises*
8. Workcheck
9. Awarding points for Workbook
10. Totaling points for the lesson

Checkout Lessons 55–125
(Every fifth lesson beginning with Lesson 55)

1. Word-Attack Skills for information passage (no points)
2. Group Reading of information passage*
3. Awarding points for Group Reading of information passage
4. Individual Reading Checkouts of an entire story*
5. Awarding points for Individual Reading Checkouts
6. Workbook Exercises*
7. Workcheck
8. Awarding points for Workbook
9. Totaling points for lesson

*Fluency Assessment**

- Record each teacher-observed 2-minute timed Individual Reading Checkout on the Fluency Assessment Summary.

*Mastery Tests**

1. Administer and score the Mastery Test.
2. Record scores on the Mastery Test Group Summary.
3. Provide remedies, retest students, record retest scores.

Comprehension Lesson Parts

Comprehension A, Comprehension A Fast Cycle

Regular Lessons

1. Thinking Operations (oral exercises)
2. Awarding points for Thinking Operations
3. Workbook Exercises*
4. Workcheck
5. Awarding points for Workbook
6. Information exercises (oral)
7. Awarding points for Information exercises
8. Totaling points for the lesson and recording point totals on the Point Summary Chart

Fact Game Lessons

1. Fact Game
2. Awarding points for Fact Game
3. Workbook Exercises*
4. Awarding points for Workbook
5. Totaling points for the lesson and recording point totals on the Point Summary Chart

Mastery Test Lessons

1. Mastery Test*
2. Teacher grading of Mastery Test
3. Awarding points for Mastery Test
4. Recording point totals on the Point Summary Chart
5. Remedies for Mastery Test

Comprehension B1, Comprehension B1 Fast Cycle, Comprehension B2

Regular Lessons

1. Oral Exercises

2. Teacher-directed Workbook Exercises

3. Awarding points for oral exercises and teacher-directed Workbook Exercises

4. Independent Workbook Exercises*

5. Workcheck

6. Awarding points for Workbook Exercises

7. Totaling points for the lesson and recording point totals on the Point Summary Chart

Fact Game Lessons

1. Fact Game

2. Awarding points for Fact Game

3. Totaling points for the lesson and recording point totals on the Point Summary Chart

Mastery Test Lessons

1. Mastery Test*

2. Teacher grading of Mastery Test

3. Awarding points for Mastery Test

4. Recording point totals on the Point Summary Chart

5. Remedies for Mastery Test

Comprehension C

Regular Lessons

1. Oral Exercises
2. Teacher-directed Workbook and Student Book Exercises
3. Independent Workbook and Student Book Exercises*
4. Workcheck
5. Awarding points for independent Workbook and Student Book exercises

Fact Game Lessons

1. Fact Game
2. Awarding points for Fact Game
3. Totaling points for the lesson and recording point totals on the Point Summary Chart

Mastery Test Lessons

1. Mastery Test*
2. Teacher grading of Mastery Test
3. Awarding points for Mastery Test
4. Recording point totals on the Point Summary Chart
5. Remedies for Mastery Test

Firm-Up Procedures

The following points summarize what the teacher can do about some unacceptable performance patterns:

- **Students continue to have trouble on a particular skill that has been taught.** The skill may not have been taught adequately. Reteach.

- **Students consistently miss items of a given type in the Workbook.** The item type should be retaught by reviewing previous exercises in the track. The teacher should not continue to permit students to make the same kinds of mistakes day after day.

- **A student (or a few students) in the group are responsible for most of the errors.** Either additional instruction should be provided or the student(s) should be moved to another group or program.

- **Mistakes seem to result from carelessness rather than from poor understanding.** The teacher can award bonus points (1 or 2) as incentives for students not to make mistakes on the type of item that is chronically missed.

- **The group consistently fails to meet criteria for earning points.** The lessons should be repeated from the point at which students began to fail to meet criteria.

PRACTICE LESSONS

This section presents sample lessons from the **Corrective Reading** Decoding and Comprehension programs. The lessons have been selected to show a range of skills taught. The contrast of early lessons with later lessons shows how the programs shift from highly structured teacher presentations to presentations that require more independent use of the skills that have been taught.

Practice teaching the sample lessons from the various programs. Repeat the formats until you can present them quite rapidly with a smooth flow from step to step. Use the appropriate signals. Move from exercise to exercise without pausing between them.

Assume that students will make mistakes at different points in the exercises. Use either the correction procedure specified in the exercise or apply the general correction procedure for correcting errors (see page 87).

Sound Pronunciation Guide

If you teach one of the Decoding programs, you should know the sound for each symbol. Practice the sounds in the Sound Pronunciation Guide on page 101. (Note that not all the sounds are taught in every program.) Make sure you can pronounce the sounds for the letters and letter combinations correctly.

Be particularly careful with the sounds that are identified as stop sounds. There should be no vowel sound audible when you say these sounds. Don't say "cuh" for **c.** The sound for **c** is unvoiced. Say the word **sack.** The last sound you say when you pronounce the word is the appropriate sound for **c** (as well as for **k** and **ck**). Similarly, the sound **b** is not pronounced "buh." If you pronounce it this way, students will have difficulty "blending" this sound with other sounds in a word. The pronunciation for **b** is the sound that occurs at the end of the word **hub.** (Whisper the rest of the word and say the **b** sound aloud.)

Although the sounds for many letter combinations are continuous, say these sounds fairly quickly. The sound for **al** is the same as if you say the word **all** aloud at a normal speaking rate, not "alllll." The sound for **ar** is the same as if you said the word **are** aloud, not "arrrrrr."

Sound Pronunciation Guide

Symbol	Sound	As in	Type
a	ăăă āāā	and ate	continuous continuous
b	b	hub	stop
c	k	sack	stop
d	d	rid	stop
e	ĕĕĕ ēēē	end me	continuous continuous
f	fff	fit	continuous
g	g	leg	stop
h	h	he	stop
i	ĭĭĭ īīī	if bite	continuous continuous
j	j	jump	stop
k	k	sack	stop
l	lll	lip	continuous
m	mmm	mat	continuous
n	nnn	not	continuous
o	ŏŏŏ ōōō	odd note	continuous continuous
p	p	sap	stop
qu	kwww	quit	continuous
r	rrr	run	continuous
s	sss	sat	continuous
t	t	got	stop
u	ŭŭŭ ūūū	up use	continuous continuous
v	vvv	van	continuous
w	www	will	continuous
x	kss	ox	continuous
y	yēēē	yell	continuous
z	zzz	zip	continuous
ai	āāā	paint	continuous
al	all	fall	continuous
ar	ar	art	continuous
au	aw	auto	continuous

Symbol	Sound	As in	Type
aw	aw	awful	continuous
ce	sss	ice	continuous
ci	sss	circle	continuous
ch	ch	chip	stop
cial	shull	special	continuous
ck	k	sack	stop
ea	ēēē ĕĕĕ	eat head	continuous continuous
ee	ēēē	feel	continuous
er	er	her	continuous
ge	j	age	stop
gi	j	giant	stop
igh	īīī	night	continuous
ing	ing	sing	continuous
ir	er	stir	continuous
kn	nnn	knot	continuous
oa	ōōō	boat	continuous
oi	oy	boil	continuous
ol	ol	cold	continuous
oo	oo	soon	continuous
or	or	fort	continuous
ou	ow	out	continuous
oul	o͝o	could	continuous
ow	oh	show	continuous
sh	shshsh	ship	continuous
tch	ch	catch	stop
th	thththth	them math	continuous continuous
tial	shull	partial	continuous
tion	shun	nation	continuous
ur	er	burn	continuous
ure	ure	pure	continuous
(w)a	aw	wash	continuous
wh	www	when	continuous

Decoding A—Lesson 6

Core skills are introduced in this early lesson. Students practice the following skills:

■ Pronouncing orally presented words so that all sounds are audible (Exercise 1)

■ Identifying the first and middle sounds in orally presented words (Exercises 1 and 5)

■ Identifying which of two orally presented words has a specified middle sound (Exercises 1 and 5)

■ Learning a new sound: **fff** (Exercise 2)

■ Identifying the eight sounds that have been introduced in earlier lessons (Exercise 2)

■ Orally saying the sounds in words (oral blending) without pausing between the sounds (Exercise 3)

■ Sounding out and reading word parts, two-sound words, and three-sound words (Exercise 4)

The Workbook Exercises provide practice on the following skills:

■ Writing the letters for sounds dictated by the teacher

■ Sounding out and reading a word part **(at)** and then writing beginning letters to complete words **(mat, sat)**

■ Sounding out and reading word parts, two-sound words, and three-sound words

■ Identifying the sounds of letters and then matching the letters

■ Matching and copying letters

■ Copying words from the list of words previously read

■ Scanning a display of letters for a specific letter that appears repeatedly in the display

Each student also reads aloud words from a Workbook Exercise as an Individual Reading Checkout.

WORD-ATTACK SKILLS

━━━━━━ **EXERCISE 1** ━━━━━━

PRONUNCIATIONS

> **Note:** Do not write the words on the board. This is an oral exercise.

Task A

1. Listen. His glasses had a gold **rim.** (Pause.) **Rim.** Say it. (Signal.) *Rim.*
2. Next word: **if.** Say it. (Signal.) *If.*
3. (Repeat step 2 for **im, reem, ram.**)
4. (Repeat all the words until firm.)

Task B It, fit, miff

1. I'll say words that have the sound ĭ́ĭ̆. What sound? (Signal.) *ĭ́ĭ̆.* Yes, ĭ́ĭ̆.
2. (Repeat step 1 until firm.)
3. Listen: **it, fit, miff.** Your turn: **it.** Say it. (Signal.) *It.* Yes, **it.**
4. Next word: **fit.** Say it. (Signal.) *Fit.* Yes, **fit.**
5. Next word: **miff.** Say it. (Signal.) *Miff.* Yes, **miff.**
6. (Repeat steps 3–5 until firm.)
7. What's the middle sound in the word **fffĭ́ĭ̆t?** (Signal.) *ĭ́ĭ̆.* Yes, ĭ́ĭ̆. (Repeat step 7 until firm.)

Task C Mat, meet

1. Listen: **mat.** Say it. (Signal.) *Mat.*
2. I'll say the first sound in the word **mmmăăăt.** (Pause.) **mmm.** What's the first sound? (Signal.) *mmm.* Yes, **mmm.**
3. Say the middle sound in the word **mmmăăăt.** Get ready. (Signal.) *ăăă.* Yes, **ăăă.**

> **To correct:**
> a. (Hold up one finger.) **mmm.**
> b. (Hold up two fingers.) **ăăă.**
> c. What's the middle sound in the word **mmmăăăt?** (Signal.) *ăăă.* Yes, **ăăă.**
> d. (Repeat step 3 until firm.)

4. Listen: **meet.** Say it. (Signal.) *Meet.*

5. I'll say the first sound in the word **mmmēēēt.** (Pause.) **mmm.** What's the first sound? (Signal.) *mmm.* Yes, **mmm.**
6. Say the middle sound in the word **mmmēēēt.** Get ready. (Signal.) *ēēē.* Yes, **ēēē.**
7. One of those words has the middle sound **ēēē.** I'll say both words again: **mat** (pause) **meet.** Which word has the middle sound **ēēē?** (Signal.) *Meet.* Yes, **meet.**

━━━━━━ **EXERCISE 2** ━━━━━━

SOUND INTRODUCTION

1. (Point to **f:**) This letter makes the sound **fff.** What sound? (Touch.) *fff.*
2. Your turn. Say each sound when I touch it.
3. (Point to **f:**) What sound? (Touch under **f:**) *fff.*
4. (Repeat step 3 for **ē, m, ĭ, r, d, ă, t, s.**)

> **To correct:**
> a. (Say the sound loudly as soon as you hear an error.)
> b. (Point to the sound:) This sound is _____. What sound? (Touch.)
> c. (Repeat the series of letters until all the students can correctly identify all the sounds in order.)

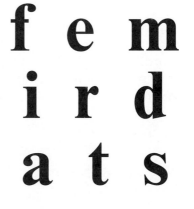

f e m
i r d
a t s

Individual test
I'll call on different students to say all the sounds. If everybody I call on can say all the sounds without making a mistake, we'll go on to the next exercise. (Call on two or three students. Touch under each sound. Each student says all the sounds.)

EXERCISE 3

NEW SAY THE SOUNDS

Note: Do not write the words on the board. This is an oral exercise.

1. Listen: **fffēēē.** (Hold up a finger for each sound.)
2. Say the sounds in (pause) **fffēēē.** Get ready. (Hold up a finger for each sound.) *fffēēē.* (Repeat until the students say the sounds without stopping.)
3. Say it fast. (Signal.) *Fee.*
4. What word? (Signal.) *Fee.* Yes, **fee.**
5. (Repeat steps 2–4 for **if, fish, sam, at, me, rim, she, we, ship, fat, miff.**)

EXERCISE 4

WORD READING

Task A Eed

1. You're going to read each word. First you sound it out; then you say it fast.
2. (Touch the ball of the arrow for the first word:) Sound it out. Get ready. (Touch under **ee, d:**) *ēēēd.* (Repeat until the students say the sounds without pausing.)

To correct sound errors:
   a. (Say the correct sound loudly as soon as you hear an error.)
   b. (Point to the sound:) What sound? (Touch.)
   c. (Repeat until firm.)
   d. (Repeat step 2.)

3. Again. Sound it out. Get ready. (Touch under **ee, d:**) *ēēēd.* (Repeat until firm.)
4. (Touch the ball of the arrow:) Say it fast. (Slash right, along the arrow:) *eed.* Yes, **eed.**

To correct say-it-fast errors:
   a. (Say the correct word:) **eed.**
   b. (Touch the ball of the arrow:) Say it fast. (Slash right:) *eed.*
   c. (Return to step 2.)

eed

Task B Seed

1. (Touch the ball of the arrow:) Sound it out. Get ready. (Touch under **s, ee, d:**) *sssēēēd.* (Repeat until the students say the sounds without pausing.)
2. Again. Sound it out. Get ready. (Touch under **s, ee, d:**) *sssēēēd.* (Repeat until firm.)
3. (Touch the ball of the arrow:) Say it fast. (Slash right:) *Seed.* Yes, **seed.**
4. (Repeat steps 1–3 for **seem, at, eet, it, if.**)

Task C Im [ĭm]

1. (Touch the ball of the arrow for the next word:) Sound it out. Get ready. (Touch under **i, m:**) *ĭĭĭmmm.* (Repeat until the students say the sounds without pausing.)
2. Again. Sound it out. Get ready. (Touch under **i, m:**) *ĭĭĭmmm.* (Repeat until firm.)
3. (Touch the ball of the arrow:) Say it fast. (Slash right:) *im.* Yes, **im.**
4. (Repeat steps 1–3 for **am, să, see, fă.**)

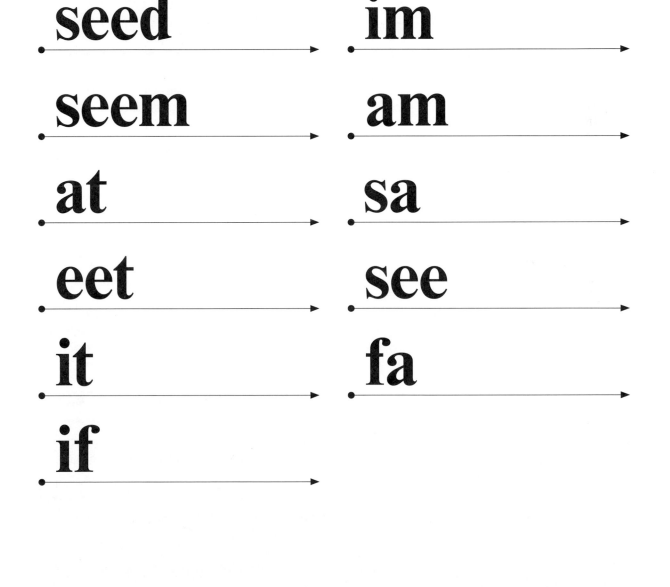

seed

seem

at

eet

it

if

im

am

sa

see

fa

Task D Fee

1. (Touch the ball of the arrow for the next word:) Sound it out. Get ready. (Touch under **f, ee**:) *fffēēē.* (Repeat until the students say the sounds without pausing.)
2. Again. Sound it out. Get ready. (Touch under **f, ee**:) *fffēēē.* (Repeat until firm.)
3. (Touch the ball of the arrow:) Say it fast. (Slash right:) *Fee.* Yes, **fee.**
4. (Repeat steps 1–3 for **fĭ, fit, fat, feet.**)

fee

fi

fit

fat

feet

PRONUNCIATIONS

> **Note:** Do not write the words on the board. This is an oral exercise.

1. Listen: **sam.** Say it. (Signal.) *Sam.*
2. I'll say the first sound in the word **sssăăămmm.** (Pause.) **sss.** What's the first sound? (Signal.) *sss.* Yes, **sss.**
3. Say the middle sound in the word **sssăăămmm.** Get ready. (Signal.) *ăăă.* Yes, *ăăă.*

> **To correct:**
> a. (Hold up one finger.) **sss.**
> b. (Hold up two fingers.) **ăăă.**
> c. What's the middle sound in **sssăăămmm?** (Signal.) *ăăă.* Yes, *ăăă.*
> d. (Repeat step 3 until firm.)

4. Listen: **seem.** Say it. (Signal.) *Seem.*
5. I'll say the first sound in the word **sssēēēmmm.** (Pause.) **sss.** What's the first sound? (Signal.) *sss.* Yes, **sss.**
6. Say the middle sound in the word **sssēēēmmm.** Get ready. (Signal.) *ēēē.* Yes, *ēēē.*
7. One of those words has the middle sound *ăăă.* I'll say both words again: **sam** (pause) **seem.** Which word has the middle sound *ăăă?* (Signal.) *Sam.* Yes, **sam.**

WORKBOOK EXERCISES

> **Note:** Pass out the Workbooks. Direct the students to open their Workbooks to Lesson 6.

(Award 6 points if the group worked well during the word attack. Then say:) Remember, you can earn up to 8 points for doing a good job on your Workbook lesson.

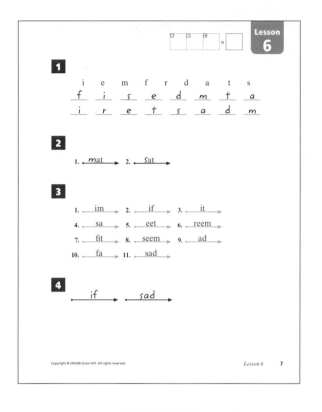

Lesson 6   **7**

EXERCISE 6
SOUND DICTATION

1. Everybody, touch part 1 in your Workbook. ✓
- These are the sounds you did before. Say all the sounds once more before you write the letters.
2. Touch the first sound. ✓
- What sound? (Clap.) *ĭĭĭ.* Yes, *ĭĭĭ.*
3. Touch the next sound. ✓
- What sound? (Clap.) *ēēē.* Yes, *ēēē.*
4. (Repeat step 3 for each remaining sound.)
5. Now you're going to write the letters for the sounds I say. First sound. (Pause.) **fff.** What sound? (Clap.) *fff.*
- Write it in the first blank. (Observe students and give feedback.)
6. Next sound. (Pause.) *ĭĭĭ.* What sound? (Clap.) *ĭĭĭ.*
- Write it in the next blank. (Observe students and give feedback.)

7. (Repeat step 6 for **sss, ēēē, d, mmm, t, ăăă, ĭĭĭ, rrr, ēēē, t, sss, ăăă, d, mmm.**)
8. (Check that students can write all the letters without errors.)

EXERCISE 7
NEW WORD COMPLETION

1. Everybody, touch word 1 in part 2. ✓
2. Sound it out. Get ready. (Clap for each sound as the students touch under **a, t:**) *ăăăt.* (Repeat until the students say the sounds without pausing.)
3. Say it fast. (Signal.) *At.* Yes, **at.**
4. You're going to change **at** to say (pause) **mat.** What will it say? (Signal.) *Mat.*
5. The first sound in **mat** is **mmm.** What sound? (Signal.) *mmm.*
- Write the letter for **mmm** before (pause) **at.** (Observe students and give feedback.)
6. You started with the word (pause) **at.** Now you have the word **mat.** What word did you start with? (Signal.) *At.* Yes, **at.**
- And what word do you have now? (Signal.) *Mat.* Yes, **mat.**
7. Touch the word on the next arrow. ✓
- That word says (pause) **at.**
8. You're going to change **at** to say (pause) **sat.** What will it say? (Signal.) *Sat.*
9. The first sound in **sat** is **sss.** So, what do you write before (pause) **at?** (Signal.) *sss.* Yes, **sss.**
- Do it. (Observe students and give feedback.)
10. You started with the word (pause) **at.** What word do you have now? (Signal.) *Sat.* Yes, **sat.**

EXERCISE 8
WORD READING: Workbook

1. Everybody, touch word 1 in part 3. ✓
2. Sound it out. Get ready. (Clap for each sound as the students touch under **i, m:**) *ĭĭĭmmm.* (Repeat until the students say the sounds without pausing.)

> **To correct sound errors:**
> a. (Say the correct sound loudly as soon as you hear an error.)
> b. Everybody, touch the sound _____. What sound? (Signal.)
> c. (Repeat step 2.)

3. Again. Sound it out. Get ready. (Clap for each sound:) *ĭĭĭmmm.*
• Say it fast. (Signal.) *im.* Yes, **im.**

> **To correct errors:**
> a. (Say the correct word:) **im.**
> b. What word? (Signal.) *im.*
> c. You're going to sound it out again. Get ready. (Clap for each sound:) *ĭĭĭmmm.*
> d. Say it fast. (Signal.) *im.*
> e. (Go to the next word.)

4. Touch word 2. ✓
5. Sound it out. Get ready. (Clap for each sound as the students touch under **i, f:**) *ĭĭĭfff.* (Repeat until the students say the sounds without pausing.)
6. Again. Sound it out. Get ready. (Clap for each sound:) *ĭĭĭfff.*
• Say it fast. (Signal.) *If.* Yes, **if.**
7. (Repeat steps 4–6 for words 3–11: **it, să, eet, reem, fit, seem, ad, fă, sad.**)

> **Individual test**
> (Call on each student to read two words in part 3.) Sound out each word and then say it fast. Remember to touch the sounds as you say them. Don't stop between the sounds.

EXERCISE 9
NEW WORD COPYING

1. Everybody, touch part 4. ✓
• You're going to write some of the words you just read.
2. The word you're going to write on the first arrow is **if.** What word? (Signal.) *If.*
3. Find **if** and write it just as it is written in part 3.
   (Observe students and give feedback.)
4. The word you're going to write on the next arrow is **sad.** What word? (Signal.) *Sad.*
5. Find **sad** and write it just as it is written in part 3.
   (Observe students and give feedback.)

EXERCISE 10
MATCHING SOUNDS

1. Everybody, touch part 5. ✓
• You're going to draw lines to match the letters. Get ready to say the sounds of the letters in the first column.
2. Touch the first letter. ✓
• What sound? (Clap.) *fff.*
3. Touch the next letter. ✓
• What sound? (Clap.) *ĭĭĭ.*
4. (Repeat step 3 for **s, r, t, ē.**)
5. Later, you'll draw lines to match the letters.

EXERCISE 11
MATCHING AND COPYING SOUNDS

1. Everybody, touch part 6. ✓
2. Later, you'll write letters in the blanks of this matching exercise.

EXERCISE 12
NEW CIRCLE GAME

1. Everybody, touch part 7. ✓
2. What will you circle in the first two lines? (Clap.) *fff.*
3. What will you circle in the next two lines? (Clap.) *t.*
4. What will you circle in the last two lines? (Clap.) *fff.*

5. Circle the sounds and finish the rest of your Workbook lesson.
(Observe students and give feedback.)

EXERCISE 13
WORKBOOK CHECK

> **Note:** See the Teacher's Guide for Workbook correction procedures.

1. (Check each student's Workbook.)
2. (Award points for Workbook performance.)
3. (Record the student's total points in Box B.)

0–1 error	8 points
2–3 errors	3 points
4 or more errors	0 points

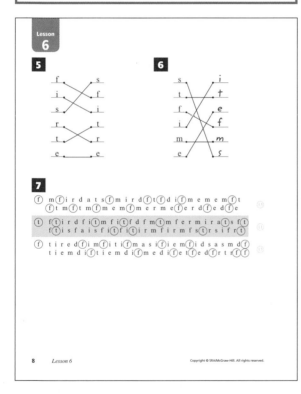

INDIVIDUAL READING CHECKOUTS

EXERCISE 14
WORD-READING CHECKOUT

- Study all the words in your Workbook. You'll each get a turn to sound out each word and say it fast. You can earn as many as 6 points for this reading.
- If you read all the words with no more than 1 error, you'll earn 6 points.
- If you make more than 1 error, you do not earn any points. But you'll have another chance to earn 6 points by studying the words some more and reading them again.
- (Check the students individually.)
- (Record either 6 or 0 points in Box C.)

Lesson point total

(Tell students to write the point total in the last box at the top of the Workbook page. Maximum for the lesson = 20 points.)

Point Summary Chart

(Tell students to write this point total in the box for Lesson 6 in the Point Summary Chart.)

END OF LESSON 6

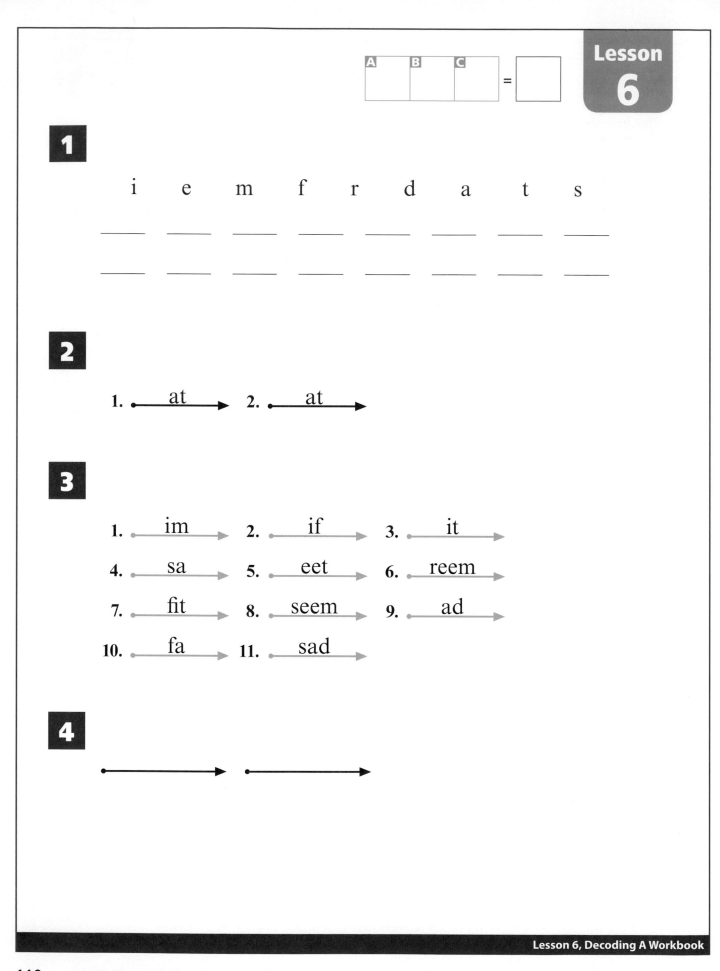

1

i e m f r d a t s

___ ___ ___ ___ ___ ___ ___ ___ ___

___ ___ ___ ___ ___ ___ ___ ___ ___

2

1. • —at→   2. • —at→

3

1. • —im→   2. • —if→   3. • —it→

4. • —sa→   5. • —eet→   6. • —reem→

7. • —fit→   8. • —seem→   9. • —ad→

10. • —fa→   11. • —sad→

4

• ————→   • ————→

5

f •	• s
i •	• f
s •	• i
r •	• t
t •	• r
e •	• e

6

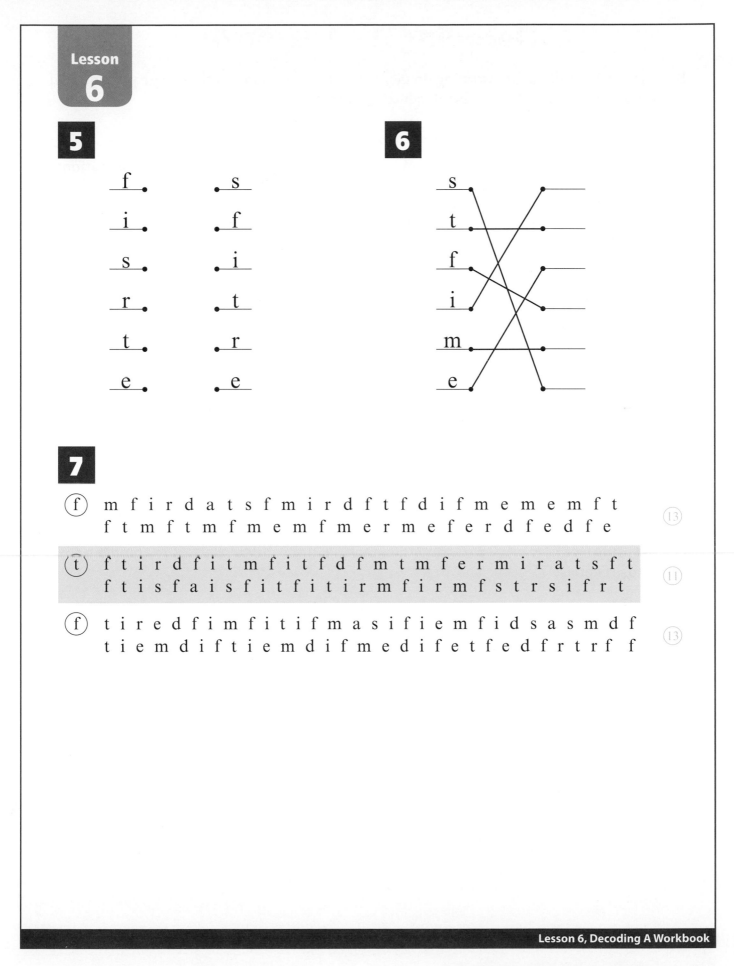

s

t

f

i

m

e

7

(f) m f i r d a t s f m i r d f t f d i f m e m e m f t
f t m f t m f m e m f m e r m e f e r d f e d f e   ⑬

(t) f t i r d f i t m f i t f d f m t m f e r m i r a t s f t
f t i s f a i s f i t f i t i r m f i r m f s t r s i f r t   ⑪

(f) t i r e d f i m f i t i f m a s i f i e m f i d s a s m d f
t i e m d i f t i e m d i f m e d i f e t f e d f r t r f f   ⑬

Decoding A—Lesson 61

By Lesson 61, students are working on more complicated examples than were presented in Lesson 6. They also review skills introduced in earlier lessons.

These skills are similar to those that were presented in Lesson 6:

■ Identifying the sounds of letters, now with thirty-four letters and letter combinations, twelve of which are reviewed in this lesson (Exercise 1)

■ Pronouncing whole words and individual sounds in words, now including the discrimination of similar vowel sounds, words with difficult consonant blends, and words with endings (Exercise 2)

■ Reading words, now without first sounding them out (Exercise 3)

■ Writing the letters and letter combinations for sounds dictated by the teacher (Exercise 4)

These skills were introduced between Lessons 7 and 60:

■ Reading words that are phonically irregular (Exercise 3)

■ Writing words the teacher dictates (Exercise 5)

■ Adding letters to word parts in the Workbook to complete words the teacher dictates (Exercise 6)

■ Matching words to word parts and then writing in the missing letters to complete the words (Exercise 7)

■ Reading sentences by identifying each word without sounding it out (Exercise 8)

■ Reading stories by identifying each word without sounding it out (Exercise 9)

■ Orally answering comprehension questions about the story after the teacher rereads it (Exercise 9)

■ Individually reading the story aloud within specified error and rate criteria (Exercise 11)

WORD-ATTACK SKILLS

PRONUNCIATIONS

EXERCISE 1

SOUND IDENTIFICATION

1. (Point to **o**:) One sound you learned for this letter is the letter name. Everybody, what's that sound? (Touch.) *ōōō.* Yes, **ōōō.**
   - What's the other sound? (Touch.) *ŏŏŏ.* Yes, **ŏŏŏ.**
2. (Point to **z**:) What sound? (Touch.) *zzz.* Yes, **zzz.**
3. (Repeat step 2 for **er, th, v, n, j, x, y, ch, ŭ, ĭ.**)

o z er
th v n
j x y
ch u i

Individual test
(Call on two or three students. Touch under each sound. Each student says all the sounds, including two sounds for **o**.)

> **Note:** Do not write the words on the board. This is an oral exercise.

Task A

1. Listen: **chances.** Say it. (Signal.) *Chances.*
2. Next word: **casts.** Say it. (Signal.) *Casts.*
3. (Repeat step 2 for **stopped, fished.**)
4. (Repeat the words until firm.)

Task B **Slum, slim, slam**

1. Listen: **slum, slim, slam.** Say those words. (Signal.) *Slum, slim, slam.* (Repeat until firm.)
2. One of those words has the middle sound *ĭĭĭ.* I'll say the words again: **slum, slim, slam.**
3. Which word has the middle sound *ĭĭĭ?* (Signal.) *Slim.* Yes, **slim.**
   - Which word has the middle sound *ăăă?* (Signal.) *Slam.* Yes, **slam.**
   - Which word has the middle sound *ŭŭŭ?* (Signal.) *Slum.* Yes, **slum.**
4. Listen: **slŭŭŭm.** What's the middle sound in the word **slum?** (Signal.) *ŭŭŭ.* Yes, **ŭŭŭ.**
   - Listen: **slĭĭĭm.** What's the middle sound in the word **slim?** (Signal.) *ĭĭĭ.* Yes, **ĭĭĭ.**
   - Listen: **slăăăm.** What's the middle sound in the word **slam?** (Signal.) *ăăă.* Yes, **ăăă.**
5. (Repeat step 4 until firm.) Good job.

Lesson 61

EXERCISE 3

WORD READING THE FAST WAY

1. You're going to read these words the fast way.
2. (For each word: Touch the ball of the arrow. Pause.) What word? (Slash right.)
3. (Repeat each list until firm.)

next

under

grabs

of

check

lost

frog

held

you

smelling

just

think

town

lift

damp

belt

after

what

hold

very

4. (For each word: Touch the ball of the arrow. Pause.) What word? (Slash right.)
5. (Repeat the column until firm.)

tramp

funny

blink

lunch

sandy

WORKBOOK EXERCISES

> **Note:** Pass out the Workbooks. Direct the students to open to Lesson 61.

(Award 6 points if the group worked well during the word attack. Remind the students of the points they can earn in their Workbook.)

━━━━━━━ **EXERCISE 4** ━━━━━━━

SOUND DICTATION

1. I'll say the sounds. You write the letters in part 1 in your Workbook.
2. First sound. Write a letter that says **www** in the first blank.
   (Observe students and give feedback.)
3. Next sound. Write two letters that go together and say **www.**
   (Observe students and give feedback.)
4. Next sound. (Pause.) **vvv.** What sound? (Signal.) *vvv.*
   • Write it.
   (Observe students and give feedback.)
5. (Repeat step 4 for **fff, ththth, shshsh, sss, ch, j, b, ooo, ăăă.**)
6. (Repeat sounds students had trouble with.)

━━━━━━━ **EXERCISE 5** ━━━━━━━

SPELLING FROM DICTATION

1. Touch part 2. ✓
   • You're going to write words that I dictate.
2. First word: **get.** What word? (Signal.) *Get.*
   • Listen again: **g . . . ĕĕĕ . . . t.** Write it in the first blank.
   (Observe students and give feedback.)
3. Next word: **cup.** What word? (Signal.) *Cup.*
   • Listen again: **c . . . ŭŭŭ . . . p.** Write it in the next blank.
   (Observe students and give feedback.)
4. (Repeat step 3 for **has, born, camp, held, fast.**)

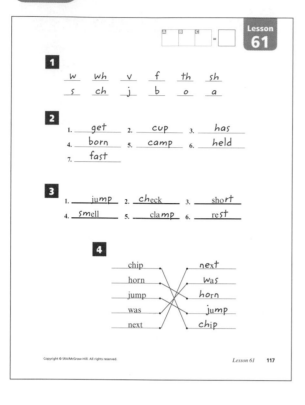

Lesson 61 **117**

EXERCISE 6

WORD COMPLETION

1. Touch the first word in part 3. ✓
- Fix it up to say (pause) **jump.** What word? (Signal.) *Jump.* Yes, **jump.**
- Fix it up.
  (Observe students and give feedback.)
2. Touch the second word. ✓
- Fix it up to say (pause) **check.** What word? (Signal.) *Check.* Yes, **check.**
- Fix it up.
  (Observe students and give feedback.)
3. (Repeat step 2 for **short, smell, clamp, rest.**)

EXERCISE 7

MATCHING COMPLETION

1. Everybody, touch part 4. ✓
2. First word. What word? (Signal.) *Chip.*
3. Next word. What word? (Signal.) *Horn.*
4. (Repeat step 3 for **jump, was, next.**)
5. Later, you'll complete the matching words.

EXERCISE 8

SENTENCE READING

1. Everybody, touch sentence 1 in part 5. ✓
2. You're going to read the fast way.
3. First word. ✓
- Get ready. (Clap for each word. Pause about 2 seconds between claps.) *Do . . . you . . . think . . . we . . . can . . . go . . . swimming . . . if . . . it . . . gets . . . sunny?*
4. (Repeat step 3 until the students until the students read the sentence without making a mistake.)
5. (Repeat steps 3 and 4 for each remaining sentence:
- **2. Check with the man at the desk.**
- **3. What did they do after dinner?**
- **4. Did she keep her hands on the wheel?**
- **5. You can not do math as well as I can.**)

Individual test
(Give each student a chance to read one of the sentences. Praise students who read accurately without long pauses.)

5

1. Do you think we can go swimming if it gets sunny?
2. Check with the man at the desk.
3. What did they do after dinner?
4. Did she keep her hands on the wheel?
5. You can not do math as well as I can.

6

An old truck did not stop well. Sandy got in the truck and went to the top of a steep hill. Then she went down the hill faster and faster. She said, "I do not think I can stop this truck." A pond was at the end of the street. Now Sandy is sitting in a wet truck with six frogs.

118 *Lesson 61*

Lesson 61, Decoding A TPB-2

===== **EXERCISE 9** =====

STORY READING

Task A

1. Everybody, touch part 6. ✓
• You're going to read this story.
2. First word. ✓
• Get ready. (Clap for each word. Pause about 2 seconds between claps.) *An . . . old . . . truck . . . did . . . not . . . stop . . . well.*
3. (Repeat step 2 until the students correctly identify all the words in the sentence in order.)
4. Next sentence. ✓
• Get ready. (Clap for each word.) *Sandy . . . got . . . in . . . the . . . truck . . . and . . . went . . . to . . . the . . . top . . . of . . . a . . . steep . . . hill.*
5. (Repeat step 4 until students correctly identify all words in the sentence in order.)
6. (Repeat steps 4 and 5 for each remaining sentence.)
7. (If students miss more than four words, repeat the story reading from the beginning.)

Task B

1. Now I'll read the story and ask questions. Follow along.
2. **An old truck did not stop well. Sandy got in the truck and went to the top of a steep hill.** (Call on a student.) Where did she go? (Idea: *To the top of a steep hill.*)
• (Call on a student.) What is wrong with the truck? (Idea: *It didn't stop well.*)
3. **Then she went down the hill faster and faster. She said, "I do not think I can stop this truck."** (Call on a student.) What did she say? *I do not think I can stop this truck.*
4. **A pond was at the end of the street. Now Sandy is sitting in a wet truck with six frogs.** (Call on a student.) Where did the truck go? (Idea: *Into the pond.*)
• (Call on a student.) What is Sandy doing now? (Idea: *Sitting in the truck in the pond with six frogs.*)

===== **EXERCISE 10** =====

WORKBOOK CHECK

1. (Check each student's Workbook.)
2. (Award points for Workbook performance.)
3. (Record the student's total points in Box B.)

0–3 errors	8 points
4–5 errors	4 points
6 errors	2 points
7 or more errors	0 points

INDIVIDUAL READING CHECKOUTS

===== **EXERCISE 11** =====

TIMED STORY-READING CHECKOUT

• Study the story. If you read the story with no more than 3 errors and read it in 1 minute or less, you'll earn 6 points.
• If you make more than 3 errors, or if you take more than 1 minute to read the story, you won't earn any points.
• If you don't earn points the first time you read the story, you can try again. If you succeed the second time you try, you'll earn 3 points.
• (Check the students individually.)
• (Record either 6, 3, or 0 points in Box C.)

Lesson point total

(Tell students to write the point total in the last box at the top of the Workbook page. Maximum = 20 points.)

Point Summary Chart

(Tell students to write this point total in the box for Lesson 61 in the Point Summary Chart.)

END OF LESSON 61

A	B	C		=	

1

_____ _____ _____ _____ _____ _____

_____ _____ _____ _____ _____ _____

2

1. _____ 2. _____ 3. _____

4. _____ 5. _____ 6. _____

7. _____

3

1. ___ju___ 2. ___eck___ 3. ___sho___

4. ___ell___ 5. ___cla___ 6. ___re___

4

chip •   • x

horn •   • a

jump •   • r

was •   • u

next •   • i

5

1. Do you think we can go swimming if it gets sunny?

2. Check with the man at the desk.

3. What did they do after dinner?

4. Did she keep her hands on the wheel?

5. You can not do math as well as I can.

6

An old truck did not stop well. Sandy got in the truck and went to the top of a steep hill. Then she went down the hill faster and faster. She said, "I do not think I can stop this truck." A pond was at the end of the street. Now Sandy is sitting in a wet truck with six frogs.

Decoding B1—Lesson 5

The first ten lessons of **Decoding B1** present the key skills taught in **Decoding A**. Students who have just completed **Decoding A** begin with Lesson 8 of B1 and do one lesson a day.

Many students who place in **Decoding B1** do not have the knowledge of sounds for letters and the sound-it-out word-reading strategies that students who complete **Decoding A** have. Therefore, students who place in **Decoding B1** start at Lesson 1 and work on those skills.

The Word-Attack Skills exercises for Lesson 5 provide practice for the following skills:

- Pronouncing words (Exercise 1) and individual sounds (first, next, last) in words (Exercises 2 and 7)

- Identifying the sounds of consonants (Exercises 3 and 4) and vowels (Exercise 4) taught in Lessons 1 through 4

- Reading words with the vowel sound **ŏ** (Exercise 5)

- Reading a list of words in which the teacher changes the medial vowel from **a** to **i** to **o** (Exercise 6)

- Saying the sounds in words with difficult consonant blends **(fr, sl, tr, pl)** and then reading the words (Exercise 8)

- Reading words with sound combinations **(or, ol, sh, th)** (Exercises 9 and 10)

Note: In Exercise 9, uppercase letters refer to letter names, and lowercase letters refer to sounds. The letters **O-L** (letter names) go together and make the sound **ol** (sound).

- Learning two irregular words, **to** and **do** (Exercise 12)

As part of the Word-Attack Skills exercises, students take turns reading rows of words (Exercise 11). The group earns points if they read at least 5 of the 6 rows with no errors.

Group Reading exercises in Lesson 5 include the following:

- Reading sentences with quotation marks, a board-work activity (Exercise 14)

- Reading sentences in the Student Book (Exercise 15)

Workbook Exercises in Lesson 5 provide practice on the following skills:

- Identifying errors the teacher makes reading aloud sentences in the Workbook (the "Fooler Game," to prepare students to catch other students' errors during Individual Reading Checkouts) (Exercise 13)

- Writing the letters and letter combinations for sounds the teacher dictates (Exercise 16)

- Matching words to word parts and then writing in the missing letters to complete the words (Exercise 17)

- Scanning a display of letters and words for a specific letter or word that appears repeatedly in the display (Exercise 18)

- Finding the first word in specific sentences in story 5 and writing those words (Exercise 19)

- Answering questions about pictures

Order of Exercises

Students who place in **Decoding B1** often are deficient in following directions. To address this problem, the early lessons in the program require students to go back and forth, in an unpredictable order, from the Student Book to the Workbook to words on the board. This practice is intentional so that students will follow frequent directions and attend to program components.

Starting in Lesson 11, the order of exercises in every lesson follows a standard pattern of four major parts.

1. Word-Attack Skills	Board work in some lessons
	Student Book in all lessons
2. Group Reading	Student Book
3. Individual Reading Checkouts	Student Book
4. Workbook Exercises	Workbook

WORD-ATTACK SKILLS

Today's Word-Attack Skills exercises are worth 8 points. Remember the rules. At the end of the Word-Attack Skills exercises, I'll call on individuals.

EXERCISE 1

PRONUNCIATION

1. I'll say some words that you're going to read. Say them just the way I say them.
2. First word: **slams.** Say it. (Signal.) *Slams.* Yes, **slams.**
3. Next word: **slips.** Say it. (Signal.) *Slips.* Yes, **slips.**
4. (Repeat step 3 for **list, send, green, drinks, grabs, shred, flags, waves.**)
5. (Repeat steps 2–4 until firm.)

EXERCISE 2

PRONUNCIATION

1. Listen: **rock.** Say it. (Signal.) *Rock.*
2. You're going to say the sounds in (pause) **rock.**
3. First sound. (Signal.) *rrr.*
   • Next sound. (Signal.) *ŏŏŏ.*
   • Last sound. (Signal.) *ck.*
4. (Repeat steps 1–3 until firm.)
5. New word: **pet.** Say it. (Signal.) *Pet.*
6. First sound. (Signal.) *p.*
   • Next sound. (Signal.) *ĕĕĕ.*
   • Last sound. (Signal.) *t.*
7. (Repeat steps 5 and 6 for **wish, with, shot.**)
8. New word: **sand.** Say it. (Signal.) *Sand.*
9. First sound. (Signal.) *sss.*
   • Next sound. (Signal.) *ăăă.*
   • Next sound. (Signal.) *nnn.*
   • Last sound. (Signal.) *d.*
10. (Repeat steps 8 and 9 until firm.)
11. New word: **he.** Say it. (Signal.) *He.*
12. First sound. (Signal.) *h.*
    • Last sound. (Signal.) *ēēē.*
13. (Repeat steps 11 and 12 until firm.)

Student Book

EXERCISE 3

LETTER SOUNDS REVIEW

1. Everybody, open your Student Book to Lesson 5. ✓

1

d l t s m f

n g h r w

2. Touch part 1. ✓
   • Say the sound for each letter.
3. First sound. (Signal.) *d.*
4. Next sound. (Signal.) *lll.*

> **To correct:**
> a. (Say the correct sound.)
> b. What sound? (Signal.)
> c. Go back to the first sound in the row.
> d. (Repeat steps 3 and 4.)

5. (Repeat step 4 for the remaining sounds.)
6. (Repeat steps 3–5 until firm.)

> **Individual test**
> (Call on individual students to say the sound for each letter in part 1.)

EXERCISE 4

VOWEL SOUNDS REVIEW

1. Touch part 2. ✓
   • You've learned the sounds for these vowels. Say the sound for each vowel letter.

2

o e a i u ee

Lesson 5

2. First sound. (Signal.) *ōōō.*
3. Next sound. (Signal.) *ēēē.*
4. (Repeat step 3 for *ăăă, ĭĭĭ, ŭŭŭ, ēēē.*)
5. (Repeat steps 2–4 until firm.)

> **Individual test**
> (Call on individual students to say the sound for each vowel in part 2.)

Board Work

EXERCISE 5
VOWEL SOUNDS

1. (Print on the board:)

> o

2. (Point to **o**:) One sound for this vowel is *ŏŏŏ.* What sound? (Signal.) *ŏŏŏ.*
3. (Print in two columns on the board:)

> on   shop
> not   rock
> rod   got

4. I'll say the sounds for each word. Then you'll tell me the word.
- (Point to **on**:) First word. (Touch under **o, n** as you say *ŏŏŏ nnn.*) What word? (Signal.) *On.*
5. (Point to **not**:) Next word. (Touch under **n, o, t** as you say *nnn ŏŏŏ t.*) What word? (Signal.) *Not.*
6. (Repeat step 5 for **rod, shop, rock, got.**)
7. This time you'll say the sounds with me. Then say the word.
- (Point to **on**:) Say the sounds. (Touch under **o** and **n** as you and the students say *ŏŏŏ nnn.*)
8. (Repeat step 7 until firm.)
9. What word? (Signal.) *On.*
10. (Point to **not**:) Say the sounds. (Touch under **n, o, t** as you and the students say *nnn ŏŏŏ t.*) What word? (Signal.) *Not.*
11. (Repeat step 10 with **rod, shop, rock, got.**)

12. This time I won't say the sounds. You'll read each word.
13. (Point to **on**:) What word? (Signal.) *On.*
14. (Repeat step 13 for **not, rod, shop, rock, got.**)

> **To correct:**
> a. The word is _____. What word? (Signal.)
> b. Say the sounds with me. (Touch under the sounds as you and the students say the sounds.)
> c. What word? (Signal.)
> d. (Repeat steps 12–14.)

EXERCISE 6
INTERNAL VOWEL CONVERSION

1. (Print in a column on board:)

> an
> tap
> hat
> lack
> pats

- You'll read each word. Then I'll change the vowel in each word.
2. (Point to the beginning of **an**. Pause.) What word? (Signal.) *An.*
3. (Repeat for **tap, hat, lack, pats.**)
4. (Replace **a** with **i** in each word:)

> in
> tip
> hit
> lick
> pits

5. (Point to the beginning of **in**. Pause.) What word? (Signal.) *In.*
• (Repeat for **tip, hit, lick, pits.**)
6. (Replace **i** with **o** in each word:)

on
top
hot
lock
pots

7. (Point to the **o** in **on**. Pause.) Remember, the **O** says ŏŏŏ.
• What word? (Signal.) *On.*
8. (Repeat step 7 for **top, hot, lock, pots.**)
9. (Repeat the column of words until firm.)

Individual test
(Repeat steps 1–8, calling on individual students to read all the words in the column.)

━━━━━ **EXERCISE 7** ━━━━━

PRONUNCIATION

1. Listen: **tree.** Say it. (Signal.) *Tree.*
2. You're going to say the sounds in (pause) **tree.**
3. First sound. (Signal.) *t.*
• Next sound. (Signal.) *rrr.*
• Last sound. (Signal.) *ēēē.*
4. (Repeat steps 1–3 until firm.)
5. New word: **plan.** Say it. (Signal.) *Plan.*
6. First sound. (Signal.) *p.*
• Next sound. (Signal.) *lll.*
• Next sound. (Signal.) *ăăă.*
• Last sound. (Signal.) *nnn.*
7. (Repeat steps 5 and 6 until firm.)
8. (Repeat steps 5–7 for: **sled [sss lll ĕĕĕ d], clip [c lll ĭĭĭ p], drag [d rrr ăăă g], best [b ĕĕĕ sss t.]**)

Individual test
(Call on individual students to say the sounds in one of these words: **green, clip, drag, tree, plan, fast.**)

━━━━━ **EXERCISE 8** ━━━━━

WORD READING

Task A

1. (Print in two columns on the board:)

free   track
drip   sleep
plan   stop

• For each word, you'll say the sounds with me. Then say the word.
2. (Point to **free:**) Say the sounds with me. (Touch under **f, r, ee** as you and the students say *fff rrr ēēē.* Repeat until firm.)
• What word? (Signal.) *Free.*

To correct:
a. The word is _____. What word? (Signal.)
b. Say the sounds with me. (Touch under the sounds as you and the students say the sounds.)
c. What word? (Signal.)
d. Go back to the first word in the row.

3. (Repeat step 2 for **drip, plan, track, sleep, stop.**)
4. This time you'll sound out the words without my help.
5. (Point to **free:**) Say the sounds. (Signal.) *fff rrr ēēē.* (Repeat until firm.)
• What word? (Signal.) *Free.*
6. (Repeat step 5 for **drip, plan, track, sleep, stop.**)

Task B

1. (Print in two columns on the board:)

milk	flag
win	seems
hand	truck

- For each word, you'll say the sounds with me. Then say the word.
2. (Point to **milk**:) Say the sounds with me. (Touch under **m, i, l, k** as you and the students say *mmm ĭĭĭ lll k.* Repeat until firm.)
- What word? *Milk.*
3. (Repeat step 2 for **win, hand, flag, seems, truck**.)
4. This time you'll sound out the words without my help.
5. (Point to **milk**:) Say the sounds. (Signal.) *mmm ĭĭĭ lll k.* (Repeat until firm.)
- What word? (Signal.) *Milk.*
6. (Repeat step 5 for **win, hand, flag, seems, truck**.)

Student Book

━━━━━━━━ **EXERCISE 9** ━━━━━━━━

SOUND COMBINATION: ol

1. Touch part 3 in your Student Book. ✓

3

ol	old told colt gold cold

2. The letters **O–L** go together and make the sound **ol**. What sound? (Signal.) *ol.*
3. You're going to read words that have the letters **O–L**.
4. Touch the first word. ✓
- What word? (Signal.) *Old.*
5. Touch the next word. ✓
- What word? (Signal.) *Told.*
6. (Repeat step 5 for each remaining word.)

Board Work

━━━━━━━━ **EXERCISE 10** ━━━━━━━━

NEW WORD READING WITH UNDERLINED PART

Task A

1. (Print in two columns on the board:)

<u>for</u>	<u>sh</u>ip
<u>fo</u>ld	tee<u>th</u>
wi<u>sh</u>	m<u>ore</u>
wi<u>th</u>	

- These words have underlined parts. You'll say the sound of each underlined part.
2. (Point to **<u>for</u>**:) What's the sound for the underlined part? (Signal.) *Or.*
3. (Repeat step 2 for **<u>fo</u>ld, wi<u>sh</u>, wi<u>th</u>, <u>sh</u>ip, tee<u>th</u>, m<u>ore</u>**.)
4. This time you'll read the words. Remember the sound the underlined part makes.
5. (Point to **<u>for</u>**:) What word? (Signal.) *For.*
6. (Repeat step 5 for **<u>fo</u>ld, wi<u>sh</u>, wi<u>th</u>, <u>sh</u>ip, tee<u>th</u>, m<u>ore</u>**.)

Task B

1. (Print in two columns on the board:)

<u>sh</u>op	<u>st</u>ore
cold	<u>th</u>at
<u>sh</u>eets	ra<u>sh</u>

- These words have underlined parts. You'll say the sound of each underlined part.
2. (Point to **<u>sh</u>op**:) What's the sound for the underlined part? (Signal.) *shshsh.*
3. (Repeat step 2 for **cold, <u>sh</u>eets, <u>st</u>ore, <u>th</u>at, ra<u>sh</u>**.)
4. This time you'll read the words. Remember the sound the underlined part makes.
5. (Point to **<u>sh</u>op**:) What word? (Signal.) *Shop.*
6. (Repeat step 5 for **cold, <u>sh</u>eets, <u>st</u>ore, <u>th</u>at, ra<u>sh</u>**.)

Student Book

━━━━━━━ **EXERCISE 11** ━━━━━━━

WORD-ATTACK SKILLS: Individual tests

1. Touch part 4 in your Student Book. ✓

4

(a) got wish cold free hand sheets

(b) shot track milk fold sleep truck

(c) seems win that told flag rock

(d) ship on plan move gold drip

(e) colt wish stop free store old

(f) teeth for drip old rash shop

2. These are words you've read. They are in a different order. I'll call on individuals to read each row. There are 6 rows. If we can read 5 rows without making a mistake—any 5 rows—everybody in the group will earn 8 points for the Word-Attack Skills exercise.

3. (Each student reads a row. Tally the rows read without error. If the group reads at least 5 rows without making errors, direct all students to record 8 points in Box A of their Point Chart.)

4. (If the group did not read at least 5 rows without errors, do not award any points for the Word-Attack Skills exercises.)

> **To correct:**
> a. The word is _____. Touch _____.
> • What word? (Signal.)
> b. Go back and read the whole row.

━━━━━━━ **EXERCISE 12** ━━━━━━━

NEW WORD READING

Task A **Irregular words**

1. Touch the first word in Part 5. ✓

5

to do

2. The vowels in these words don't make the sound you think they should make.

3. The first word is **to.** I'll spell the first word: **T–O.**
• What word did I spell? (Signal.) *To.* Yes, **to.**

4. The next word is **do.** I'll spell **do: D–O.** What word did I spell? (Signal.) *Do.* Yes, **do.**

5. Spell the first word. (Signal.) *T–O.*
• What word? (Signal.) *To.*

6. Spell the next word. (Signal.) *D–O.*
• What word? (Signal.) *Do.*

7. (Repeat steps 5 and 6 until firm.)

Workbook: Teacher Directed

━━━━━━━ **EXERCISE 13** ━━━━━━━

THE FOOLER

1. Open your Workbook to Lesson 5. ✓
• We're going to play the Fooler Game. Find Part 1.

2. I'll read each sentence. Follow along. I'll say some words wrong in some sentences, but not all of them. Pencils down. ✓

3. Sentence 1 (read slowly): **If** (pause and ✓) **he** (pause) **freeze** (pause) **to** (pause) **go** (pause) **for** (pause) **us?**
• Once more: **If** (pause) **he** (pause) **freeze** (pause) **to** (pause) **go** (pause) **for** (pause) **us?**

4. Circle any words I didn't read correctly. Pencils down when you're finished. ✓

5. I missed three words. Tell me the first word I missed. (Signal.) *Is.* Yes, **is.**
• Tell me another word I missed. (Signal.) *Free.* Yes, **free.**
• Tell me another word I missed. (Signal.) *With.* Yes, **with.**
• Everybody, you should have circled **is, free,** and **with.**
(Observe students and give feedback.)

1
1. (Is) he (free) to go (with) us?

6. (Call on a student to read sentence 1.) *Is he free to go with us?*

7. Pencils down. ✓

- Sentence 2: **If** (pause and ✓) **it** (pause) **is** (pause) **the** (pause) **last** (pause) **meet,** (pause) **we** (pause) **will** (pause) **go.**
- Once more: **If** (pause) **it** (pause) **is** (pause) **the** (pause) **last** (pause) **meet,** (pause) **we** (pause) **will** (pause) **go.**

8. Circle any words I did not read correctly. Pencils down when you're finished. ✓

9. I missed one word. Tell me the word I missed. (Signal.) *This.* Yes, **this.**

- Everybody, you should have circled **this.** (Observe students and give feedback.)

1   2. If ⬭this⬭ is the last meet, we will go.

- (Call on a student to read sentence 2.) *If this is the last meet, we will go.*

10. Pencils down. ✓

- Sentence 3: **Our** (pause and ✓) **junk** (pause) **could** (pause) **not** (pause) **fit** (pause) **in** (pause) **that** (pause) **trunk.**
- Once more: **Our** (pause) **junk** (pause) **could** (pause) **not** (pause) **fit** (pause) **in** (pause) **that** (pause) **trunk.**

11. Circle any words I did not read correctly. Pencils down when you're finished. ✓

12. I missed three words. Tell me the first word I missed. (Signal.) *The.* Yes, **thuh.**

- Tell me another word I missed. (Signal.) *Did.* Yes, **did.**
- Everybody, tell me the other word I missed. (Signal.) *Truck.* Yes, **truck.**

1   3. ⬭The⬭ junk ⬭did⬭ not fit in that ⬭truck⬭

- (Call on a student to read sentence 3.) *The junk did not fit in that truck.*

Board Work

━━━━━━━━━━ **EXERCISE 14** ━━━━━━━━━━

NEW **SENTENCE READING: Quotations**

1. (Print on the board:)

   He said, "Go to the shop."

2. Here's a sentence with quote marks. (Touch both quotation marks.) The words inside the quote marks tell what the person said.

3. (Underline the words between the quotation marks: **He said, "Go to the shop."**)

4. I'll read the sentence: **He said, "Go to the shop."**

5. Here's what he said. (Pause.) **Go to the shop.**

6. Say the whole sentence. (Call on a student.) *He said, "Go to the shop."*

- Now say the words he said. (Signal.) *Go to the shop.*

7. (Repeat step 6 until firm.)

GROUP READING

Student Book

━━━━━━━━━━ **EXERCISE 15** ━━━━━━━━━━

SENTENCE READING

1. Open your Student Book to Lesson 5, part 6.

2. Everybody, touch part 6. ✓

- I'll read the first four sentences slowly. Touch each word I read and try to remember it.
- Sentence 1: **We** (pause and ✓) **will** (pause) **go** (pause) **for** (pause) **more** (pause) **fish** (pause) **at** (pause) **the** (pause) **store.**
- Sentence 2: **Stick** (pause and ✓) **with** (pause) **me** (pause) **and** (pause) **we** (pause) **will** (pause) **have** (pause) **fun.**
- Sentence 3: **She** (pause and ✓) **sat** (pause) **with** (pause) **me** (pause) **at** (pause) **the** (pause) **track** (pause) **meet.**
- Sentence 4 **She** (pause and ✓) **had** (pause) **a** (pause) **fun** (pause) **trip.**

6

1. We will go for more fish at the store.
2. Stick with me and we will have fun.
3. She sat with me at the track meet.
4. She had a fun trip.
5. Is he free to go with us?
6. If this is the last meet, we will go.
7. The junk did not fit in that truck.

3. I'll call on individual students to read the sentences. Here are the rules that you are to follow:
    One: Point to each word that is read.
    Two: Read loudly when I call on you.
- If the group reads the sentences without making more than 3 errors, everybody in the group earns 6 points.
4. Read sentence 1. (Call on a student.) *We will go for more fish at the store.*
5. (Call on different students to read sentences 2–7. Praise students who read without making errors.)

To correct:
   a. The word is _____. Touch _____.
   • What word? (Signal.)
   b. Go back and read the whole sentence.

WORKBOOK EXERCISES

Workbook: Teacher Directed

=== **EXERCISE 16** ===
WRITING LETTERS FOR SOUNDS

1. Open your Workbook to Lesson 5. ✓
- Touch the first space in part 2. ✓
2. You're going to write the letter or letters for each sound I say.
3. The first sound is (pause) **or**. What sound? (Signal.) *or.*
- Write the letters for **or**. (Observe students and give feedback.)

4. Touch the next space. ✓
- The sound is (pause) **ol**. What sound? (Signal.) *ol.*
- Write the letters for **ol**. (Observe students and give feedback.)
5. Touch the next space. ✓
- The sound is (pause) ĭĭĭ. What sound? (Signal.) ĭĭĭ.
- Write the letter for ĭĭĭ. (Observe students and give feedback.)
6. (Repeat step 5 for **rrr, ŏŏŏ, d, j, ăăă, nnn, g.**)

Individual test
(Call on a student.) Read the letters that you wrote, starting with the first space.

=== **EXERCISE 17** ===
MATCHING COMPLETION

1. Find part 3. ✓
- You're going to read the words in the first column.
2. Touch the top word. ✓
- What word? (Signal.) *Track.*
3. Touch the next word. ✓
- What word? (Signal.) *Rash.*
4. (Repeat step 3 for **creek, sheets.**)
5. Later, you'll draw lines to the parts in the second column and complete the words in the second column.

=== **EXERCISE 18** ===
CIRCLE GAME

1. Find part 4. ✓
2. Read the part you'll circle in the first line. (Call on a student.) *ol.*
- How many are there? (Signal.) *5.*
3. Read the word you'll circle in the second line. (Call on another student.) *Do.*
- How many are there? (Signal.) *5.*
4. Read the word you'll circle in the third line. (Call on another student.) *Was.*
- How many are there? (Signal.) *4.*

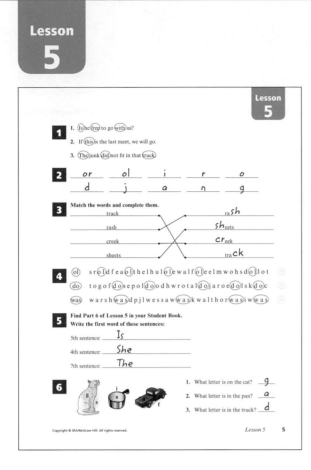

EXERCISE 19

NEW **SENTENCE IDENTIFICATION**

1. Find part 5. ✓
- I'll read the instructions: **Find part 6 of Lesson 5 in your Student Book.** ✓
- **Write the first word of these sentences.**

2. You're going to write the first word of the fifth sentence. Touch the fifth sentence in part 6 of your Student Book. ✓
3. What's the first word of the fifth sentence? (Call on a student.) *Is.*
4. Everybody, write the word **is** in your Workbook in the blank for the fifth sentence.
   (Observe students and give feedback.)
5. Now you are going to write the first word of another sentence. Which sentence? (Call on a student.) *The fourth sentence.*
6. Everybody, touch the fourth sentence in part 6 of your Student Book. ✓
7. What's the first word of the fourth sentence? (Call on a student.) *She.*
8. Write the word **she** in your Workbook in the blank for the fourth sentence.
   (Observe students and give feedback.)
9. Now you're going to write the first word of another sentence. Which sentence? (Call on a student.) *The seventh sentence.*
10. Everybody, touch the seventh sentence in part 6 of your Student Book. ✓
11. What's the first word of the seventh sentence? (Call on a student.) *The.*
12. Everybody, write the word **the** in your Workbook in the blank for the seventh sentence.
   (Observe students and give feedback.)

NEW **Independent Student Work**

1. Complete your Workbook lesson. You'll see a new kind of activity in part 6. You'll look at the picture and answer the questions.
2. Remember, if you make no more than 4 errors, you earn 6 points.
3. (After checking the Workbooks, direct students who made no more than 4 errors to record 6 points in Box C of their Point Chart.)

Point schedule for Lesson 5

Box	Lesson part	Points
A	Word Attack	0 or 8
B	Sentence reading	0 or 6
C	Workbook	0 or 6
Bonus	(Teacher option)	—

NEW **Five-lesson point summary**

- (For **letter grades** based on points for Lessons **1** through **5,** tell students to compute the total for the blue boxes [C, D, and Bonus] and write the number in the Total box at the end of each row in their Point Chart. Students then add the totals and write the sum in the green box.)
- (For **rewards** based on points, tell students to compute the total for all boxes [A, B, C, D, and Bonus] and write the number in the Total box at the end of each row. Students then add the totals and write the sum in the green box.)

END OF LESSON 5

1

d l t s m f

n g h r w

2

o e a i u ee

3

| ol | old told colt gold cold

4

(a) got wish cold free hand sheets

(b) shot track milk fold sleep truck

(c) seems win that told flag rock

(d) ship on plan move gold drip

(e) colt wish stop free store old

(f) teeth for drip old rash shop

5

to do

6

1. We will go for more fish at the store.
2. Stick with me and we will have fun.
3. She sat with me at the track meet.
4. She had a fun trip.
5. Is he free to go with us?
6. If this is the last meet, we will go.
7. The junk did not fit in that truck.

Lesson 5   **5**

1

1. Is he free to go with us?

2. If this is the last meet, we will go.

3. The junk did not fit in that truck.

2

_____ _____ _____ _____ _____

_____ _____ _____ _____ _____

3 **Match the words and complete them.**

track	ra
rash	eets
creek	eek
sheets	tra

4

(ol) s r o l d f e a o l t h e l h u l o l e w a l f o l e e l m w o h s d o l l o t ⑤

(do) t o g o f d o s e p o l d o o d h w r o t a l d o j a r o e d o l s k d o c ⑤

(was) w a r s h w a s d p j l w e s s a w w a s k w a l t h o r w a s i w w a s ④

5 **Find Part 6 of Lesson 5 in your Student Book.**
Write the first word of these sentences:

5th sentence: _____

4th sentence: _____

7th sentence: _____

6

g
s
i
a
d
f

1. What letter is on the cat? _____

2. What letter is in the pan? _____

3. What letter is in the truck? _____

Decoding B1—Lesson 26

By this lesson, the Word-Attack Skills and Group Reading exercises in each lesson have provided practice for the following skills:

- Identifying the short sounds for the vowels **a, e, i, o, u**

- Identifying two sounds for the vowels **o** and **e**

- Identifying the sounds of most common consonants

- Identifying the sounds of various letter combinations, including **ee, th, sh, or, ol, ing, ch, wh, er, oo, ea, oa**

- Identifying the sounds of letters and letter combinations in words and reading words containing them

- Reading common, phonically irregular words, such as **said, was, give, to, what**

- Reading silent-**E** words, such as **hope, time, ride**

- Reading words with endings, such as **hopped, fatter, mopping, poles, liking, broken, handed**

- Reading aloud stories that provide cumulative practice on all the word types introduced, including discriminating between minimally different words **(camp, clamp, champ, tamp)**

- Reading story segments aloud within a specified error limit for each segment

- Orally answering comprehension questions about the stories

The Workbook Exercises have provided practice on the following skills:

- Writing the letters and letter combinations for sounds the teacher dictates

- Matching words to word parts and then writing in the missing letters to complete the words

- Reading words with endings and doubled consonants **(hopped, fitting)** and writing the words without endings **(hop, fit)**

- Reading silent-**E** words with endings **(rider, saving)** and writing the words without endings **(ride, save)**

- Writing answers to questions about pictures related to the content of a story

- Writing answers to comprehension questions about a story

- Copying sentences based on the story

Daily oral reading checkouts have provided practice on reading aloud passages within specified error and rate criteria. Minimum reading rates began at 60 words per minute in Lesson 16 and increased to 70 words per minute by Lesson 26.

The Word-Attack Skills exercises for Lesson 26 provide practice on the following skills:

- Reading a short word list on the board that focuses on minimal changes in the words presented (Exercise 1)

- Identifying the sounds of letters or letter combinations in words and then reading the words (Exercise 2)

- Reading silent-**E** words (Exercise 3)

- Reading and spelling aloud new, phonically irregular words and then reading a mixed list of phonically regular and irregular words (Exercise 4)

The Group Reading activity provides practice on reading in context silent-**E** words, words with endings, words containing letter combinations, and phonically irregular words. Immediately after reading each part of the story within a specified error criterion, the students orally answer questions the teacher asks about that part.

Following the reading of the story, students work in pairs and orally read a passage from Lesson 26 within a specified error limit (no more than 2 errors) and a passage from Lesson 25 within specified error and rate criteria (no more than 3 errors, 70 words per minute). Students record points for Lesson 26 Individual Reading Checkouts in Box C-1 (first checkout points) and Box C-2 (second checkout points) of their Point Chart for Lesson 26. (See the sample Point Charts on pages 79 and 80.) Students also keep a record of their performance on the Individual Reading Checkout (second checkout, timed reading) on the Individual Reading Progress Chart at the back of the Workbook. (See the sample chart on page 143.)

The Workbook Exercises provide practice on the following skills:

- Writing the letters and letter combinations for sounds the teacher dictates (part 1)

- Reading words with endings and doubled consonants and writing the correctly spelled words without endings (part 2)

- Writing answers to comprehension questions about a story (part 3)

- Matching words to word parts and then writing in the missing letters to complete the words (part 4)

- Copying a sentence based on the story (part 5)

Correction Procedures

Board Work

> **To correct all word-identification errors during Board Work exercises, follow these steps:**
> a. The word is _____.
> b. What word? (Signal.)
> c. Spell _____. (Signal for each letter.)
> • What word? (Signal.)
> d. (Go back to the first word and present the words in order.)

Word-Attack Skills in the Student Book

> **To correct word-identification errors:**
> a. The word is _____.
> b. What word? (Signal.)
> c. Spell _____. (Signal for each letter.)
> • What word? (Signal.)
> d. Go back to the first word in the (row/column). ✓
> • What word? (Signal.)

Group Reading

> **To correct word-reading errors:**
> a. (As soon as the student misidentifies a word, say:) The word is _____.
> • Touch _____. ✓
> • What word? (Signal.)
> b. Go back and read the sentence again.

Lesson 26

WORD-ATTACK SKILLS

Board Work

—————— **EXERCISE 1** ——————

INTERNAL VOWEL CONVERSIONS: ea, oa

1. (Print in a column on the board:)

> rear
> leaf
> mean
> ears

2. (Point to **rear.** Pause.) What word?
   (Signal.) *Rear.*
   • (Repeat for **leaf, mean, ears.**)
3. (Replace **ea** with **oa** in each word:)

> roar
> loaf
> moan
> oars

4. (Point to **roar.** Pause.) What word?
   (Signal.) *Roar.*
   • (Repeat for **loaf, moan, oars.**)
5. (Change the list to:)

> rear
> loaf
> mean
> ears

6. (Point to **rear.** Pause.) What word?
   (Signal.) *Rear.*
   • (Repeat for **loaf, mean, ears.**)
7. (Change to the original list:)

> rear
> leaf
> mean
> ears

• (Repeat steps 2–6 until firm.)

> **Individual test**
> (Repeat steps 1–6, calling on individual students to read all the words in the column.)

Student Book

—————— **EXERCISE 2** ——————

WORD READING WITH UNDERLINED PART

1. Open your Student Book to Lesson 26. ✓

1

> ranch faster chopped
> goats checked horses
> bent slap leave heels
> loafers swam swim jab

• Touch part 1. ✓
• You're going to say the sound for the underlined part and then read the word.
2. First word. ✓
• What sound? (Signal.) *ch.*
• What word? (Signal.) *Ranch.*
3. Next word. ✓
• What sound? (Signal.) *er.*
• What word? (Signal.) *Faster.*
4. (Repeat step 3 for each remaining word.)
5. (Repeat steps 2–4 until firm.)

—————— **EXERCISE 3** ——————

WORD READING

1. Touch the first word in part 2. ✓

2

> rode named rider safe
> makes side tame time

2. What word? (Signal.) *Rode.*
3. Next word. ✓
• What word? (Signal.) *Named.*
4. (Repeat step 3 for each remaining word.)

EXERCISE 4

WORD READING

Task A Irregular words

1. Touch the first word in part 3. ✓

3

Emma anyone nobody good
because let's boss didn't
ready their Flop woman
women milked herself station
question biggest stayed Branch

2. That word is **Emma.** What word? (Signal.) *Emma.*
- Spell **Emma.** (Signal for each letter.) *E–M–M–A.*
- What word? (Signal.) *Emma.*
3. The next word is **anyone.** What word? (Signal.) *Anyone.*
- Spell **anyone.** (Signal for each letter.) *A–N–Y–O–N–E.*
- What word? (Signal.) *Anyone.*
4. The next word is **nobody.** What word? (Signal.) *Nobody.*
- Spell **nobody.** (Signal for each letter.) *N–O–B–O–D–Y.*
- What word? (Signal.) *Nobody.*
5. The next word is **good.** What word? (Signal.) *Good.*
- Spell **good.** (Signal for each letter.) *G–O–O–D.*
- What word? (Signal.) *Good.*

Task B

1. Go back to the first word. ✓
- What word? (Signal.) *Emma.*
2. Next word. ✓
- What word? (Signal.) *Anyone.*
3. (Repeat step 2 for each remaining word.)

EXERCISE 5

WORD-ATTACK SKILLS: Individual tests

1. (Call on individual students. Each student reads a row. Tally the rows read without error. If the group reads at least 9 rows without making errors, direct all students to record 4 points in Box A of their Point Chart. Criterion is 80 percent of rows read without error.)
2. (If the group did not read at least 9 rows without errors, do not award any points for the Word-Attack Skills exercises.)

GROUP READING

EXERCISE 6

STORY READING

1. Everybody, touch part 4. ✓
2. After you read each part without making more than 3 errors, I'll ask questions about that part.

4

The Rancher

3. (Call on a student to read the title.) *The Rancher.*
- What do you think this story is about? (Accept reasonable responses.)
4. (Use the following procedures for each part of the story.)
a. (Call on individual students. Each is to read one or two sentences. Praise students who read without making errors.)
b. (At the end of the part, tell the students the number of errors the group made and whether the group earned points for that part.)
c. (If the group made more than 3 errors, direct the group to reread the part.)
d. (After the group reads a part with no more than 3 errors, call on individual students to answer the comprehension questions for that part.)

There was a big ranch in the West. The rancher who ran this ranch was named Emma Branch. She rode a horse well. She chopped fast, and she swam faster. The men and women who worked for Emma Branch liked her. They said, "She is the best in the West." On her ranch she had sheep, and she had cows. There were goats and horses. There was a lot of grass.

The rancher had a lot of women and men working for her. They worked with the sheep and the goats, and they milked the cows. Each worker had a horse. But the rancher's horse was the biggest and the best. It was a big, black horse named Flop.

[1]

First-part questions:

a. What was the name of the rancher? *Emma Branch.*
b. Name some things she did well. (Ideas: *Rode a horse well, chopped fast, swam faster.*)
c. What kind of animals did she have on her ranch? (Idea: *Sheep, cows, goats, horses.*)
d. Who had the biggest horse? (Ideas: *The rancher; Emma Branch.*)
e. What was its name? *Flop.*

Flop got its name because it reared up. When Flop reared up, any rider on it fell down and went "flop" in the grass. But Flop did not rear up when the rancher rode it. Emma Branch bent near Flop's ear and said, "Let's go, Flop." And they went. She did not have to slap the horse. She didn't have to jab her heels and yell at Flop. She just said, "Let's go," and they went like a shot.

Every day, she checked up on the workers to see what they were doing. She checked to see that they were working well and that they were not loafing.

[1]

Second-part questions:

a. Why did Flop have the name Flop? (Idea: *When anyone tried to ride Flop, Flop reared up and the rider went "flop" in the grass.*)
b. Did Flop give Emma a hard time? *No.*
c. What did Emma do every day? (Idea: *Checked on the workers.*)

If a worker was loafing, Emma told the worker, "I will say this for the last time: 'Do not loaf on this ranch any more.' " If a worker was loafing the next time she checked, she said, "Go from my ranch. We do not need loafers here."

The women and men who worked on the ranch said, "When you hear Flop running, you had better be working. If you are not working, you had better get ready to leave this ranch."

But the workers that stayed at the ranch liked to work for Emma Branch. They said, "We like to have Emma on our side. We can see how mean Flop is, and he is very tame when Emma rides him. So it's good to have Emma on your side."

[2]

Third-part questions:

a. What would Emma do if she found a worker loafing for the first time? (Idea: *Tell the worker not to loaf on the ranch anymore.*)
b. What would she do the next time? (Idea: *Tell the worker to leave the ranch.*)
c. Why did the workers think it was good to have Emma on their side? (Accept reasonable responses.)

5. (After the group has completed reading the story and answering the comprehension questions, tell the students the total number of points to record in Box B of their Point Chart. Maximum = 4 points.)

FLUENCY ASSESSMENT

―――――― **EXERCISE 7** ――――――

NEW) READING CHECKOUTS

> **Note:** The rate criterion for Lessons 26–30 is 70 words per minute.

1. (For this part of the lesson, assigned pairs of students work together during the checkouts.)
2. (Each student does two checkouts.)
- (First checkout: Students can earn 3 points by making no more than 2 errors on the first part of story 26. Students record points in Box C-1 of their Point Chart.)
- (Second checkout: 1-minute timed reading. Students can earn 3 points by reading at least **70 words** and making no more than 3 errors on the first part of story 25. Students record points in Box C-2 of their Point Chart.)
3. (During each checkout, observe at least two pairs of students. Make notes on mistakes. Give checkers feedback.)
4. (Direct all students to plot their reading rate—the number of words they read in 1 minute—on the Individual Reading Progress Chart at the end of their Workbook.)
- (Next, direct students to circle the number of errors they made during the timed reading.)
5. (Record on the Fluency Assessment Summary form the timed reading checkout performance for each student you observed.)

WORKBOOK EXERCISES

Workbook: Teacher Directed

―――――― **EXERCISE 8** ――――――
WRITING LETTERS FOR SOUNDS

1. Open your Workbook to Lesson 26. ✓
- Find part 1. ✓
- You're going to write the letter or letters for each sound that I say.
2. First sound: **er.** What sound? (Signal.) *er.*
- Write it.
3. Next sound: **or.** What sound? (Signal.) *or.*
- Write it.
4. (Repeat step 3 for ĭĭĭ, **sss, fff, b,** ăăă, ĕĕĕ, ŏŏŏ, **p.**)

> **Individual test**
> (Call on a student.) Read the letters you wrote, starting with the first blank.

Lesson 26

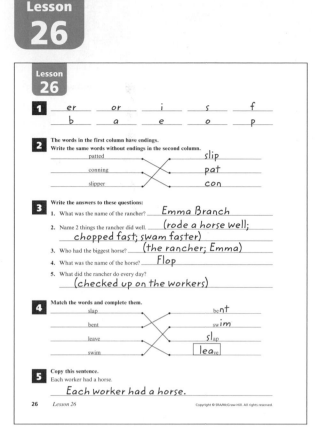

Independent Student Work

1. Complete all the other parts of your Workbook lesson. If you make no more than 4 errors, you earn 6 points.
2. (After checking the Workbooks, direct students who made no more than 4 errors to record 6 points in Box D of their Point Chart.)

Point schedule for Lesson 26

Box	Lesson part	Points
A	Word Attack	0 or 4
B	Group Reading	0 to 4
C-1	1st Reading Checkout (not timed)	0 or 3
C-2	2nd Reading Checkout (timed)	0 or 3
D	Workbook	0 or 6
Bonus	(Teacher option)	—

END OF LESSON 26

EXERCISE 9

WRITING WORDS WITHOUT ENDINGS

1. Find part 2. ✓
• The words in the first column have endings.
2. First word. ✓
• What word? (Signal.) *Patted.*
3. Next word. ✓
• What word? (Signal.) *Conning.*
4. (Repeat step 3 for **slipper.**)
5. Later, you're going to write the same words without endings in the second column.

1

ra<u>n</u>ch fas<u>ter</u> <u>ch</u>opped

<u>g</u>o<u>a</u>ts <u>ch</u>e<u>ck</u>ed h<u>or</u>ses

<u>b</u>ent <u>sl</u>ap <u>l</u>e<u>a</u>ve heels

<u>l</u>o<u>a</u>fers <u>sw</u>am <u>sw</u>i<u>m</u> <u>j</u>ab

2

rode named rider safe

makes side tame time

3

<u>Emma</u> <u>anyone</u> <u>nobody</u> <u>good</u>

because let's boss didn't

ready their Flop woman

women milked herself station

question biggest stayed Branch

4

The Rancher

There was a big ranch in the West. The rancher who ran this   13
ranch was named Emma Branch. She rode a horse well. She   24
chopped fast, and she swam faster. The men and women who   35
worked for Emma Branch liked her. They said, "She is the best   47
in the West." On her ranch she had sheep, and she had cows.   60
There were goats and horses. There was a lot <u>of</u> grass.   71

The rancher had a lot of women and men working for her.   83
They worked with the sheep and the goats, and they milked the   95

Lesson 26   **55**

cows. Each worker had a horse. But the rancher's horse was the 107
biggest and the best. It was a big, black horse named Flop. 119

[1]

Flop got its name because it reared up. When Flop reared 130
up, any rider on it fell down and went "flop" in the grass. But 144
Flop did not rear up when the rancher rode it. Emma Branch 156
bent near Flop's ear and said, "Let's go, Flop." And they went. 168
She did not have to slap the horse. She didn't have to jab her 182
heels and yell at Flop. She just said, "Let's go," and they went 195
like a shot. 198

Every day, she checked up on the workers to see what they 210
were doing. She checked to see that they were working well and 222
that they were not loafing. 227

[1]

If a worker was loafing, Emma told the worker, "I will say 239
this for the last time: 'Do not loaf on this ranch any more.' " If 253
a worker was loafing the next time she checked, she said, "Go 265
from my ranch. We do not need loafers here." 274

The women and men who worked on the ranch said, "When 285
you hear Flop running, you had better be working. If you are 297
not working, you had better get ready to leave this ranch." 308

But the workers that stayed at the ranch liked to work for 320
Emma Branch. They said, "We like to have Emma on our side. 332
We can see how mean Flop is, and he is very tame when Emma 346
rides him. So it's good to have Emma on your side." 357

[2]

1 _____ _____ _____ _____ _____

_____ _____ _____ _____ _____

2 **The words in the first column have endings.**
Write the same words without endings in the second column.

_____ patted   _____

_____ conning   _____

_____ slipper   _____

3 **Write the answers to these questions:**

1. What was the name of the rancher? _____

2. Name 2 things the rancher did well. _____

   _____

3. Who had the biggest horse? _____

4. What was the name of the horse? _____

5. What did the rancher do every day?

   _____

4 **Match the words and complete them.**

_____ slap   •   •   be _____

_____ bent   •   •   sw _____

_____ leave   •   •   ap _____

_____ swim   •   •   ve _____

5 **Copy this sentence.**
Each worker had a horse.

_____

Individual Reading Progress Chart
Decoding B1: LESSONS 16–35

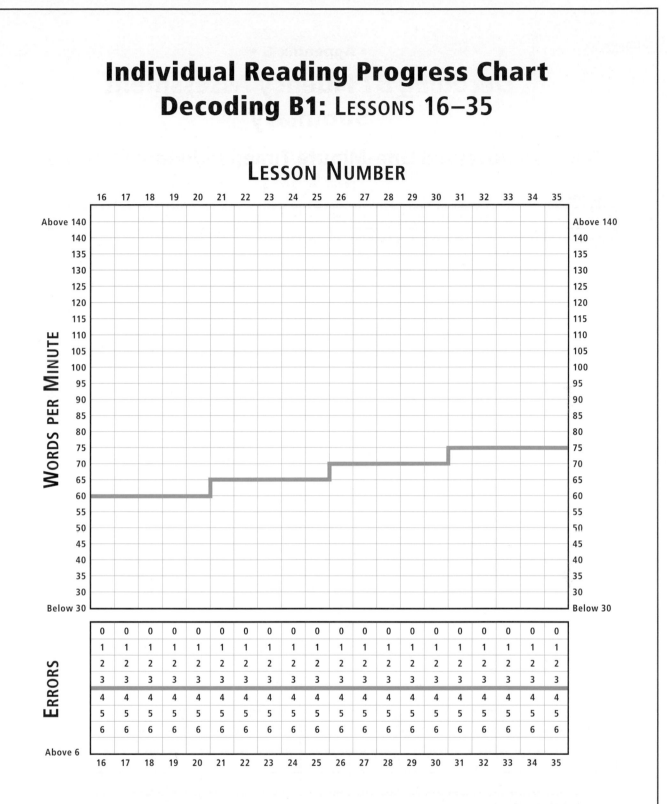

LESSON NUMBER

| | 16 | 17 | 18 | 19 | 20 | 21 | 22 | 23 | 24 | 25 | 26 | 27 | 28 | 29 | 30 | 31 | 32 | 33 | 34 | 35 |

WORDS PER MINUTE

Above 140, 140, 135, 130, 125, 120, 115, 110, 105, 100, 95, 90, 85, 80, 75, 70, 65, 60, 55, 50, 45, 40, 35, 30, Below 30

ERRORS

0	0	0	0	0	0	0	0	0	0	0	0	0	0	0	0	0	0	0	0
1	1	1	1	1	1	1	1	1	1	1	1	1	1	1	1	1	1	1	1
2	2	2	2	2	2	2	2	2	2	2	2	2	2	2	2	2	2	2	2
3	3	3	3	3	3	3	3	3	3	3	3	3	3	3	3	3	3	3	3
4	4	4	4	4	4	4	4	4	4	4	4	4	4	4	4	4	4	4	4
5	5	5	5	5	5	5	5	5	5	5	5	5	5	5	5	5	5	5	5
6	6	6	6	6	6	6	6	6	6	6	6	6	6	6	6	6	6	6	6

Above 6

| 16 | 17 | 18 | 19 | 20 | 21 | 22 | 23 | 24 | 25 | 26 | 27 | 28 | 29 | 30 | 31 | 32 | 33 | 34 | 35 |

• Appendix G •

Decoding B1 Fluency Assessment Summary

Teacher-Observed One-Minute Timed Individual Checkouts

Teacher:

Student name:	*Lesson range:*	16–20		21–25		26–30		31–35	
	Criteria:	words	errors	words	errors	words	errors	words	errors
		60	3	65	3	70	3	75	3
1.									
2.									
3.									
4.									
5.									
6.									
7.									
8.									
9.									
10.									
11.									
12.									
13.									
14.									
15.									
16.									
17.									
18.									
19.									
20.									
21.									
22.									
23.									
24.									
25.									
Total not at criteria:									
Percent not at criteria:									

Decoding B2—Lesson 32

The Word-Attack Skills exercises for this lesson provide practice on the following skills:

■ Reading a short word list on the board that focuses on changes in the endings of the words presented (Exercise 1)

■ Reading pairs of words that have minimal differences (Exercise 2)

■ Identifying the sounds of letters or letter combinations in words and then reading the words (Exercise 3)

■ Reading and orally spelling a new, phonically irregular word and then reading a mixed list of phonically regular and irregular words (Exercise 4)

The story contains a number of words with letter combinations (including **oi,** which is relatively new), words with endings, and compound words. Compared to the story from **Decoding B1** Lesson 26, this story is longer, contains more conventional syntax, and has a more detailed plot. Before they read the story, students answer questions that involve recalling details and summarizing events in the preceding story.

Following the reading of the story, students work in pairs and read aloud a passage from Lesson 32 within a specified error limit (no more than 2 errors) and a passage from Lesson 31 within specified error and rate criteria (no more than 3 errors, 105 words per minute).

The Workbook Exercises provide practice on the following skills:

■ Sequencing story events (part 1)

■ Writing answers to comprehension questions about a story (part 2)

■ Reading words with endings and then writing the words without endings (part 3)

Correction Procedures

Board Work

To correct word-identification errors during Board Work exercises, follow these steps:
- a. The word is _____.
- b. What word? (Signal.)
- c. Spell _____. (Signal for each letter.)
- • What word? (Signal.)
- d. (Return to the first word in the column and present the words in order.)

Word-Attack Skills in the Student Book

To correct word-identification errors:
- a. The word is _____.
- b. What word? (Signal.)
- c. Spell _____. (Signal for each letter.)
- • What word? (Signal.)
- d. Go back to the first word in the (row/column). ✓
- • What word? (Signal.)

Group Reading

To correct word-reading errors:
(As soon as a student misidentifies a word, say:)
- • The word is _____.
- • Touch under that word. ✓
- • What word? (Signal.)
- • Go back to the beginning of the sentence and read that sentence again.

WORD-ATTACK SKILLS

Board Work

——— EXERCISE 1 ———
ENDINGS BUILDUP

1. (Print in a column on the board:)

> wash
> spill
> join

2. (Point to **wash**. Pause.) What word?
   (Signal.) *Wash.*
   • (Repeat for **spill, join.**)
3. (Change the list to:)

> wash es
> spill s
> join s

4. (Point to **washes**. Pause.) What word?
   (Signal.) *Washes.*
   • (Repeat for **spills, joins.**)
5. (Change the list to:)

> wash ed
> spill ed
> join ed

6. (Point to **washed**. Pause.) What word?
   (Signal.) *Washed.*
   • (Repeat for **spilled, joined.**)
7. (Change the list to:)

> wash ing
> spill ing
> join ing

8. (Point to **washing**. Pause.) What word?
   (Signal.) *Washing.*
   • (Repeat for **spilling, joining.**)

9. (Change to the original list:)

> wash
> spill
> join

• (Repeat steps 2–8 until firm.)

> **Individual test**
> (Repeat steps 1–8, calling on individual
> students to read all the words in the
> column.)

Student Book

——— EXERCISE 2 ———
WORD CONVERSIONS

1. Open your Student Book to Lesson 32. ✓

1

A	B	C	D	E
food	burn	benches	pointed	load
fold	barn	beaches	painted	loud

• Touch part 1. ✓
2. Touch the first word in column A. ✓
• What word? (Signal.) *Food.*
3. Next word. ✓
• What word? (Signal.) *Fold.*
4. (Repeat steps 2 and 3 for the words in
   columns B–E.)

——— EXERCISE 3 ———
WORD READING

1. Touch the first word in part 2. ✓

2

soiled   cooled   eaten   watched   pounded

• What sound? (Signal.) *oy.*
• What word? (Signal.) *Soiled.*
2. Next word. ✓
• What sound? (Signal.) *oo.*
• What word? (Signal.) *Cooled.*
3. (Repeat step 2 for each remaining word.)

EXERCISE 4

WORD READING

1. Touch the first word in part 3. ✓

3

> listened tests invisible copper
>
> silver glass flatter visible
>
> grime lazy removes relatives
>
> freezer stomped floor stove
>
> gallon realize shook

2. That word is **listened.** What word? (Signal.) *Listened.*
- Spell **listened.** (Signal for each letter.) *L–I–S–T–E–N–E–D.*
- What word? (Signal.) *Listened.*
3. Next word. ✓
- What word? (Signal.) *Tests.*
4. (Repeat step 3 for each remaining word.)

EXERCISE 5

WORD-ATTACK SKILLS: Individual tests

1. (Call on individual students. Each student reads a row or column. Tally the rows and columns read without error. If the group reads at least 9 rows and columns without making errors, direct all students to record 4 points in Box A of their Point Chart. Criterion is 80 percent of rows and columns read without error.)
2. (If the group did not read at least 9 rows and columns without errors, do not award any points for the Word-Attack Skills exercises.)

GROUP READING

EXERCISE 6

STORY READING

1. (Call on individual students to answer these questions.)
- Irma was trying to invent a particular kind of paint. What did she want that paint to do? (Idea: *Be super hard so that it would not wear out.*)
- What kind of paint did she actually invent? (Idea: *Paint that makes things invisible.*)
- What happened to make her think that the paint made things invisible? (Accept reasonable summaries.)
2. Everybody, touch part 4. ✓
3. After you read each part of the story without making more than 2 errors, I'll ask questions about that part.

4   **Irma Tests the Invisible Paint**

4. (Call on a student to read the title.) *Irma Tests the Invisible Paint.*
- What do you think this story is about? (Accept reasonable responses.)
5. (Use the following procedures for each part of the story.)
a. (Call on individual students. Each is to read one or two sentences. Praise students who read without making errors.)
b. (At the end of the part, tell the students the number of errors the group made and whether the group earned points for that part.)
c. (If the group made more than 2 errors, direct the group to reread the part.)
d. (After the group reads a part with no more than 2 errors, call on individual students to answer the comprehension questions for that part.)

Irma had left a nail on the hard paint. When she came back to her lab, the nail was invisible. Slowly she began to realize that the paint had made the nail invisible.

She said to herself, "I will test that paint." She took a coin from her purse and dropped the coin on the paint. Then she watched and waited. After a while, she saw that the coin was starting to turn invisible. It now looked like a glass coin. She could still see it, but it did not look like a copper coin or a silver coin. It looked like a glass coin.

[1]

First-part questions:

a. How did she test the paint? (Idea: *She dropped a coin on the paint.*)
b. How did the appearance of the coin change after a while? (Idea: *It looked like a glass coin.*)

She dropped it on the floor. "Clink," it went. It sounded like a coin. She took a hammer and hit the coin ten times. She wanted to see what would happen to it now. The coin got flatter and bigger, but it still looked like glass. She said, "I don't believe what is happening."

She set the coin on the paint again and waited. Soon the coin was invisible. Now it didn't look like glass. It didn't look like anything.

"I don't believe it," Irma said to herself. She felt the coin. She could feel the dents that had been made by the hammer.

[1]

Second-part questions:

a. How did the coin change when she hit it with a hammer? (Idea: *It became flatter and bigger.*)
b. When she returned the coin to the paint, what happened to it? (Idea: *It became invisible.*)

Irma closed her eyes and picked up the coin. "It feels like it should feel," she said to herself. Then she opened her eyes and looked at the coin in her hand. It was invisible.

She said, "I must see how this invisible paint works." She got a pot of water and heated it on the stove in her lab. When the water began to boil, she dropped the coin into it. Then she watched to see what would happen.

Slowly she could see the coin begin to form at the bottom of the boiling water. Slowly it became visible. At first it looked like glass. Then it began to look like a coin that had been pounded with a hammer.

[1]

Third-part question:

a. How did she make the coin reappear? (Idea: *She dropped the coin into boiling water.*)

She lifted the coin from the boiling water and set it on a sheet of foil. When the coin had cooled, she picked it up and looked at it. She said, "I know that I can remove the invisible paint with boiling water. Now I will try something else."

She took a soiled rag and tore off a small bit. She set the bit of rag on the hard paint. Then she watched as the rag became invisible.

"Now I will see if something else will remove that invisible paint." She took the bit of soiled rag and dropped it in the washtub. Then she turned on the cold water and let it run over the rag.

[2]

Fourth-part questions:

a. She found one way to make the invisible things visible again. What was that? (Idea: *To drop them in boiling water.*)

b. She was going to test another way, so she made something else invisible. What was that? (Idea: *A bit of soiled rag.*)

c. What did she do with the rag when it was invisible? (Idea: *Put it in the washtub and ran cold water on it.*)

The water washed away bits of grime. As each bit of grime left the rag, a spot became visible. But the rest of the rag was still invisible. "Cold water does not seem to work too well," Irma said.

Then she took a can of motor oil from the shelf. She filled a cup with oil and dropped the rag into the cup of oil. Slowly the rag became visible. Irma smiled. She said, "Oil removes the invisible paint."

Now Irma had to think. She could hardly believe what had happened. She went over everything five times. Then she shook her head and said, "It must have happened. I must have made a paint that turns things invisible."

[2]

Fifth-part questions:

a. How did the water change the rag? (Idea: *Where it washed away bits of grime, spots became visible.*)

b. What did she soak the rag in next? (Idea: *Motor oil.*)

c. What happened to the rag? (Idea: *It became visible.*)

"Irma," Berta called from upstairs, "what happened to that gallon of ice cream that was in the freezer?"

Irma said, "If it's not in the freezer, you must have eaten it."

Berta yelled, "Well, why didn't you get more? How can we watch TV if we don't have ice cream?"

Irma said, "You'll just have to do the best you can."

Berta did not say anything. She stomped back to the living room. As Irma listened to her lazy boarder walking across the floor, she got an idea. She smiled and said to herself, "I think I can have a lot of fun with this invisible paint."

[1]

Sixth-part questions:

a. What was Berta complaining about? (Idea: *She wanted ice cream.*)

b. What was Irma thinking at the end of this story? (Idea: *That she could have fun with the paint.*)

c. How could she have fun with that paint? (Accept reasonable responses.)

6. (After the group has completed reading the story and answering the comprehension questions, tell the students the total number of points to record in Box B of their Point Chart. Maximum = 8 points.)

FLUENCY ASSESSMENT

═══════ **EXERCISE 7** ═══════

READING CHECKOUTS

1. (For this part of the lesson, assigned pairs of students work together during the checkouts.)

2. (Each student does two checkouts.)

- (First checkout: Students can earn 2 points by making no more than 2 errors on the first part of story 32. Students record points in Box C-1 of their Point Chart.)

- (Second checkout: 1-minute timed reading. Students can earn 2 points by reading at least 105 words and making no more than 3 errors on the first part of story 31. Students record points in Box C-2 of their Point Chart.)

3. (During each checkout, observe at least two pairs of students. Make notes on mistakes. Give checkers feedback.)

4. (Direct all students to plot their reading rate—the number of words they read in 1 minute—on the Individual Reading Progress Chart at the end of their Workbook.)

- (Direct students to circle the number of errors they made during the timed reading.)

5. (Record on the Fluency Assessment Summary form the timed reading checkout performance for each student you observed.)

WORKBOOK EXERCISES

Independent Student Work

1. Open your Workbook to Lesson 32. ✓
- Complete all parts of your Workbook lesson. If you make no more than 3 errors, you earn 4 points.
2. (After checking the Workbooks, direct students who made no more than 3 errors to record 4 points in Box D of their Point Chart.)

END OF LESSON 32

1

A	B	C	D	E
food	burn	benches	pointed	load
fold	barn	beaches	painted	loud

2 s<u>oi</u>led c<u>oo</u>led <u>ea</u>ten wat<u>ch</u>ed p<u>ou</u>nded

3 <u>listen</u>ed tests invisible copper

silver glass flatter visible

grime lazy removes relatives

freezer stomped floor stove

gallon realize shook

4

Irma Tests the Invisible Paint

Irma had left a nail on the hard paint. When she came back   13
to her lab, the nail was invisible. Slowly she began to realize   25
that the paint had made the nail invisible.   33

She said to herself, "I will test that paint." She took a coin   46
from her purse and dropped the coin on the paint. Then she   58
watched and waited. After a while, she saw that the coin was   70
starting to turn invisible. It now looked like a glass coin. She   82
could still see it, but it did not look like a copper coin or a   97
silver coin. It looked like a glass <u>coin</u>.   105

[1]

She dropped it on the floor. "Clink," it went. It sounded like   117
a coin. She took a hammer and hit the coin ten times. She   130

Lesson 32 **109**

wanted to see what would happen to it now. The coin got   142
flatter and bigger, but it still looked like glass. She said, "I don't   155
believe what is happening."   159

She set the coin on the paint again and waited. Soon the coin   172
was invisible. Now it didn't look like glass. It didn't look like   184
anything.   185

"I don't believe it," Irma said to herself. She felt the coin. She   198
could feel the dents that had been made by the hammer.   209

[1]

Irma closed her eyes and picked up the coin. "It feels like it   222
should feel," she said to herself. Then she opened her eyes and   234
looked at the coin in her hand. It was invisible.   244

She said, "I must see how this invisible paint works." She got   256
a pot of water and heated it on the stove in her lab. When the   271
water began to boil, she dropped the coin into it. Then she   283
watched to see what would happen.   289

Slowly she could see the coin begin to form at the bottom of   302
the boiling water. Slowly it became visible. At first it looked   313
like glass. Then it began to look like a coin that had been   326
pounded with a hammer.   330

[1]

She lifted the coin from the boiling water and set it on a   343
sheet of foil. When the coin had cooled, she picked it up and   356
looked at it. She said, "I know that I can remove the invisible   369
paint with boiling water. Now I will try something else."   379

She took a soiled rag and tore off a small bit. She set the bit   394
of rag on the hard paint. Then she watched as the rag became   407
invisible.   408

110   *Lesson 32*

"Now I will see if something else will remove that invisible 419 paint." She took the bit of soiled rag and dropped it in the washtub. 433 Then she turned on the cold water and let it run over the rag. 447

[2]

The water washed away bits of grime. As each bit of grime left 460 the rag, a spot became visible. But the rest of the rag was still 474 invisible. "Cold water does not seem to work too well," Irma said. 486

Then she took a can of motor oil from the shelf. She filled a 500 cup with oil and dropped the rag into the cup of oil. Slowly the 514 rag became visible. Irma smiled. She said, "Oil removes the 524 invisible paint." 526

Now Irma had to think. She could hardly believe what had 537 happened. She went over everything five times. Then she shook 547 her head and said, "It must have happened. I must have made a 560 paint that turns things invisible." 565

[2]

"Irma," Berta called from upstairs, "what happened to that 574 gallon of ice cream that was in the freezer?" 583

Irma said, "If it's not in the freezer, you must have eaten it." 596

Berta yelled, "Well, why didn't you get more? How can we 607 watch TV if we don't have ice cream?" 615

Irma said, "You'll just have to do the best you can." 626

Berta did not say anything. She stomped back to the living 637 room. As Irma listened to her lazy boarder walking across the 648 floor, she got an idea. She smiled and said to herself, "I think I 662 can have a lot of fun with this invisible paint." 672

[1]

Lesson 32   **111**

Lesson 32

1 Write **1, 2,** or **3** in front of each sentence to show when these things happened in the story. Then write the sentences in the blanks.

_____ **Irma took a coin from her purse and dropped the coin on the paint.**

_____ **Irma dropped the coin in the boiling water.**

_____ **The coin became invisible.**

1. _____

_____

2. _____

_____

3. _____

_____

2 **Write the answers to these questions:**

1. What happened to the coin when Irma hit it with a hammer?

_____

2. How did Irma make the rag become visible again?

_____

3. What did Berta want? _____

4. What was Irma thinking at the end of this story? _____

_____

3 **The words in the first column have endings. Write the same words without endings in the second column.**

boarder _____

eaten _____

washing _____

flatter _____

waved _____

Individual Reading Progress Chart
Decoding B2: LESSONS 2–35

LESSON NUMBER

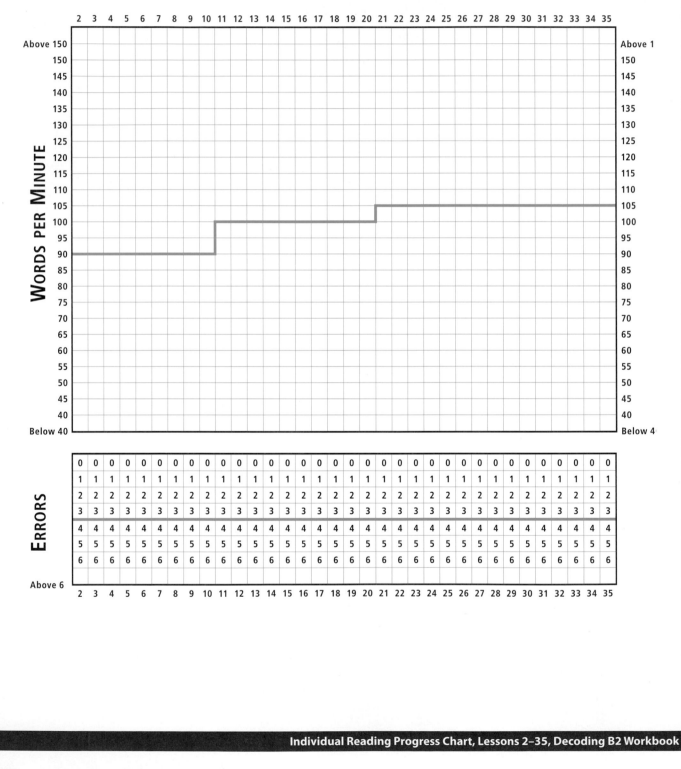

Decoding C—Lesson 26

The vocabulary for stories 1 through 25 consolidates the skills presented in **Decoding B1** and **B2,** providing a review for students who completed **Decoding B2** and an introduction for new students.

In Lessons 6 through 25, students practice a strategy for reading multipart words. Some words are relatively easy to break into parts because they are made up of a word base with affixes. For example, **disagreement** has **agree** in the middle, with **dis** in front and **ment** after it. Unfortunately, most of the longer words students read do not have a word base. For the words **insulation, generate,** and **tremendous,** there is no "middle part" that is a word base. The strategy used for the multipart-words exercises in Lessons 6 through 25 involves breaking words into three parts, which are somewhat arbitrary and do not always correspond to syllables.

New affixes **ex** and **un** are introduced (Exercises 1 and 2) in Lesson 26. Previously taught sound combinations are reviewed (Exercise 3). Vocabulary exercises present meanings for familiar words such as **tunnel** and words such as **canopy** that are probably unfamiliar to many students (Exercise 4). New informational words **(sequoia, foliage)** are included in a word list (Exercise 5).

This story is the first factual selection in **Decoding C.** The vocabulary and sentence structure are not particularly complex; however, the selection presents a great deal of information. Specified comprehension items (numbered 1 through 3) are presented after students read each section of the story (Exercise 7). If the group makes more than 12 decoding errors during the oral reading of the story, they are to read the story again either immediately or during the next lesson.

Following the reading of the story, students work together in pairs. Each student reads aloud for 2 minutes and can earn points by meeting the specified rate and accuracy criteria (240 words in 2 minutes, making no more than 5 total errors).

As the last activity of the lesson, students work independently in their Workbooks. The Workbook Exercises include ten comprehension items on story 26 (part 1), vocabulary items (part 2), and word-analysis items that require students to write affixes and the root words of multisyllabic words (part 3).

Correction Procedures

Word-Attack Skills

> **To correct word-identification errors:**
> a. The word is _____.
> b. What word? (Signal.)
> c. Spell _____. (Signal for each letter.)
> • What word? (Signal.)
> d. Go back to the first word in the (row/column). ✓
> • (Present the words in order.)

Group Reading

> **To correct word-reading errors:**
> (As soon as a student misidentifies a word, say:)
> a. The word is _____.
> b. Touch under that word. ✓
> c. What word? (Signal.)
> d. Go back to the beginning of the sentence and read that sentence again.

Comprehension errors during Group Reading

> **To correct comprehension errors:**
> a. (Call on a student to reread the passage that answers the question.)
> b. (Repeat the question for the student who made the error.)
> c. (Require that student to give an appropriate answer before proceeding with the story reading.)

Lesson 26

WORD-ATTACK SKILLS

Board Work

─────── **EXERCISE 1** ───────

NEW **AFFIX: ex**

1. (Print in a column on the board:)

> tend
> cite
> ample
> plain
> pose

2. (Point to **tend**. Pause.) What word? (Signal.) *Tend.*
- (Repeat for **cite, ample, plain, pose**.)
- (Repeat the list until firm.)
3. (Add **ex** to the beginning of each word:)

> extend
> excite
> example
> explain
> expose

4. (Point to **extend**. Pause.) What word? (Signal.) *Extend.*
- (Repeat for **excite, example, explain, expose**.)
- (Repeat the list until firm.)

Student Book

─────── **EXERCISE 2** ───────

NEW **AFFIX: un**

1. Open your Student Book to Lesson 26. ✓

1

un

A	B
unreal	unable
unseen	unlimited
unbelievable	unfortunate
uncertain	

- Touch the letters **U–N** in part 1. ✓
- When those letters appear at the beginning of a word, they usually mean **not**. What does **un** mean? (Signal.) *Not.*
2. Touch the first word in column A. ✓
- What word? (Signal.) *Unreal.*
- What does **unreal** mean? (Signal.) *Not real.*
3. Touch the next word. ✓
- What word? (Signal.) *Unseen.*
- What does **unseen** mean? (Signal.) *Not seen.*
4. (Repeat step 3 for each remaining word.)
5. (Repeat the list until firm.)
6. (Repeat steps 2–5 for the words in column B.)

─────── **EXERCISE 3** ───────

WORD PRACTICE

1. Touch the first word in part 2. ✓

2

bright easily interesting contained
distance gigantic although falter
fifteenth branches approaches flights
matches floating frightened

- What sound? (Signal.) *īīī.*
- What word? (Signal.) *Bright.*
2. Touch the next word. ✓
- What sound? (Signal.) *ēēē.*
- What word? (Signal.) *Easily.*
3. (Repeat step 2 for each remaining word.)
4. (Repeat each row of words until firm.)

======= **EXERCISE 4** =======
VOCABULARY

1. Touch part 3. ✓

3

1. tunnel
2. fluttered
3. snaked
4. drizzly
5. canopy

- We're going to talk about what those words mean.
2. Touch word 1. ✓
- What word? (Signal.) *Tunnel.*
- Who can tell me what a **tunnel** is? (Call on a student.) (Idea: *A passage through water or mountains.*)
3. Everybody, touch word 2. ✓
- What word? (Signal.) *Fluttered.*
- **Flutter** is another way of saying **move back and forth rapidly.** What's another way of saying "The leaves **moved back and forth rapidly** in the breeze"? (Signal.) *The leaves fluttered in the breeze.*
4. Touch word 3. ✓
- What word? (Signal.) *Snaked.*
- **Snaked** is another way of saying **twisted.** Everybody, what's another way of saying "The road **twisted** between the mountains"? (Signal.) *The road snaked between the mountains.*
5. Touch word 4. ✓
- What word? (Signal.) *Drizzly.*
- Who knows what a **drizzly** rain is like? (Call on a student.) (Idea: *Like a light, quiet rain.*)
6. Everybody, touch word 5. ✓
- What word? (Signal.) *Canopy.*
- A **canopy** is like a **roof** above something. Everybody, what's another way of saying "The branches were a **roof** above the forest"? (Signal.) *The branches were a canopy above the forest.*

======= **EXERCISE 5** =======
WORD PRACTICE

1. Touch the first word in part 4. ✓

4

sequoia foliage building cousin
swirled* darkness drifted develop
survive* through swayed* Pacific
November create covered among
suggested neither extended
constructed parent rapidly

- What word? (Signal.) *Sequoia.*
2. Next word. ✓
- What word? (Signal.) *Foliage.*
3. (Repeat step 2 for each remaining word.)
4. (Repeat each row of words until firm.)
5. What does **swirled** mean? (Call on a student.)
- (Repeat for **survive, swayed.**)

======= **EXERCISE 6** =======
NEW WORD-ATTACK SKILLS: Individual tests

1. (Call on individual students. Each student reads a row or column. Tally the rows and columns read without error. If the group reads at least 10 rows and columns without making errors, direct all students to record 5 points in Box A of their Point Chart. Criterion is 80 percent of rows and columns read without error.)
2. (If the group did not read at least 10 rows and columns without errors, do not award any points for the Word-Attack Skills exercises.)

SELECTION READING

━━━━━━ **EXERCISE 7** ━━━━━━

STORY READING

1. Everybody, touch part 5. ✓
2. The error limit for this story is 12. If the group reads the story with 12 errors or less, you earn 5 points.

5 | **The Redwood Tree**

3. (Call on a student to read the title.) *The Redwood Tree.*
- What do you think this story is about? (Accept reasonable responses.)
4. (Call on individual students. Each is to read two to four sentences.)
5. (Call on individual students to answer the specified questions during the story reading.)

This is the story of a redwood tree that is living today in northern California. That redwood, like many others, has had an interesting life.

Its life began with a seed contained in a cone. A redwood cone is about as big as a quarter. The cone starts to grow in early summer. By late summer it is full-sized and bright green with many seeds inside. The cone is not yet full grown, however. As fall approaches, the cone begins to change color, turning brown. Small flaps on all sides of the cone open, and as they do, the tiny seeds fall out. The seeds are so small that ten of them would easily fit on the end of your finger. If you wanted a pound of these seeds, you would have to collect about 120 thousand of them. ❶

1. How big is a redwood cone? (Idea: *About as big as a quarter.*)
1. How big are the redwood seeds? (Ideas: *Very small; so small that ten could fit on the end of your finger.*)

It seems strange that a seed so small can grow into the world's tallest tree, but it's true. Redwoods are the tallest trees, although a cousin of the redwood—the giant sequoia—has a thicker trunk than the redwood. Some giant sequoias have trunks so thick that people have constructed tunnels through them, and these tunnels are so big that cars can pass through them. The giant sequoia, however, does not grow as tall as the redwood. To get an idea of how tall the bigger redwoods are, imagine what it would be like to climb a flight of stairs as high as these redwoods. Imagine climbing five flights of stairs. Imagine how far down it is when you are five stories high. A big redwood is much taller than a five-story building, however. So imagine going up to the tenth floor, the fifteenth floor, the twentieth floor. From up here you can see a long distance, and it's a long, long way down. However, if you were on the twentieth floor of a building, you would not be near the top of a big redwood. You would probably be tired from climbing twenty flights of stairs, however, to reach the top of a big redwood, you would have to climb another fifteen flights of stairs. That's right. A very tall redwood is about as tall as a thirty-five-story building. A person standing down at the base of the tree would look like an ant. The base of the redwood's trunk is so big that eight people could stand next to each other and hide behind the trunk. And that gigantic tree develops from a seed smaller than a grain of wheat. ❷

2. Which kinds of trees are the tallest? *Redwoods.*
2. Which kinds of trees have the thickest trunks? *Giant sequoias.*
2. How tall is a very tall redwood? (Idea: *About as tall as a thirty-five-story building.*)

FLUENCY ASSESSMENT

It was on a sunny November day that the seed of the redwood tree in this story fluttered from the cone. The parent tree stood on the bank of a small creek that snaked among the giant redwoods. The weather had been cold, and a drizzly rain had been falling for days. During the rain, the flaps of the redwood cone swelled up and closed. But now the sun emerged, and a brisk wind swirled through the tops of the redwoods, bending their tops to the south. As the top of the parent tree swayed in the cool wind, the cones began to dry out, and the flaps began to open. Below, the forest was deeply shaded by the foliage of the giant redwoods, which formed a canopy of green that extended as far as one could see. In the distance was the sound of the Pacific Ocean.

Late that afternoon, a sudden gust of wind pushed through the forest, bending branches of the redwoods. When that wind hit the parent tree, six of the cone's forty seeds fluttered down and drifted down, down, into the dark forest below. One of those seeds would develop into a giant. The others would not survive. ❸

3. When did the seeds from the redwood tree flutter from the cone? (Idea: *On a very sunny November day.*)

3. How many seeds fluttered down? *Six.*

3. How many seeds survived? *One.*

6. (Award points quickly.)

7. (If the group makes more than 12 errors, repeat the reading immediately or on the next day.)

■━━━━━━━ EXERCISE 8 ━━━━━━━■

TIMED READING CHECKOUTS

1. (For this part of the lesson, assigned pairs of students work together during the checkouts.)

• (If one student does not have a checkout partner, arrange another time when you can give the checkout.)

2. (Each student does a 2-minute timed reading. Students earn 5 points by reading at least 240 words and making no more than 5 errors on the first part of story 26. Students record points in Box C of their Point Chart and plot their reading rate and errors on the Individual Reading Progress Chart.)

• (During each timed checkout, observe one pair of students for 2 minutes. Make notes on any mistakes the reader makes.)

3. (Record the timed reading checkout performance for each student you observed on the Fluency Assessment Summary form.)

WORKBOOK EXERCISES

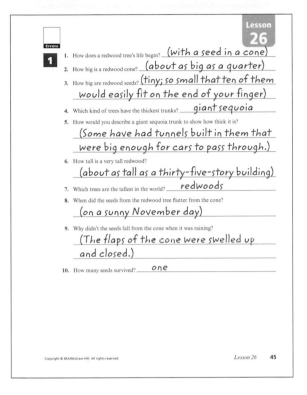

Lesson 26

Errors [ ]

1

1. How does a redwood tree's life begin? *(with a seed in a cone)*
2. How big is a redwood cone? *(about as big as a quarter)*
3. How big are redwood seeds? *(tiny; so small that ten of them would easily fit on the end of your finger)*
4. Which kind of trees have the thickest trunks? *giant sequoia*
5. How would you describe a giant sequoia trunk to show how thick it is? *(Some have had tunnels built in them that were big enough for cars to pass through.)*
6. How tall is a very tall redwood? *(about as tall as a thirty-five-story building)*
7. Which trees are the tallest in the world? *redwoods*
8. When did the seeds from the redwood tree flutter from the cone? *(on a sunny November day)*
9. Why didn't the seeds fall from the cone when it was raining? *(The flaps of the cone were swelled up and closed.)*
10. How many seeds survived? *one*

Lesson 26 **45**

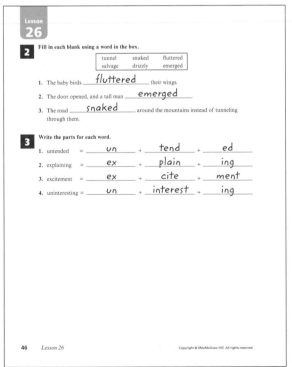

Lesson 26

2 Fill in each blank using a word in the box.

| tunnel | snaked | fluttered |
| salvage | drizzly | emerged |

1. The baby birds *fluttered* their wings.
2. The door opened, and a tall man *emerged*
3. The road *snaked* around the mountains instead of tunneling through them.

3 Write the parts for each word.

1. untended = *un* + *tend* + *ed*
2. explaining = *ex* + *plain* + *ing*
3. excitement = *ex* + *cite* + *ment*
4. uninteresting = *un* + *interest* + *ing*

46 *Lesson 26*

Independent Student Work

Task A

- Open your Workbook to Lesson 26. ✓
- Complete all the parts of your Workbook lesson using a pencil. If you make no errors, you will earn 5 points.

Task B

1. (Before presenting Lesson 27, check student Workbooks for Lesson 26.)
- (Call on individual students to read the items and answers in each part. Students mark errors using a pen.)
2. (Direct the students to count the number of errors and write the number in the Errors box at the top of the Workbook page.)
3. (Award points and direct students to record points in Box D of their Point Chart.)

   0 errors....................................5 points
   1 error ....3 points
   2 or 3 errors ....1 point
   more than 3 errors ....0 points

END OF LESSON 26

1

un

A	B
unreal	unable
unseen	unlimited
unbelievable	unfortunate
uncertain	

2

bright   easily   interesting   contained

distance   gigantic   although   falter

fifteenth   branches   approaches   flights

matches   floating   frightened

3

1. tunnel
2. fluttered
3. snaked
4. drizzly
5. canopy

4

sequoia   foliage   building   cousin

swirled   darkness   drifted   develop

survive   through   swayed   Pacific

November   create   covered   among

suggested   neither   extended

constructed   parent   rapidly

82   *Lesson 26*

5   The Redwood Tree

This is the story of a redwood tree that is living today in   13
northern California. That redwood, like many others, has had an   23
interesting life.   25

Its life began with a seed contained in a cone. A redwood cone is   39
about as big as a quarter. The cone starts to grow in early summer. By   54
late summer it is full-sized and bright green with many seeds inside.   66
The cone is not yet full grown, however. As fall approaches, the cone   79
begins to change color, turning brown. Small flaps on all sides of the   92
cone open, and as they do, the tiny seeds fall out. The seeds are so   107
small that ten of them would easily fit on the end of your finger. If you   123
wanted a pound of these seeds, you would have to collect about 120   136
thousand of them. ❶   139

It seems strange that a seed so small can grow into the world's   152
tallest tree, but it's true. Redwoods are the tallest trees, although a   164
cousin of the redwood—the giant sequoia—has a thicker trunk than   176
the redwood. Some giant sequoias have trunks so thick that people   187
have constructed tunnels through them, and these tunnels are so big   198
that cars can pass through them. The giant sequoia, however, does not   210
grow as tall as the redwood. To get an idea of how tall the bigger   225
redwoods are, imagine what it would be like to climb a flight of stairs   239
<u>as</u> high as these redwoods. Imagine climbing five flights of stairs.   250
Imagine how far down it is when you are five stories high. A big   264
redwood is much taller than a five-story building, however. So   274
imagine going up to the tenth floor, the fifteenth floor, the twentieth   286
floor. From up here you can see a long distance, and it's a long, long   301
way down. However, if you were on the twentieth floor of a building,   314
you would not be near the top of a big redwood. You would probably   328

Lesson 26   **83**

be tired from climbing twenty flights of stairs; however, to reach the 340
top of a big redwood, you would have to climb another fifteen flights 353
of stairs. That's right. A very tall redwood is about as tall as a 367
thirty-five-story building. A person standing down at the base of the 378
tree would look like an ant. The base of the redwood's trunk is so big 393
that eight people could stand next to each other and hide behind the 406
trunk. And that gigantic tree develops from a seed smaller than a 418
grain of wheat. ❷ 421

It was on a sunny November day that the seed of the redwood tree 435
in this story fluttered from the cone. The parent tree stood on the 448
bank of a small creek that snaked among the giant redwoods. The 460
weather had been cold, and a drizzly rain had been falling for days. 473
During the rain, the flaps of the redwood cone swelled up and closed. 486
But now the sun emerged, and a brisk wind swirled through the tops 499
of the redwoods, bending their tops to the south. As the top of the 573
parent tree swayed in the cool wind, the cones began to dry out, and 587
the flaps began to open. Below, the forest was deeply shaded by the 600
foliage of the giant redwoods, which formed a canopy of green that 612
extended as far as one could see. In the distance was the sound of the 627
Pacific Ocean. 629

Late that afternoon, a sudden gust of wind pushed through the 640
forest, bending branches of the redwoods. When that wind hit the 651
parent tree, six of the cone's forty seeds fluttered down and drifted 663
down, down, into the dark forest below. One of those seeds would 675
develop into a giant. The others would not survive. ❸ 684

84 *Lesson 26*

Errors

1

1. How does a redwood tree's life begin? _____

2. How big is a redwood cone? _____

3. How big are redwood seeds? _____

   _____

4. Which kind of trees have the thickest trunks? _____

5. How would you describe a giant sequoia trunk to show how thick it is?

   _____

   _____

6. How tall is a very tall redwood?

   _____

7. Which trees are the tallest in the world? _____

8. When did the seeds from the redwood tree flutter from the cone?

   _____

9. Why didn't the seeds fall from the cone when it was raining?

   _____

   _____

10. How many seeds survived? _____

2 **Fill in each blank using a word in the box.**

tunnel	snaked	fluttered
salvage	drizzly	emerged

1. The baby birds _____ their wings.

2. The door opened, and a tall man _____.

3. The road _____ around the mountains instead of tunneling through them.

3 **Write the parts for each word.**

1. untended   = _____ + _____ + _____

2. explaining   = _____ + _____ + _____

3. excitement   = _____ + _____ + _____

4. uninteresting = _____ + _____ + _____

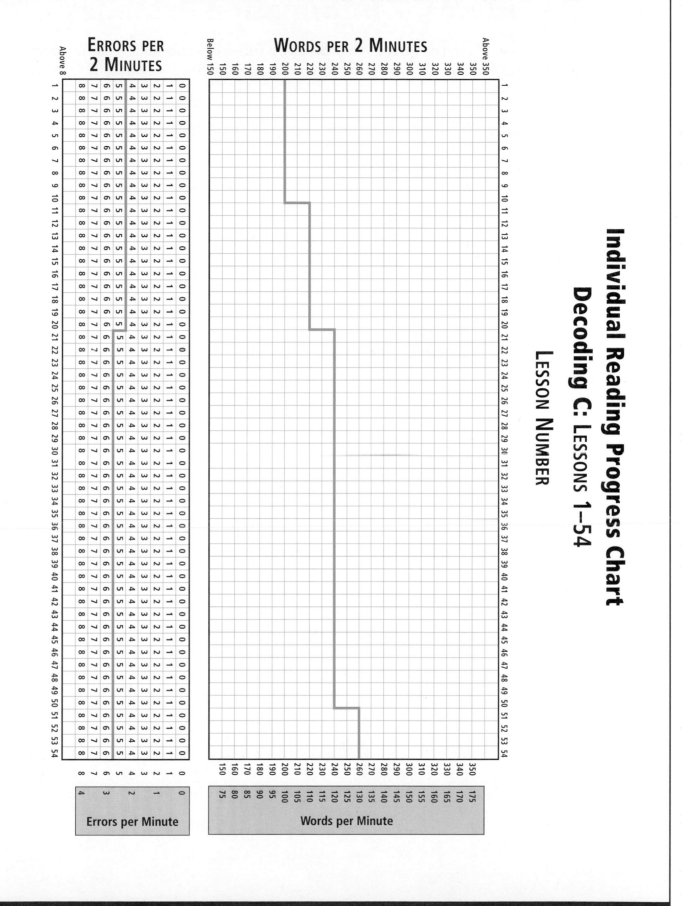

Individual Reading Progress Chart
Decoding C: Lessons 1–54
Lesson Number

Errors per 2 Minutes

Words per 2 Minutes

Errors per Minute

Words per Minute

Decoding C—Information Passages

Starting with Lesson 55, in the lessons that involve a full-story checkout (that is, every fifth lesson), the students read an information passage in the Student Book. This passage is read before the checkout.

Information passages differ from the regular selections in the following ways:

1 They are shorter—only 300 to 400 words.

2 They are unrelated to preceding selections of vocabulary sequences.

3 They present new information in a variety of styles, from typical newspaper and magazine approaches to textbook language.

In brief, these passages help form a transition from **Decoding C** to a variety of reading material.

The procedures for teaching information passages are the same as those for the group reading of other selections. You present word-attack exercises, and then the group reads the information passage. Individual students read two to four sentences. You ask oral comprehension questions.

Bonus Information Passages

In addition to the short information passages students read as part of the full-story checkout lessons, students read "bonus" passages. These passages are part of the regular lessons, starting at Lesson 58 and continuing on a schedule that presents two bonus information passages in every ten lessons. There are fourteen bonus information passages.

Students read these selections after they complete the regular parts of the lesson and the Workbook has been checked. The selections have a carefully controlled vocabulary and are written so that the sentence structures are more complicated than those used in the regular reading sentences. The bonus passages present information that is interesting, and they provide practice in reading passages that have difficult words.

INFORMATION PASSAGE

> **Note:** This Information Passage is not part of the regular 35- to 45-minute lesson activities. Schedule 15 to 20 minutes for presenting the passage.

NEW **INFORMATION-PASSAGE READING**

Task A

1. Turn to page 196 in your Student Book. ✓
- This selection is a bonus information passage. It's something like the information passage you read in Lesson 55, but you don't receive points for reading this passage. The passage is interesting and gives you good practice reading selections that have some difficult words.
- The words in the box are words that you will read in the information passage.

Fresnel	vandals	technology
lenses	columns	engineers

2. Touch the first word. ✓
- That word is a French name, and the English pronunciation is FREZ-nell. What word? (Signal.) *Fresnel.*
3. Next word. ✓
- That word is **vandals.** What word? (Signal.) *Vandals.*
4. (Repeat step 3 for each remaining word.)
5. Go back to the first word. ✓
- What word? (Signal.) *Fresnel.*
6. Next word. ✓
- What word? (Signal.) *Vandals.*
7. (Repeat step 6 for each remaining word.)

Task B

1. (Call on a student to read the title.) *Lighthouses.*
- What is this passage about? (Call on a student.) (Idea: *Lighthouses.*)
2. (Call on individual students. Each is to read two to four sentences.)
3. (Call on individual students to answer comprehension questions during the passage reading.)

Lighthouses

Lighthouses have a bright light that warns ships and boats about getting too close to dangerous areas. At one time, lighthouses were the only means for alerting ships about dangerous places. Today, lighthouses are not necessary because ships have radar and depth finders. Some ships also use messages from Global Positioning System (GPS) to provide information about exactly where the ship is on a map. If the GPS message shows the ship in a particular location, the ship is within 10 to 20 feet of where the message indicates it is. **❶**

1. Why are lighthouses located where they are? (Idea: *They were needed in dangerous areas to alert ships.*)
1. Why are lighthouses not necessary today? (Idea: *Ships use radar, depth finders, and GPS for guidance.*)
1. What does GPS stand for? *Global Positioning System.*

The early lighthouses were designed so that they were about 40 miles apart. The light from one lighthouse cannot be seen for more than about 20 miles because Earth is curved, but the light travels in a straight line. If a ship is 20 miles down the coast from one lighthouse, the ship's captain can probably see the light from the next lighthouse.

If the engineers who built lighthouses made them taller, the light would be visible from a greater distance. The problem with making them taller is that fog is common along a coast line. Often there are low clouds not more than 100 feet above the ocean. If the light from a lighthouse came from much more than 100 feet above the ocean, it would often be in the clouds, and the light would not be visible to ships. In some places, lighthouses are only about 30 feet tall. A short lighthouse tells you there are frequent fogs in the area. ❷

2. Why can't the light from a lighthouse be seen for more than 20 miles? (Idea: *Earth is curved, but light travels in a straight line.*)
2. Why aren't lighthouses taller than they are so they could be seen from farther distances? (Idea: *If lighthouses were more than 100 feet above the ocean, the light would often be in clouds and would not be visible to ships.*)
2. What do you know about an area that has a very short lighthouse tower? (Idea: *The area often has fog.*)

The most powerful lenses for lighthouses were built in France and were designed by a man named Fresnel. The Fresnel lens has a very complicated design. It has columns of glass with fins on them. A lighthouse in Oregon had one of the largest Fresnel lenses ever built. This lens, which was over six feet tall, was damaged by vandals in the 1990s. Several experts in glass and lenses decided to make replacements for the columns that were damaged. They worked for three years on this project. Even though they had equipment and technology far more advanced than Fresnel had, they could not make parts as good as those of the original lens. ❸

3. What is the name of the most powerful lighthouse lens? *Fresnel lens.*
3. How long did scientists work on trying to make lenses to replace the damaged Fresnel lenses? *Three years.*
3. Were scientists able to make lenses as effective as the original Fresnel lenses? *No.*

END OF LESSON 58

INFORMATION PASSAGE

Fresnel	vandals	technology
lenses	columns	engineers

Lighthouses

Lighthouses have a bright light that warns ships and boats about getting too close to dangerous areas. At one time, lighthouses were the only means for alerting ships about dangerous places. Today, lighthouses are not necessary because ships have radar and depth finders. Some ships also use messages from Global Positioning System (GPS) to provide information about exactly where the ship is on a map. If the GPS message shows the ship in a particular location, the ship is within 10 to 20 feet of where the message indicates it is. ❶

The early lighthouses were designed so that they were about 40 miles apart. The light from one lighthouse cannot be seen for more than about 20 miles because Earth is curved, but the light travels in a straight line. If a ship is 20 miles down the coast from one lighthouse, the ship's captain can probably see the light from the next lighthouse.

If the engineers who built lighthouses made them taller, the light would be visible from a greater distance. The problem with making them taller is that fog is common along a coast line. Often there are low clouds not more than 100 feet above the ocean. If the light from a

196 *Lesson 58*

lighthouse came from much more than 100 feet above the ocean, it would often be in the clouds, and the light would not be visible to ships. In some places, lighthouses are only about 30 feet tall. A short lighthouse tells you there are frequent fogs in the area. ❷

The most powerful lenses for lighthouses were built in France and were designed by a man named Fresnel. The Fresnel lens has a very complicated design. It has columns of glass with fins on them. A lighthouse in Oregon had one of the largest Fresnel lenses ever built. This lens, which was over six feet tall, was damaged by vandals in the 1990s. Several experts in glass and lenses decided to make replacements for the columns that were damaged. They worked for three years on this project. Even though they had equipment and technology far more advanced than Fresnel had, they could not make parts as good as those of the original lens. ❸

Lesson 58   **197**

Decoding C—Lesson 118

By Lesson 118, students have learned eleven affixes. The word-attack portion of the lesson is shorter. The meanings of the affixes **sub, able, dis, re,** and **ly** are reviewed (Exercise 1). Word parts are reviewed (Exercise 2). Fairly sophisticated words are presented (Exercise 3), and vocabulary words are presented (Exercise 4).

The reading selection is longer than the redwood selection in Lesson 26. The writing style is similar to typical text material, using complex sentences and conveying a great deal of information.

After the group reading of the selection, students work in pairs doing a 2-minute oral reading of story 118 (reading a minimum of 150 words per minute with no more than 5 total errors in 2 minutes).

Students write answers to the comprehension items and vocabulary items presented in the Workbook.

WORD-ATTACK SKILLS

Student Book

═══════ **EXERCISE 1** ═══════

AFFIX REVIEW

1. Open your Student Book to Lesson 118. ✓

> **1**
>
> sub able dis re ly

- Touch part 1. ✓
- Let's see if you remember a meaning for each of those affixes.
2. Touch the letters **S–U–B.** ✓
- What's one meaning of **sub?** (Call on a student. Accept **under** or **less than.**)
- What's another meaning of **sub?** (Call on another student.)
3. Everybody, touch the letters **A–B–L–E.** ✓
- What's one meaning of **able?** (Signal.) *Able to be.*
4. Touch the letters **D–I–S.** ✓
- What's one meaning of **dis?** (Call on a student. Accept **not, the opposite of,** or **away from.**)
- What's another meaning of **dis?** (Call on another student.)
5. Everybody, touch the letters **R–E.** ✓
- What's one meaning of **re?** (Signal.) *Again.*
6. Touch the letters **L–Y.** ✓
- What's one meaning of **ly?** (Signal.) *How something happened.*

═══════ **EXERCISE 2** ═══════

WORD PRACTICE

1. Touch the first word in part 2. ✓

> **2**
>
> spe<u>c</u>ial <u>sub</u>stance extr<u>a</u>ct* de<u>ser</u>ve* ac<u>cep</u>ted

- What's the underlined part? (Signal.) *shull.*
- What word? (Signal.) *Special.*
2. Touch the next word. ✓
- What's the underlined part? (Signal.) *sub.*
- What word? (Signal.) *Substance.*
3. (Repeat step 2 for each remaining word.)
4. (Repeat the words until firm.)
5. What does **extract** mean? (Call on a student.)
- (Repeat for **deserve.**)

═══════ **EXERCISE 3** ═══════

WORD PRACTICE

1. Touch the first word in part 3. ✓

> **3**
>
> treatments   submarine   eventually
>
> devices*   conditions   filthy   corpses
>
> dissected   sponge   anatomist
>
> patients   completed   battlefield
>
> muscles   amputate*   contribution
>
> arteries   achievements   publish

- What word? (Signal.) *Treatments.*
2. Next word. ✓
- What word? (Signal.) *Submarine.*
3. (Repeat step 2 for each remaining word.)
4. (Repeat each row of words until firm.)
5. What does **devices** mean? (Call on a student.)
- (Repeat for **amputate.**)

EXERCISE 4

VOCABULARY

1. Touch part 4. ✓

4

1. selection
2. sketches
3. masterpieces
4. anatomy
5. dressings
6. limbs

- We're going to talk about what those words mean.
2. Touch word 1. ✓
- What word? (Signal.) *Selection.*
- A **selection** is a **portion of something.** Everybody, what do we call **a portion of something?** (Signal.) *A selection.*
3. Touch word 2. ✓
- What word? (Signal.) *Sketches.*
- What are **sketches?** (Call on a student.) (Idea: *Rough, quick drawings.*)
4. Everybody, touch word 3. ✓
- What word? (Signal.) *Masterpieces.*
- **Masterpieces** are **fine works of art.** Everybody, what's another way of saying "The painting was a **fine work of art**"? (Signal.) *The painting was a masterpiece.*
5. Touch word 4. ✓
- What word? (Signal.) *Anatomy.*
- **Anatomy** is **the study of the body.** Everybody, what is **the study of the body** called? (Signal.) *Anatomy.*
6. Touch word 5. ✓
- What word? (Signal.) *Dressings.*
- **Bandages that cover a wound** are called **dressings.** Everybody, what do we call **bandages that cover a wound?** (Signal.) *Dressings.*
7. Touch word 6. ✓
- What word? (Signal.) *Limbs.*
- Arms and legs are **limbs.** Everybody, what are **arms and legs?** (Signal.) *Limbs.*

EXERCISE 5

WORD-ATTACK SKILLS: Individual tests

1. (Call on individual students. Each student reads a row or column. Tally the rows and columns read without error. If the group reads at least 7 rows and columns without making errors, direct all students to record 5 points in Box A of their Point Chart. Criterion is 80 percent of rows and columns read without error.)
2. (If the group did not read at least 7 rows and columns without errors, do not award any points for the Word-Attack Skills exercises.)

SELECTION READING

EXERCISE 6

STORY READING

1. Everybody, touch part 5. ✓
2. The error limit for this story is 12. If the group reads the story with 12 errors or less, you earn 5 points.

5 The Early Study of Anatomy and Surgery

3. (Call on a student to read the title.) *The Early Study of Anatomy and Surgery.*
- What do you think this story is about? (Accept reasonable responses.)
4. (Call on individual students. Each is to read two to four sentences.)
5. (Call on individual students to answer the specified questions during the story reading.)

After you read this selection, look up some of the paintings of Leonardo da Vinci. When you examine these paintings, look at the way Leonardo drew the human body. Leonardo understood the structure of the human body probably as well as anybody who had ever lived. And he reached this understanding of the body by studying its inner structure. He worked with corpses (dead bodies), and he dissected them (cut parts away so that he could study other parts). He recorded his findings by making sketches of the body parts. He made detailed drawings of muscles, bones, even nerves. He hoped to publish a great work on the anatomy of the human body. Unfortunately, he died before he completed the book. All that he left behind were hundreds of notes and sketches. Many of these were lost after his death, but some were saved. These notes and sketches found their way to different parts of Europe. ❶

1. How did Leonardo learn so much about human anatomy? (Idea: *By dissecting and studying human corpses.*)
1. What had he hoped to publish? (Idea: *A great work on human anatomy.*)

Leonardo also left sketches of another kind. Among them were details for building a submarine, an airplane, and other devices that would not be "invented" for hundreds of years. Besides the devices that remained on paper, he did invent machines that were actually used to construct buildings, make statues, and create special effects for plays. He created paintings that are considered masterpieces. He helped open the door to the study of human anatomy. But he never saw some of his greatest achievements accepted by the world. ❷

2. What were some of Leonardo's achievements? (Ideas: *He drew plans for building a submarine, an airplane, and other inventions; he built machines that were used in construction; he painted masterpieces.*)
2. Why might Leonardo have felt like a failure? (Idea: *Because he never saw some of his greatest achievements accepted by the world.*)

A very different kind of contribution to medicine in the 1500s was made by a man named Ambroise Paré. Paré was not an anatomist or an artist. He began as a helper to a barber-surgeon in a hospital of more than one thousand beds. Conditions in that hospital were terrible even by the standards of that time. Rats could be seen in every part of the building. The bedding and the dressings of the wounds were filthy. The odor was so bad that the attendants could not enter the sickroom unless they held a sponge dipped in vinegar over their nose and mouth. The patients were not fed regularly. ❸

3. How did Paré begin his work in medicine? (Idea: *As a helper to a barber-surgeon in a hospital.*)
3. What were the conditions in the hospital in which Paré worked? (Ideas: *Terrible; there were rats; it was filthy; it smelled awful.*)

After three years of working in the hospital, Paré became an army surgeon. Conditions for treating soldiers on the battlefield were as bad as those in the hospital. The surgeons would amputate limbs or try to extract bullets from gunshot wounds. Bullets were new in warfare, and the surgeons did not know how to treat the wounds bullets caused. Some cut out the bullet and then poured hot oil into the wound. These surgeons used the slogan: "If the wound is not curable by using the knife, use fire." (*Fire* meant "hot oil.") ❹

4. Where did Paré work after he left the hospital? (Idea: *In the army.*)
4. How did surgeons treat bullet wounds? (Idea: *By cutting out the bullet and pouring hot oil into the wound.*)

Paré changed two things. First, he discovered how to tie off arteries in amputations so that the patient did not bleed to death. Second, he discovered that wounds healed better without boiling oil. Instead, he used clean cloth and mild substances like egg whites to cover the wounds. Paré's methods worked. Many of the soldiers that Paré treated lived. Many didn't suffer as much as they would have if they had received the usual treatments. They usually didn't develop fevers, and the wounds healed more quickly. ❺

5. Name the two changes Paré made in treating wounds. (Ideas: *He tied off arteries in amputations, and he didn't treat wounds with boiling oil.*)

People began to become aware of the work of Paré. He became court surgeon to three kings. In his day, many other doctors thought surgery was below their dignity. Paré helped raise the standing of surgery. But many physicians and surgeons resented Paré. They didn't believe in his

methods. They thought he was an ignorant man because he didn't even know Latin.

Paré did a lot of things to advance medicine. He developed new methods for delivering babies and cut down the number of deaths among mothers and newborn babies. The methods that Paré developed were eventually adopted by others. In fact, when he died, his methods were being used in the hospital where he had begun as a barber's assistant. ❻

6. Why didn't other doctors respect Paré? (Ideas: *They thought he was ignorant because he didn't speak Latin; they didn't believe in his methods.*)
6. What did Paré do to help women? (Ideas: *He developed new methods for delivering babies; he cut down on the number of deaths among mothers and newborn babies.*)
6. (Award points quickly.)
7. (If the group makes more than 12 errors, repeat the reading immediately or on the next day.)

FLUENCY ASSESSMENT

━━━━━ **EXERCISE 7** ━━━━━
TIMED READING CHECKOUTS

1. (For this part of the lesson, assigned pairs of students work together during the checkouts.)
- (If one student does not have a checkout partner, arrange another time when you can give the checkout.)

2. (Each student does a 2-minute timed reading. Students earn 5 points by reading at least 300 words and making no more than 5 errors on the first part of story 118. Students record points in Box C of their Point Chart and plot their reading rate and errors on the Individual Reading Progress Chart.)

- (During each timed checkout, observe one pair of students for 2 minutes. Make notes on any mistakes the reader makes.)

3. (Record the timed reading checkout performance for each student you observed on the Fluency Assessment Summary form.)

WORKBOOK EXERCISES

Independent Student Work

Task A

- Open your Workbook to Lesson 118. ✓
- Complete all the parts of your Workbook lesson using a pencil. If you make no errors, you will earn 5 points.

Task B

1. (Before presenting Lesson 119, check student Workbooks for Lesson 118.)

- (Call on individual students to read the items and answers in each part. Students mark errors using a pen.)

2. (Direct the students to count the number of errors and write the number in the Errors box at the top of the Workbook page.)

3. (Award points and direct students to record points in Box D of their Point Chart.)

0 errors	5 points
1 error	3 points
2 or 3 errors	1 point
more than 3 errors	0 points

> **Note:** The bonus Information Passage on the next page is not part of the regular 35- to 45-minute lesson activities. Schedule 15 to 20 minutes for presenting the passage.

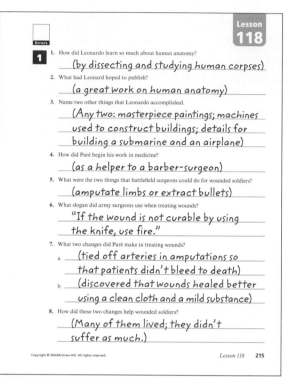

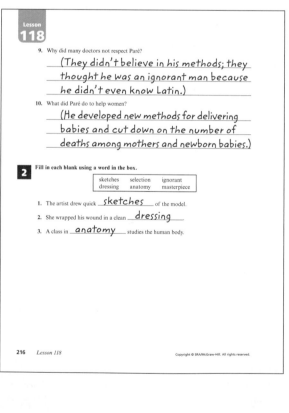

INFORMATION PASSAGE

INFORMATION-PASSAGE READING

Task A

1. Turn to page 432 in your Student Book. ✓
- The words in the box are words that you will read in the information passage.

| occupation electrician frequent repairer |
| electrocution |

2. Touch the first word. ✓
- That word is **occupation.** What word? (Signal.) *Occupation.*
3. Next word. ✓
- That word is **electrician.** What word? (Signal.) *Electrician.*
4. (Repeat step 3 for each remaining word.)
5. Go back to the first word. ✓
- What word? (Signal.) *Occupation.*
6. Next word. ✓
- What word? (Signal.) *Electrician.*
7. (Repeat step 6 for each remaining word.)

Task B

1. (Call on a student to read the title.) *The Most Dangerous Occupations—Part 1.*
- What is this passage about? (Call on a student.) (Idea: *The most dangerous occupations.*)
2. (Call on individual students. Each is to read two to four sentences.)
3. (Call on individual students to answer comprehension questions during the passage reading.)

The Most Dangerous Occupations—Part 1

Some occupations are dangerous. People who work in an office or at home are far less likely to have an accident that is related to the job than somebody who works outside. The reason that outdoor jobs are more dangerous than indoor jobs is that some kinds of weather make an outdoor job dangerous. A worker who is trying to repair electrical power lines during a wind storm or thunderstorm is in far more danger of being injured or killed than the worker who does the same job during good weather.

Truck driving is a dangerous occupation. In fact, the trucking industry has the largest number of work-related deaths of any occupation. That doesn't mean that truck driving is the most dangerous job. There are a lot more truck drivers than there are workers in some of the other dangerous occupations. The most common cause of death for truck drivers is highway crashes, often in bad weather. ❶

1. Which is safer, working indoors or outdoors? *Working indoors.*
1. What are some reasons outdoor work is more dangerous? (Ideas: *Bad weather makes some outdoor occupations dangerous; highway accidents are a common cause of work-related death for truck drivers.*)
1. Name some situations that may result in the death of a worker who is repairing electric power lines. (Idea: *Wind storms and thunderstorms are dangerous weather for workers.*)
1. Which occupation has the largest number of work-related deaths? *Truck driving.*

If you look at 100,000 workers in each dangerous occupation and see how many deaths there are per 100,000, truck driving is the fifth most dangerous job. In the trucking industry, about 26 of every 100,000 workers are killed in work-related accidents. That's over five times the number of deaths compared to the average job.

For workers who install or repair electric power lines, 28 per 100,000 are killed. Almost all are the result of being electrocuted. Farming is also a dangerous job, almost as dangerous as trucking. The reason is that the machinery is dangerous. Farmers use dangerous machinery to harvest crops, mow fields, or plant seed. ❷

2. Which occupation has more work-related deaths per 100,000 workers, truck drivers or workers who install or repair electric power lines? *Workers who install or repair electric power lines.*
2. Why is farming dangerous? (Idea: *Farmers use dangerous machinery.*)

For some jobs, the greatest cause of death is falling. These jobs include roofing and working on the construction of tall buildings or bridges. These jobs are more dangerous than either trucking or repairing electrical power lines.

The table below shows the top ten most dangerous occupations. The most dangerous are fishers and loggers, followed by airline pilots.

The third column of the table shows the most common causes of death. The most frequent cause of death for electricians is electrocution. The most frequent cause of death for airplane pilots is crashing. ❸

The top ten most dangerous occupations		
	Occupation	Most frequent cause of work-related deaths
1.	Fishers	Drowning
	Loggers	Struck by object
2.	Airline pilots	Airplane crash
3.	Taxicab drivers	Violence
	Construction workers and roofers	Falling
4.	Electric-power-line repairers	Electrocution
5.	Truck drivers	Highway crashes
6.	Farm occupations	Machinery
7.	Police	Violence, highway crashes
8.	Factory workers	Machinery
9.	Electricians	Electrocution
10.	Welders	Falling, fire

3. What is the most common work-related cause of death for electricians? *Electrocution.*
3. What is the most common work-related cause of death for factory workers? *Machinery.*
3. Touch number 1 in the left column of the table. ✓
- The table shows that two occupations are tied for the most dangerous. What are they? *Fishers and loggers.*
3. What's the most frequent cause of death for fishers? *Drowning.*
- Why do you think that happens? (Ideas: *Fishing boats can capsize in very bad weather; fishers can fall overboard in bad weather and high waves.*)
3. What's the most frequent cause of death for loggers? *Struck by object.*
- What kind of objects might strike loggers? (Idea: *Trees, large limbs of trees.*)

END OF LESSON 118

1   **sub   able   dis   re   ly**

2   spe<u>cial</u>   <u>sub</u>stance   <u>ex</u>tract   des<u>er</u>ve   ac<u>c</u>epted

3   treatments   submarine   eventually

      devices   conditions   filthy   corpses

      dissected   sponge   anatomist

      patients   completed   battlefield

      muscles   amputate   contribution

      arteries   achievements   publish

4   1. selection
      2. sketches
      3. masterpieces
      4. anatomy
      5. dressings
      6. limbs

Lesson 118   **429**

5 The Early Study of Anatomy and Surgery

After you read this selection, look up some of the paintings of 12
Leonardo da Vinci. When you examine these paintings, look at the way 24
Leonardo drew the human body. Leonardo understood the structure of 34
the human body probably as well as anybody who had ever lived. And he 48
reached this understanding of the body by studying its inner structure. 59
He worked with corpses (dead bodies), and he dissected them (cut parts 71
away so that he could study other parts). He recorded his findings by 84
making sketches of the body parts. He made detailed drawings of 95
muscles, bones, even nerves. He hoped to publish a great work on the 108
anatomy of the human body. Unfortunately, he died before he completed 119
the book. All that he left behind were hundreds of notes and sketches. 132
Many of these were lost after his death, but some were saved. These 145
notes and sketches found their way to different parts of Europe. ❶ 156

Leonardo also left sketches of another kind. Among them were 166
details for building a submarine, an airplane, and other devices that 177
would not be "invented" for hundreds of years. Besides the devices 188
that remained on paper, he did invent machines that were actually 199
used to construct buildings, make statues, and create special effects 209
for plays. He created paintings that are considered masterpieces. He 219
helped open the door to the study of human anatomy. But he never 232
saw some of his greatest achievements accepted by the world. ❷ 242

A very different kind of contribution to medicine in the 1500s was 254
made by a man named Ambroise Paré. Paré was not an anatomist or 267
an artist. He began as a helper to a barber-surgeon in a hospital of 281
more than one thousand beds. Conditions in that hospital were 291
terrible even by the standards of that time. <u>Rats</u> could be seen in every 305
part of the building. The bedding and the dressings of the wounds 317

430 *Lesson 118*

were filthy. The odor was so bad that the attendants could not enter 330
the sickroom unless they held a sponge dipped in vinegar over their 342
nose and mouth. The patients were not fed regularly. ❸ 351

After three years of working in the hospital, Paré became an army 363
surgeon. Conditions for treating soldiers on the battlefield were as bad 374
as those in the hospital. The surgeons would amputate limbs or try to 387
extract bullets from gunshot wounds. Bullets were new in warfare, and 398
the surgeons did not know how to treat the wounds bullets caused. 410
Some cut out the bullet and then poured hot oil into the wound. These 424
surgeons used the slogan: "If the wound is not curable by using the 437
knife, use fire." (*Fire* meant "hot oil.") ❹ 444

Paré changed two things. First, he discovered how to tie off arteries 456
in amputations so that the patient did not bleed to death. Second, he 469
discovered that wounds healed better without boiling oil. Instead, he 479
used clean cloth and mild substances like egg whites to cover the 491
wounds. Paré's methods worked. Many of the soldiers that Paré 501
treated lived. Many didn't suffer as much as they would have if they 514
had received the usual treatments. They usually didn't develop fevers, 524
and the wounds healed more quickly. ❺ 530

People began to become aware of the work of Paré. He became 542
court surgeon to three kings. In his day, many other doctors thought 554
surgery was below their dignity. Paré helped raise the standing of 565
surgery. But many physicians and surgeons resented Paré. They didn't 575
believe in his methods. They thought he was an ignorant man because 587
he didn't even know Latin. 592

Paré did a lot of things to advance medicine. He developed new 604
methods for delivering babies and cut down the number of deaths among 616
mothers and newborn babies. The methods that Paré developed were 626
eventually adopted by others. In fact, when he died, his methods were 638
being used in the hospital where he had begun as a barber's assistant. ❻ 651

Lesson 118   **431**

INFORMATION PASSAGE

occupation   electrician   frequent   repairer   electrocution

The Most Dangerous Occupations—Part 1

Some occupations are dangerous. People who work in an office or at home are far less likely to have an accident that is related to the job than somebody who works outside. The reason that outdoor jobs are more dangerous than indoor jobs is that some kinds of weather make an outdoor job dangerous. A worker who is trying to repair electrical power lines during a wind storm or thunderstorm is in far more danger of being injured or killed than the worker who does the same job during good weather.

Truck driving is a dangerous occupation. In fact, the trucking industry has the largest number of work-related deaths of any occupation. That doesn't mean that truck driving is the most dangerous job. There are a lot more truck drivers than there are workers in some of the other dangerous occupations. The most common cause of death for truck drivers is highway crashes, often in bad weather. ❶

If you look at 100,000 workers in each dangerous occupation and see how many deaths there are per 100,000, truck driving is the fifth most dangerous job. In the trucking industry, about 26 of every 100,000 workers are killed in work-related accidents. That's over five times the number of deaths compared to the average job.

For workers who install or repair electric power lines, 28 per 100,000 are killed. Almost all are the result of being electrocuted. Farming is also a dangerous job, almost as dangerous as trucking.

432   *Lesson 118*

The reason is that the machinery is dangerous. Farmers use dangerous machinery to harvest crops, mow fields, or plant seed. ❷

For some jobs, the greatest cause of death is falling. These jobs include roofing and working on the construction of tall buildings or bridges. These jobs are more dangerous than either trucking or repairing electrical power lines.

The table below shows the top ten most dangerous occupations. The most dangerous are fishers and loggers, followed by airline pilots.

The third column of the table shows the most common causes of death. The most frequent cause of death for electricians is electrocution. The most frequent cause of death for airplane pilots is crashing. ❸

The top ten most dangerous occupations	
Occupation	**Most frequent cause of work-related deaths**
1. Fishers	Drowning
Loggers	Struck by object
2. Airline pilots	Airplane crash
3. Taxicab drivers	Violence
Construction workers and roofers	Falling
4. Electric-power-line repairers	Electrocution
5. Truck drivers	Highway crashes
6. Farm occupations	Machinery
7. Police	Violence, highway crashes
8. Factory workers	Machinery
9. Electricians	Electrocution
10. Welders	Falling, fire

Lesson 118   **433**

Lesson
118

1

1. How did Leonardo learn so much about human anatomy?

_____

2. What had Leonard hoped to publish?

_____

3. Name two other things that Leonardo accomplished.

_____

_____

_____

4. How did Paré begin his work in medicine?

_____

5. What were the two things that battlefield surgeons could do for wounded soldiers?

_____

6. What slogan did army surgeons use when treating wounds?

_____

_____

7. What two changes did Paré make in treating wounds?

   a. _____

   _____

   b. _____

   _____

8. How did these two changes help wounded soldiers?

_____

_____

9. Why did many doctors not respect Paré?

_____

_____

_____

10. What did Paré do to help women?

_____

_____

_____

2 **Fill in each blank using a word in the box.**

sketches	selection	ignorant
dressing	anatomy	masterpiece

1. The artist drew quick _____ of the model.

2. She wrapped his wound in a clean _____.

3. A class in _____ studies the human body.

Comprehension A Fast Cycle—Lesson 8

The following core skills that will later be incorporated in more sophisticated applications are introduced and reviewed in this lesson:

- Deductions involving **all** and **every, no** and **don't** (Exercises 1 through 3)

- Review of how objects are the same (Exercise 4)

- An information game in which clues are provided for identifying an object (Exercises 5 and 6)

- Statement inferences (Exercise 7)

- Definitions and substituting new words for familiar ones in specified sentences (Exercise 8)

- Review of previously taught definitions (Exercise 9)

The Workbook includes the following activities:

- True–False (Exercise 10)

- Classification (Exercise 11)

- Same (Exercise 12)

- Some, All, None (Exercise 13)

- Identifying an object from a description of the object (Exercise 14)

The final part of the lesson deals with information—seasons of the year, a poem, and facts about animal classification.

Correction Procedures

Follow these steps to correct errors:

1. (Say the answer.)
2. (Repeat the task [the instructions or question].)
3. (Back up in the exercise and present the steps in order.)
4. (Finish the remaining steps in the exercise.)
5. (Repeat the entire exercise if students made more than 1 or 2 mistakes.)

THINKING OPERATIONS

═══ EXERCISE 1 ═══
DEDUCTIONS: With *all* and *every*

The first Thinking Operation today is **Deductions.**

1. I'll say rules with **all** or **every.** You say them the other way. What two words are we going to use? (Hold up one finger.) *All.*
- (Hold up two fingers.) *Every.*
2. Listen. **All** people learn. Say that. (Signal.) *All people learn.*
- Now say it the other way. Get ready. (Signal.) *Every person learns.*
- (Repeat step 2 until firm.)
3. Here's a new rule: **Every** person eats. Say that. (Signal.) *Every person eats.*
- Now say it the other way. Get ready. (Signal.) *All people eat.*
- (Repeat step 3 until firm.)
4. Here's a new rule: **Every** year is fifty-two weeks long. Say that. (Signal.) *Every year is fifty-two weeks long.*
- Now say it the other way. Get ready. (Signal.) *All years are fifty-two weeks long.*
- (Repeat step 4 until firm.)

═══ EXERCISE 2 ═══
DEDUCTIONS: With *no* and *don't*

Task A

1. I'll say a rule one way with the word **no.** Then I'll say it another way with the word **don't.**
2. Listen. Babies **don't** read. Say that. (Signal.) *Babies don't read.*
- Now I'll say the same rule with **no. No** babies read. Say that. (Signal.) *No babies read.*

Task B

1. Here's a new rule: **No** chairs eat. Say that. (Signal.) *No chairs eat.*
- Now you're going to say the rule that starts with **chairs.** (Pause.) Get ready. (Signal.) *Chairs don't eat.*

- Now you're going to say the rule that starts with **no chairs.** (Pause.) Get ready. (Signal.) *No chairs eat.*
- (Repeat step 1 until firm.)
2. Here's a new rule: Trees **don't** read. Say that. (Signal.) *Trees don't read.*
- Now you're going to say the rule that starts with **no trees.** (Pause.) Get ready. (Signal.) *No trees read.*
- Now you're going to say the rule that starts with **trees.** (Pause.) Get ready. (Signal.) *Trees don't read.*
- (Repeat step 2 until firm.)

> **Individual test**
> (Call on individuals to do one step in Task B.)

═══ EXERCISE 3 ═══
NEW DEDUCTIONS: With *don't*

1. Listen to this rule. Dogs **don't** have wings. Everybody, say that. (Signal.) *Dogs don't have wings.*
2. Retrievers are dogs. So (pause; signal), *retrievers don't have wings.*
- How do you know that retrievers don't have wings? (Signal.) *Because dogs don't have wings.*
3. Listen. Dogs **don't** have wings. Beagles are dogs. So (pause; signal), *beagles don't have wings.*
- How do you know that beagles don't have wings? (Signal.) *Because dogs don't have wings.*
4. Listen. Dogs **don't** have wings. Poodles are dogs. So (pause; signal), *poodles don't have wings.*
- How do you know that poodles don't have wings? (Signal.) *Because dogs don't have wings.*
5. (Repeat steps 2–4 until firm.)

━━━━━━━━ **EXERCISE 4** ━━━━━━━

NEW **SAME: Objects**

The next Thinking Operation is **Same.**

1. Anything you can point to is an object. What do we call anything you can point to? (Signal.) *An object.*
- I'll name some objects. A box, a flower, a rock. When I call on you, name three more objects. (Call on individual students.)
2. I'll name three ways that a banana and a rock are the same. (Hold up one finger.) They are objects.
- (Hold up two fingers.) They take up space.
- (Hold up three fingers.) You find them in **some** place.
3. Do it with me. Name those three ways that a banana and a rock are the same. (Respond with the students. Hold up one finger.) *They are objects.*
- (Hold up two fingers.) *They take up space.*
- (Hold up three fingers.) *You find them in* **some** *place.*
- (Repeat until the students are responding with you.)
4. All by yourselves. Name those three ways that a banana and a rock are the same.
- (Hold up one finger.) *They are objects.*
- (Hold up two fingers.) *They take up space.*
- (Hold up three fingers.) *You find them in some place.*
- (Repeat until the students say the facts in order.)
5. Anything you can point to is an object. Can you point to a horse and a ladder? (Signal.) *Yes.*
- So, are a horse and a ladder objects? (Signal.) *Yes.*
- So, name three ways that a horse and a ladder are the same. (Hold up one finger.) *They are objects.*

- (Hold up two fingers.) *They take up space.*
- (Hold up three fingers.) *You find them in some place.*
- (Repeat until the students say the facts in order.)

━━━━━━━━ **EXERCISE 5** ━━━━━━━

DESCRIPTION

The next Thinking Operation is **Description.**

1. I'm going to tell you about an object you know. But I'm going to call it a funny name. See if you can figure out what object I'm talking about.
2. (Hold up one finger.) A lat is made of metal.
- (Hold up two fingers.) A lat has a point and a head.
- (Hold up three fingers.) You pound a lat with a hammer.
3. Let's say the three things we know about a lat. (Respond with the students. Hold up one finger.) *A lat is made of metal.*
- (Hold up two fingers.) *A lat has a point and a head.*
- (Hold up three fingers.) *You pound a lat with a hammer.*
- (Repeat until the students are responding with you.)
4. You say the three things you know about a lat. (Hold up one finger.) *A lat is made of metal.*
- (Hold up two fingers.) *A lat has a point and a head.*
- (Hold up three fingers.) *You pound a lat with a hammer.*
- (Repeat until the students say the statements in order.)
5. Everybody, tell me what I'm calling a lat. (Signal.) *A nail.*
- Yes, it's really a nail.

EXERCISE 6

DESCRIPTION

1. Here's the rule. **Yum** is a funny word that we'll use for pencil. What word are we using for **pencil?** (Signal.) *Yum.*
2. Listen to this sentence. A yum is used to cut meat. Is that statement true or false? (Signal.) *False.*
3. Next sentence. You can wear a yum on your foot. Is that statement true or false? (Signal.) *False.*
4. Next sentence. Most yums have a point and an eraser. Is that statement true or false? (Signal.) *True.*
5. Next sentence. You can write with a yum. Is that statement true or false? (Signal.) *True.*
6. Next sentence. A yum can walk. Is that statement true or false? (Signal.) *False.*

EXERCISE 7

STATEMENT INFERENCE

The next Thinking Operation is **Statement Inference.**

Task A

1. Listen. Most reptiles sleep during the day. Say that statement. (Signal.) *Most reptiles sleep during the day.* (Repeat until firm.)

> **Individual test**
> (Call on individual students to say the statement.)

2. Everybody, listen. Most reptiles sleep during the day.
- How many reptiles sleep during the day? (Signal.) *Most.*
- What do most reptiles do during the day? (Signal.) *Sleep.*
- When do most reptiles sleep? (Signal.) *During the day.*
- Where do most reptiles sleep during the day? (Signal.) *I don't know.*
- What sleeps during the day? (Signal.) *Most reptiles.*

- What kind of reptiles sleep during the day? (Signal.) *I don't know.*
- What do most reptiles do? (Signal.) *Sleep during the day.*
- (Repeat step 2 until firm.)

> **Individual test**
> (Call on individual students to answer a question from step 2.)

Task B

1. Listen. His sister saved money to buy hiking shoes. Say that statement. (Signal.) *His sister saved money to buy hiking shoes.* (Repeat until firm.)

> **Individual test**
> (Call on individual students to say the statement.)

2. Everybody, listen. His sister saved money to buy hiking shoes. What did his sister do? (Signal.) *Saved money to buy hiking shoes.*
- Why did his sister save money? (Signal.) *To buy hiking shoes.*
- What did his sister save? (Signal.) *Money.*
- How much money did his sister save? (Signal.) *I don't know.*
- What did his sister save money to buy? (Signal.) *Hiking shoes.*
- What kind of shoes did his sister save money to buy? (Signal.) *Hiking.*
- How many hiking shoes did his sister save money to buy? (Signal.) *I don't know.*
- Who saved money to buy hiking shoes? (Signal.) *His sister.*
- (Repeat step 2 until firm.)

> **Individual test**
> (Call on individual students to answer a question from step 2.)

━━━━━━ **EXERCISE 8** ━━━━━━

DEFINITIONS

The next Thinking Operation is **Definitions.**

1. Amble. What does **amble** mean? (Signal.) *Walk slowly.*
- What word means **walk slowly?** (Signal.) *Amble.*
- (Repeat step 1 until firm.)
2. Listen. Ambling is fun. Say that. (Signal.) *Ambling is fun.* (Repeat until firm.)
- Now you're going to say that sentence with different words for **ambling.** (Pause.) Get ready. (Signal.) *Walking slowly is fun.* (Repeat until firm.)
- (Repeat step 2 until firm.)
3. Listen. The pig ambled next to the fence. Say that. (Signal.) *The pig ambled next to the fence.* (Repeat until firm.)
- Now you're going to say that sentence with different words for **ambled.** (Pause.) Get ready. (Signal.) *The pig walked slowly next to the fence.* (Repeat until firm.)
- (Repeat step 3 until firm.)

━━━━━━ **EXERCISE 9** ━━━━━━

DEFINITIONS

1. **Indolent.** (Pause.) What's a synonym for **indolent?** (Signal.) *Lazy.*
- And what's a synonym for **lazy?** (Signal.) *Indolent.*
- (Repeat step 1 until firm.)
2. Listen. When it is sunny, I feel lazy. Say that. (Signal.) *When it is sunny, I feel lazy.* (Repeat until firm.)
- Now you're going to say that sentence with a synonym for **lazy.** (Pause.) Get ready. (Signal.) *When it is sunny, I feel indolent.* (Repeat until firm.)
- (Repeat step 2 until firm.)
3. **Canine.** (Pause.) What's a synonym for **canine?** (Signal.) *Dog.*
- And what's a synonym for **dog?** (Signal.) *Canine.*
- (Repeat step 3 until firm.)
4. Listen. His canine has a wet nose. Say that. (Signal.) *His canine has a wet nose.* (Repeat until firm.)

- Now you're going to say that sentence with a synonym for **canine.** (Pause.) Get ready. (Signal.) *His dog has a wet nose.* (Repeat until firm.)
- (Repeat step 4 until firm.)
5. **Complete.** (Pause.) What's a synonym for **complete?** (Signal.) *Finish.*
- And what's a synonym for **finish?** (Signal.) *Complete.*
- (Repeat step 5 until firm.)
6. Listen. I can't finish this work. Say that. (Signal.) *I can't finish this work.* (Repeat until firm.)
- Now you're going to say that sentence with a synonym for **finish.** (Pause.) Get ready. (Signal.) *I can't complete this work.* (Repeat until firm.)
- (Repeat step 6 until firm.)

Points

(Pass out the Workbooks. Award points for Thinking Operations.)

WORKBOOK EXERCISES

We're going to do the Workbooks now. Remember to follow my instructions carefully.

━━━━━━ **EXERCISE 10** ━━━━━━

NEW SOME, ALL, NONE

1. Everybody, touch part A in your Workbook. ✓
- I'll say statements about the picture. Some of these statements are true, some are false, and some **may be** true or **may be** false.
- Here's a **maybe** statement about the picture: Some of the trees are five years old. That **may be** true or **may be** false. We don't know.
- Here's another **maybe** statement: All the trees belong to Mr. Jones. That **may be** true or **may be** false. We don't know.
2. Get ready to make a box around **true, false,** or **maybe.** Item 1. **None** of the trees are twenty years old. Make a box around **true, false,** or **maybe** for item 1. ✓

3. Item 2. **All** of the trees are peach trees. Make a box around **true, false,** or **maybe** for item 2. ✓
4. Item 3. **Some** of the trees have leaves. Make a box around **true, false,** or **maybe** for item 3. ✓
5. Item 4. **All** of the trees have leaves. Make a box around **true, false,** or **maybe** for item 4. ✓
6. Let's check your answers. Mark any item you missed with an **X.** Everybody, tell me **true, false,** or **maybe.**
  - Item 1. **None** of the trees are twenty years old. (Signal.) *Maybe.*
  - Item 2. **All** of the trees are peach trees. (Signal.) *Maybe.*
  - Item 3. **Some** of the trees have leaves. (Signal.) *True.*
  - Item 4. **All** of the trees have leaves. (Signal.) *False.*

EXERCISE 11
CLASSIFICATION

1. Pencils down. Don't write anything yet. Everybody, touch the instructions for part B in your Workbook. ✓
  - I'll read the first instruction. Listen. Underline the furniture. What are you going to do to every piece of furniture? (Signal.) *Underline it.*
2. I'll read the next instruction. Make a box around the containers. What are you going to do to every container? (Signal.) *Make a box around it.*
  - Everybody, do it. Underline the furniture and make a box around the containers. ✓
3. Get ready to mark your papers. Put an **X** by any object you got wrong.
4. What class is a **glass** in? (Signal.) *Containers.*
  - How did you mark the **glass?** (Signal.) *Made a box around it.*
5. (Repeat step 4 for **bowl, stool, garbage can, chest of drawers, bookcase, vase, jug, easy chair,** and **table.**)

EXERCISE 12
SAME

1. Everybody, touch part C in your Workbook. ✓
  - Some of the objects in Box 1 are made of the same material. **Circle** all the objects that are made of the same material. Do it. ✓
2. Some of the objects in Box 2 are usually found in the same room. **Put a 2 on** all the objects that are usually found in the same room. Do it. ✓
3. Some of the objects in Box 3 are in the same class. **Draw a box around** each object that's in the same class. Do it. ✓
4. Everybody, get ready to check part C. You're going to name the material of the objects you marked in Box 1. (Pause.) Get ready. (Signal.) *Metal.*
  - You're going to name the place of the objects you marked in Box 2. (Pause.) Get ready. (Signal.) *Living room.*
  - You're going to name the class of the objects you marked in Box 3. (Pause.) Get ready. (Signal.) *Food.*

5. Make an **X** next to any item you miss. Which objects did you mark in Box 1? (Call on one student.) *Can, nail, scissors.*

- What is the same about those objects? (Call on one student.) *They are made of metal.*

- How did you mark each of those objects? (Call on one student.) *Circled it.*

6. (Repeat step 5 for Boxes 2 and 3.)

EXERCISE 13
NEW SOME, ALL, NONE

1. Everybody, touch part D in your Workbook. ✓

- I'll say statements that are true of one of the pictures. You write the letter of the right picture. Don't get fooled, because I may say statements about the same picture twice.

2. Item 1. **Only some** of the bottles are full. Write the letter of that picture on line 1. ✓

3. Item 2. **All** the bottles are empty. Write the letter of that picture on line 2. ✓

4. Item 3. **Only some** of the bottles are empty. Write the letter of that picture on line 3. ✓

5. Item 4. **None** of the bottles are empty. Write the letter of that picture on line 4. ✓

6. Let's check your answers. Mark any items you missed with an **X**. Tell me the letter of the right picture.

7. Item 1. **Only some** of the bottles are full. (Signal.) *E.*

8. (Repeat step 7 for items 2–4.)

EXERCISE 14
NEW DESCRIPTION

1. Everybody, touch part E in the Workbook. ✓

- Figure out which woman I describe.

2. Item 1. This woman is smiling. This woman has black hair. This woman is wearing glasses. Listen again. (Repeat the description.)

- Write the letter for item 1. ✓

3. Item 2. This woman is smiling. This woman is not wearing glasses. This woman has light hair. Listen again. (Repeat the description.)

- Write the letter for item 2. ✓

4. Item 3. This woman has black hair. This woman is wearing glasses. This woman is wearing earrings. Listen again. (Repeat the description.)

- Write the letter for item 3. ✓

5. Let's check your answers. Mark any items you missed with an **X**.

6. Item 1. This woman is smiling. This woman has black hair. This woman is wearing glasses. Everybody, what letter? (Signal.) *D.*

7. (Repeat step 6 for items 2 and 3.)

Points

(Award points for Workbooks.)

INFORMATION

We're going to work on Information now.

EXERCISE 15
CALENDAR: Seasons in a Year

1. There are four seasons in a year. How many seasons are in a year? (Signal.) *Four.*
- Tell me the fact about how many seasons are in a year. (Signal.) *There are four seasons in a year.*
2. My turn to name the seasons in a year. Winter, spring, summer, fall. Your turn. Name the seasons in a year. (Signal.) *Winter, spring, summer, fall.* (Repeat until firm.)
3. You named the four (pause; signal) *seasons in a year.*
4. How many seasons are in a year? (Signal.) *Four.*

> **Individual test**
> (Call on individual students to do one of the following tasks:)
> a. Tell me the fact about how many seasons are in a year.
> b. Name the seasons in a year.

EXERCISE 16
MEMORIZATION: Poem

Task A

1. Let's see if you remember some information. What does a mechanic do? (Call on a student. Accept reasonable responses.)
- Yes, a mechanic fixes cars.
2. What does an astronomer do? (Call on a student. Accept reasonable responses.)
- Yes, an astronomer looks at stars.
3. How would you recognize a captain in the army? (Call on a student. Accept reasonable responses.)
- Yes, a captain has two bars on each shoulder.

4. What is sparring? (Call on a student. Accept reasonable responses.)
- Yes, sparring is light boxing. Boxers spar a lot when they are getting in shape for a fight.

Task B

1. Here's that poem that tells about the things we've talked about before. Listen.
A mechanic fixes cars,
An astronomer looks at stars,
A captain has two bars,
And a boxer spars and spars.
2. Here's the first line. Listen. A mechanic fixes cars.
- Your turn. Say it. (Signal.) *A mechanic fixes cars.* (Repeat until firm.)
3. An astronomer looks at stars.
- Your turn. Say it. (Signal.) *An astronomer looks at stars.* (Repeat until firm.)
4. A mechanic fixes cars, an astronomer looks at stars. Say it with me. (Signal. Respond with the students.) *A mechanic fixes cars, an astronomer looks at stars.* (Repeat until the students are responding with you.)
- Your turn. (Signal.) *A mechanic fixes cars, an astronomer looks at stars.* (Repeat until firm.)
5. A captain has two bars. Say it. (Signal.) *A captain has two bars.* (Repeat until firm.)
6. A mechanic fixes cars, an astronomer looks at stars, a captain has two bars. Say it with me. (Signal. Respond with the students.) *A mechanic fixes cars, an astronomer looks at stars, a captain has two bars.* (Repeat until students are responding with you.)
- Your turn. (Signal.) *A mechanic fixes cars, an astronomer looks at stars, a captain has two bars.* (Repeat until firm.)
7. And a boxer spars and spars. Say it. (Signal.) *And a boxer spars and spars.* (Repeat until firm.)

8. Here's the whole poem.
   A mechanic fixes cars,
   An astronomer looks at stars,
   A captain has two bars,
   And a boxer spars and spars.
   Say it with me. (Signal. Respond with the students. Repeat until students respond with you.)

9. All by yourselves. Say the poem. (Signal. The students say the poem. Repeat until firm.)

=========== **EXERCISE 17** ===========

NEW **INFORMATION: Animals**

1. You're learning about animals that have a backbone. How many classes of those animals are there? (Signal.) *Five.*

   • You've learned facts about two of those classes. Which classes? (Signal.) *Mammals and reptiles.* (Repeat until firm.)

2. Name a mammal. (Call on individual students. The group is to name at least five mammals.)

   • You learned two facts about **all mammals.** Everybody, tell me those two facts. (Hold up one finger.) First fact. *All mammals have hair.*

   • (Hold up two fingers.) Second fact. *All mammals are warm-blooded.*

   • (Repeat until the students say the facts in order.)

3. Name a reptile. (Call on individual students. The group is to name at least four reptiles.)

   • You learned two facts about **all reptiles.** Everybody, tell me those two facts. (Hold up one finger.) First fact. *All reptiles are cold-blooded.*

   • (Hold up two fingers.) Second fact. *All reptiles are born on land.*

   • (Repeat until the students say the facts in order.)

4. What class are monkeys in? (Signal.) *Mammals.*

   • So, tell me the two facts you know about **monkeys.** (Hold up one finger.) First fact. *Monkeys have hair.*

   • (Hold up two fingers.) Second fact. *Monkeys are warm-blooded.*

   • (Repeat until the students say the facts in order.)

5. What class are alligators in? (Signal.) *Reptiles.*

   • So, tell me the two facts you know about **alligators.** (Hold up one finger.) First fact. *Alligators are cold-blooded.*

   • (Hold up two fingers.) Second fact. *Alligators are born on land.*

   • (Repeat until the students say the facts in order.)

=========== **EXERCISE 18** ===========

NEW **INFORMATION: Animals**

1. You're going to learn about another class of animals that have a backbone.

2. Eagles are not mammals or reptiles. They are birds. Name another bird. (Call on individual students. The group is to name at least four birds.)

3. Here's the first fact about **all birds.** Listen. All birds have feathers. Say that fact. (Signal.) *All birds have feathers.* (Repeat until firm.)

   • Yes, even birds that can't fly have feathers.

4. Here's that fact again: All birds have feathers. Eagles are birds. So, eagles (pause; signal) *have feathers.*

   • Robins are birds. So, robins (pause; signal) *have feathers.*

   • Ducks are birds. So, ducks (pause; signal) *have feathers.*

5. Everybody, tell me the first fact about **all birds.** (Signal.) *All birds have feathers.*

   • Here's the second fact about **all birds.** Listen. All birds are warm-blooded. Say that fact. (Signal.) *All birds are warm-blooded.* (Repeat until firm.)

6. Here are the two facts you've learned about **all birds.** (Hold up one finger.) First fact. All birds have feathers.

- (Hold up two fingers.) Second fact. All birds are warm-blooded.

- Your turn. Tell me the two facts about **all birds.** (Hold up one finger.) First fact. *All birds have feathers.*

- (Hold up two fingers.) Second fact. *All birds are warm-blooded.*

- (Repeat until the students say the facts in order.)

7. Penguins are birds. So, tell me the two facts you know about **penguins.** (Hold up one finger.) First fact. *Penguins have feathers.*

- (Hold up two fingers.) Second fact. *Penguins are warm-blooded.*

- (Repeat until the students say the facts in order.)

8. Ostriches are birds. So, tell me the two facts you know about **ostriches.** (Hold up one finger.) First fact. *Ostriches have feathers.*

- (Hold up two fingers.) Second fact. *Ostriches are warm-blooded.*

- (Repeat until the students say the facts in order.)

Individual test
(Call on individual students to do one of the following tasks:)
  a. Robins are birds. What two facts do you know about robins?
  b. Sparrows are birds. What two facts do you know about sparrows?
  c. Name three mammals.
  d. Name three reptiles.
  e. Name three birds.

Points

(Award points for Information. Direct the students to total their points for the lesson and enter the total on the Point Summary Chart.)

END OF LESSON 8

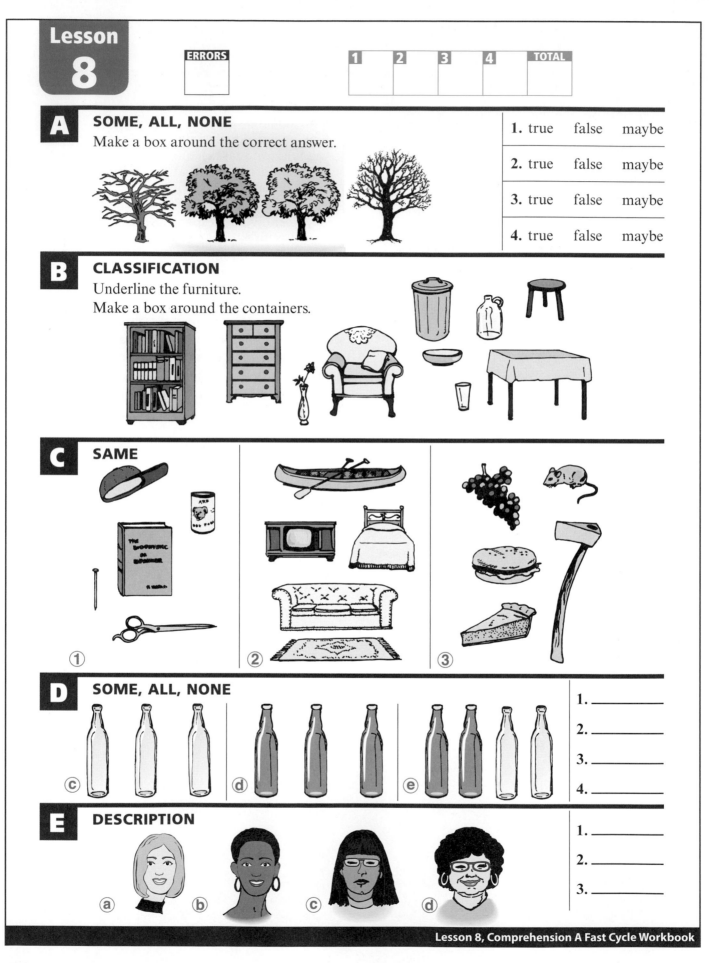

Lesson 8

ERRORS

1	2	3	4	TOTAL

A SOME, ALL, NONE
Make a box around the correct answer.

1. true	false	maybe
2. true	false	maybe
3. true	false	maybe
4. true	false	maybe

B CLASSIFICATION
Underline the furniture.
Make a box around the containers.

C SAME

① ② ③

D SOME, ALL, NONE

ⓒ ⓓ ⓔ

1. _____
2. _____
3. _____
4. _____

E DESCRIPTION

ⓐ ⓑ ⓒ ⓓ

1. _____
2. _____
3. _____

Comprehension A—Lesson 52

More sophisticated variations of the skills that were introduced in Fast Cycle Lesson 8 appear in regular Lesson 52. The following thinking operations are included:

■ Statement inference involving a fairly complex sentence (Exercise 1)

■ Deductions in which students are tested on the limitations of information conveyed by a rule (Exercise 2)

■ Constructing deductions (Exercise 3)

■ Definitions with new and review words—**construct, majority, inquire, consume** (Exercises 4 and 5)

■ The use of basic evidence to explain different outcomes (Exercise 6)

■ Review of same, opposites (Exercises 7 through 10)

■ Analyzing analogies based on synonyms, opposites, and classes (Exercises 11 through 13)

■ Inductions (Exercise 14)

The Workbook includes these activities:

■ Drawing deductions (Exercise 15)

■ Classifying things as objects, actions, or adjectives (Exercise 16)

■ Analogies based on information about holidays (Exercise 17)

■ Descriptions (Exercise 18)

The information activities deal with the review of two poems.

THINKING OPERATIONS

EXERCISE 1

STATEMENT INFERENCE

The first Thinking Operation today is
Statement Inference.

1. Listen. Pollution in the air increases every
   year. Say that statement. (Signal.)
   Pollution in the air increases every year.
   (Repeat until firm.)

> **Individual test**
> (Call on individual students to say the
> statement.)

2. Everybody, listen. Pollution in the air
   increases every year. When does pollution
   increase in the air? (Signal.) *Every year.*
   - What increases in the air every year?
     (Signal.) *Pollution.*
   - Where does pollution increase every
     year? (Signal.) *In the air.*
   - How does pollution in the air increase
     every year? (Signal.) *I don't know.*
   - What does pollution in the air do every
     year? (Signal.) *Increases.*
   - Does the pollution in the air get greater
     every year? (Signal.) *Yes.*
   - (Repeat step 2 until firm.)

> **Individual test**
> (Call on individual students to answer a
> question from step 2.)

EXERCISE 2

DEDUCTIONS: With *no*

The next Thinking Operation is **Deductions.**

1. Listen to this rule. No amphibians are
   warm-blooded. Say the rule. (Signal.) *No
   amphibians are warm-blooded.*

2. **Henrietta** had a scary dream. What does
   the rule let you know about Henrietta?
   (Signal.) *Nothing.*

3. Listen. No amphibians are warm-
   blooded. A salamander is an **amphibian.**
   What does the rule let you know about a
   salamander? (Signal.) *A salamander isn't
   warm-blooded.*
   - How do you know that a salamander
     isn't warm-blooded? (Signal.) *Because no
     amphibians are warm-blooded.*

4. Listen. No amphibians are warm-
   blooded. A frog is an **amphibian.** What
   does the rule let you know about a frog?
   (Signal.) *A frog isn't warm-blooded.*
   - How do you know that a frog isn't warm-
     blooded? (Signal.) *Because no
     amphibians are warm-blooded.*

5. Listen. No amphibians are warm-
   blooded. **Bill** looked for a tiger. What
   does the rule let you know about Bill?
   (Signal.) *Nothing.*

6. (Repeat steps 2–5 until firm.)

EXERCISE 3

DEDUCTIONS

1. Get ready to make a deduction.

2. Listen. Some planets have many moons.
   Saturn is a planet. So (pause; signal),
   maybe Saturn has many moons. (Repeat
   until firm.)

3. My turn to say the whole deduction.
   Some planets have many moons. Saturn
   is a planet. So, maybe Saturn has many
   moons.

4. Your turn. Say the whole deduction.
   (Signal.) *Some planets have many moons.
   Saturn is a planet. So, maybe Saturn has
   many moons.* (Repeat until firm.)

> **Individual test**
> (Call on individual students to say the
> whole deduction.)

===== **EXERCISE 4** =====

DEFINITIONS

The next Thinking Operation is **Definitions.**

1. **Construct** means **to make** or **to build.** What word means **to make** or **to build?** (Signal.) *Construct.*

2. Listen. He will build his house on a hill. Say that. (Signal.) *He will build his house on a hill.* (Repeat until firm.)

• Now you're going to say that sentence with a different word for **build.** (Pause.) Get ready. (Signal.) *He will construct his house on a hill.* (Repeat until firm.)

• (Repeat step 2 until firm.)

3. Listen. That building is made of concrete. Say that. (Signal.) *That building is made of concrete.* (Repeat until firm.)

• Now you're going to say that sentence with a different word for **made.** (Pause.) Get ready. (Signal.) *That building is constructed of concrete.* (Repeat until firm.)

• (Repeat step 3 until firm.)

4. Listen. She will build her own furniture. Say that. (Signal.) *She will build her own furniture.* (Repeat until firm.)

• Now you're going to say that with a different word for **build.** (Pause.) Get ready. (Signal.) *She will construct her own furniture.* (Repeat until firm.)

• (Repeat step 4 until firm.)

===== **EXERCISE 5** =====

DEFINITIONS

1. **Majority.** (Pause.) What does **majority** mean? (Signal.) *More than half.*

• What word means **more than half?** (Signal.) *Majority.*

• (Repeat step 1 until firm.)

2. Listen. The **majority** of the class voted for Joyce. Say that. (Signal.) *The majority of the class voted for Joyce.* (Repeat until firm.)

• Now you're going to say that sentence with different words for **majority.** (Pause.) Get ready. (Signal.) *More than half of the class voted for Joyce.* (Repeat until firm.)

• (Repeat step 2 until firm.)

3. **Inquire.** (Pause.) What's a synonym for **inquire?** (Signal.) *Ask.*

• And what's a synonym for **ask?** (Signal.) *Inquire.*

• (Repeat step 3 until firm.)

4. Listen. "Where is the meeting?" he asked. Say that. (Signal.) *"Where is the meeting?" he asked.* (Repeat until firm.)

• Now you're going to say that sentence with a synonym for **asked.** (Pause.) Get ready. (Signal.) *"Where is the meeting?" he inquired.* (Repeat until firm.)

• (Repeat step 4 until firm.)

5. **Consume.** (Pause.) What does **consume** mean? (Signal.) *Use up.*

• What word means **use up?** (Signal.) *Consume.*

• (Repeat step 5 until firm.)

6. Listen. Every bath uses up thirty gallons of water. Say that. (Signal.) *Every bath uses up thirty gallons of water.* (Repeat until firm.)

• Now you're going to say that sentence using a different word for **uses up.** (Pause.) Get ready. (Signal.) *Every bath consumes thirty gallons of water.* (Repeat until firm.)

• (Repeat step 6 until firm.)

===== **EXERCISE 6** =====

BASIC EVIDENCE: Using Facts

The next Thinking Operation is **Basic Evidence.**

1. You're going to use two facts to explain things that happen. (Hold up one finger.) First fact. It takes many years to become a doctor. Say it. (Signal.) *It takes many years to become a doctor.* (Repeat until firm.)

• (Hold up two fingers.) Second fact. Doctors work in hospitals. Say it. (Signal.) *Doctors work in hospitals.* (Repeat until firm.)

2. Everybody, say those facts again. (Hold up one finger.) First fact. *It takes many years to become a doctor.*
- (Hold up two fingers.) Second fact. *Doctors work in hospitals.*
- (Repeat until the students say the facts in order.)

> **Individual test**
> (Call on individual students to say the facts.)

3. Here's what happens: They have to read hundreds of books. You're going to tell me the fact that explains **why** that happens. (Pause.) Get ready. (Signal.) *It takes many years to become a doctor.*
4. Listen. First fact. It takes many years to become a doctor. Second fact. Doctors work in hospitals.
5. Here's what happens: There are no eighteen-year-old doctors. You're going to tell me the fact that explains **why** that happens. (Pause.) Get ready. (Signal.) *It takes many years to become a doctor.*
6. Here's what happens: There are many nurses where doctors work. You're going to tell me the fact that explains **why** that happens: (Pause.) Get ready. (Signal.) *Doctors work in hospitals.*
7. Here's what happens: Doctors hear ambulances every day. You're going to tell me the fact that explains **why** that happens. (Pause.) Get ready. (Signal.) *Doctors work in hospitals.*
8. (Repeat steps 5–7 until firm.)

━━━━━━━━ **EXERCISE 7** ━━━━━━━━
SAME: Review

The next Thinking Operation is **Same.**
1. I'll name some things. When I call on you, name ways those things are the same.
2. A cow and a horse. Name eight ways they are the same. (Call on one student. Praise the student if he or she names eight ways.)

3. A television and a radio. Name eight ways they are the same. (Call on one student. Praise the student if he or she names eight ways.)
4. Skating and dancing. Name four ways they are the same. (Call on one student. Praise the student if he or she names four ways.)
5. A snake and a lizard. Name eight ways they are the same. (Call on one student. Praise the student if he or she names eight ways.)

━━━━━━━━ **EXERCISE 8** ━━━━━━━━
NEW OPPOSITES

The next Thinking Operation is **Opposites.**
1. (Draw a straight line on the board. Draw a jagged line below it. Point to the straight line.) This is straight.
- (Point to the crooked line.) This is crooked.
2. What's the opposite of **crooked?** (Signal.) *Straight.*
- What's the opposite of **straight?** (Signal.) *Crooked.*
- (Repeat step 2 until firm.)

━━━━━━━━ **EXERCISE 9** ━━━━━━━━
OPPOSITES

1. **Straight.** (Pause.) What's the opposite of **straight?** (Signal.) *Crooked.*
- **Crooked.** (Pause.) What's the opposite of **crooked?** (Signal.) *Straight.*
- (Repeat step 1 until firm.)
2. **Fuller.** (Pause.) What's the opposite of **fuller?** (Signal.) *Emptier.*
- Having a **noisy** party. (Pause.) What's the opposite of having a **noisy** party? (Signal.) *Having a quiet party.*
- (Repeat step 2 until firm.)
3. **Dead.** (Pause.) What's the opposite of **dead?** (Signal.) *Alive.*
- **Hardest.** (Pause.) What's the opposite of **hardest?** (Signal.) *Softest.*
- (Repeat step 3 until firm.)
4. **Straight.** (Pause.) What's the opposite of **straight?** (Signal.) *Crooked.*
5. (Repeat steps 2–4 until firm.)

Lesson 52

═══════ **EXERCISE 10** ═══════

OPPOSITES

1. You're going to say sentences with **opposites.**
2. Listen. Summer is usually the driest season. Say that. (Signal.) *Summer is usually the driest season.* (Repeat until firm.)
  - Now you're going to say that sentence with the opposite of **driest.** (Pause.) Get ready. (Signal.) *Summer is usually the wettest season.* (Repeat until firm.)
  - (Repeat step 2 until firm.)
3. Listen. Oak bark is rougher than beech bark. Say that. (Signal.) *Oak bark is rougher than beech bark.* (Repeat until firm.)
  - Now you're going to say that sentence with the opposite of **rougher.** (Pause.) Get ready. (Signal.) *Oak bark is smoother than beech bark.* (Repeat until firm.)
  - (Repeat step 3 until firm.)
4. Listen. Stoplights make driving safe. Say that. (Signal.) *Stoplights make driving safe.* (Repeat until firm.)
  - Now you're going to say that sentence with the opposite of **safe.** (Pause.) Get ready. (Signal.) *Stoplights make driving dangerous.* (Repeat until firm.)
  - (Repeat step 4 until firm.)
5. Listen. Some people are sad when they lose money. Say that. (Signal.) *Some people are sad when they lose money.* (Repeat until firm.)
  - Now you're going to say that sentence with the opposite of **sad.** (Pause.) Get ready. (Signal.) *Some people are happy when they lose money.* (Repeat until firm.)
  - (Repeat step 5 until firm.)
6. Listen. Good fruit is hard to find in winter. Say that. (Signal.) *Good fruit is hard to find in winter.* (Repeat until firm.)
  - Now you're going to say that sentence with the opposite of **good.** (Pause.) Get ready. (Signal.) *Bad fruit is hard to find in winter.* (Repeat until firm.)
  - (Repeat step 6 until firm.)
7. Listen. Most rivers are crooked. Say that. (Signal.) *Most rivers are crooked.* (Repeat until firm.)
  - Now you're going to say that sentence with the opposite of crooked. (Pause.) Get ready. (Signal.) *Most rivers are straight.* (Repeat until firm.)
  - (Repeat step 7 until firm.)

═══════ **EXERCISE 11** ═══════

ANALOGIES: Synonyms

The next Thinking Operation is **Analogies.**
1. Here's an analogy about words: **Lazy** is to **indolent** as **complete** is to…(Pause 2 seconds.) Get ready. (Signal.) *Finish.*
  - Everybody, say that analogy. (Signal.) *Lazy is to indolent as complete is to finish.* (Repeat until firm.)
2. What are **lazy** and **complete?** (Signal.) *Words.*

  To correct students who say *Synonyms:*
  a. **Lazy** and **complete** are **words.**
  b. (Repeat step 2.)
  - **Lazy** is to **indolent** as **complete** is to **finish.** That analogy tells something about those words. (Pause.) What does that analogy tell about those words? (Signal.) *What synonyms those words have.* (Repeat until firm.)
3. Say the analogy. (Signal.) *Lazy is to indolent as complete is to finish.* (Repeat until firm.)
4. And what does that analogy tell about those words? (Signal.) *What synonyms those words have.*
5. (Repeat steps 3 and 4 until firm.)

EXERCISE 12
ANALOGIES: Opposites

1. Here's an analogy about words: **Short** is to **long** as **fast** is to...(Pause 2 seconds.) Get ready. (Signal.) *Slow.*
- Everybody, say the analogy. (Signal.) *Short is to long as fast is to slow.* (Repeat until firm.)
2. What are **short** and **fast?** (Signal.) *Words.*
- **Short** is to **long** as **fast** is to **slow.** That analogy tells something about those words. (Pause.) What does that analogy tell about those words? (Signal.) *What opposites those words have.* (Repeat until firm.)
3. Say the analogy. (Signal.) *Short is to long as fast is to slow.* (Repeat until firm.)
4. And what does that analogy tell about those words? (Signal.) *What opposites those words have.*
5. (Repeat steps 3 and 4 until firm.)

EXERCISE 13
ANALOGIES

> **Note:** Praise all reasonable responses in steps 1, 3, and 4, but have the group repeat the responses specified in the exercise.

Task A

1. Here's an analogy: A spoon is to metal as a toothbrush is to...(Pause 2 seconds.) Get ready. (Signal.) *Plastic.*
- Everybody, say that analogy. (Signal.) *A spoon is to metal as a toothbrush is to plastic.* (Repeat until firm.)
2. What class are a spoon and a toothbrush in? (Signal.) *Tools.*
3. A spoon is to metal as a toothbrush is to plastic. The analogy tells something about those tools. (Pause.) What does that analogy tell about those tools? (Signal.) *What material those tools are made of.* (Repeat until firm.)
4. Say the analogy. (Signal.) *A spoon is to metal as a toothbrush is to plastic.* (Repeat until firm.)

Task B

1. Here's an analogy: A ladder is to climbing as a shovel is to...(Pause 2 seconds.) Get ready. (Signal.) *Digging.*
- Everybody, say that analogy. (Signal.) *A ladder is to climbing as a shovel is to digging.* (Repeat until firm.)
2. What class are a ladder and a shovel in? (Signal.) *Tools.*
3. A ladder is to climbing as a shovel is to digging. The analogy tells something about those tools. (Pause.) What does that analogy tell about those tools? (Signal.) *What you do with those tools.*
- (Repeat step 3 until firm.)
4. Say the analogy. (Signal.) *A ladder is to climbing as a shovel is to digging.* (Repeat until firm.)

EXERCISE 14
INDUCTIONS

The next Thinking Operation is **Inductions.**

1. I'm going to tell you facts about the sun and the temperature on planets. See if you can figure out the rules.
2. Listen. On Mercury the sun is near and the planet is hot. On Saturn the sun is far and the planet is cold. On Venus the sun is near and the planet is hot. On Neptune the sun is far and the planet is cold. On Jupiter the sun is far and the planet is cold.
3. You're going to tell me the rule about what happens when the sun is far. (Pause.) Get ready. (Signal.) *When the sun is far, the planet is cold.*
4. You're going to tell me the rule about what happens when the sun is near. (Pause.) Get ready. (Signal.) *When the sun is near, the planet is hot.*
5. (Repeat steps 3 and 4 until firm.)

> **Individual test**
> (Call on individual students to do step 3 or step 4.)

Points

(Pass out the Workbooks. Award points for Thinking Operations.)

WORKBOOK EXERCISES

We're going to do Workbooks now.

━━━━━━━ **EXERCISE 15** ━━━━━━━

DEDUCTIONS

1. Everybody, touch part A in your Workbook. ✓
- Read the sentences in the box with me. Get ready. (Signal.) *Here's the only thing Sue did. Sue wore some of the white shirts.*
- What's the **only** thing Sue did? (Signal.) *Wore some of the white shirts.* (Repeat until firm.)
2. Everybody, read item 1 with me. Get ready. (Signal.) *Sue wore object A.*
- Write the answer. ✓
3. Read item 2 with me. Get ready. (Signal.) *Sue did not wear object C.*
- Write the answer. ✓
4. Read item 3 with me. Get ready. (Signal.) *Sue wore object D.*
- Write the answer. ✓
5. Get ready to check your answers. Make an **X** next to any item that's wrong. I'll read the items. You say **true, false,** or **maybe.** Item 1. Sue wore object A. (Signal.) *Maybe.*
- Item 2. Sue did not wear object C. (Signal.) *True.*
- Item 3. Sue wore object D. (Signal.) *False.*

━━━━━━━ **EXERCISE 16** ━━━━━━━

SAME

1. Everybody, find part B in your Workbook. ✓
- You're going to make a box around the answer at the end of each row.

2. Now, I'll read the words in each row. You make a box around the answer.
3. Row 1. **Motorcycle, ink, lamp.** Make a box around the answer. ✓
4. Row 2. **Hot, sticky, lumpy.** Make a box around the answer. ✓
5. Row 3. **Skates, water, picture.** Make a box around the answer. ✓
6. Row 4. **Mean, happy, quick.** Make a box around the answer. ✓
7. Row 5. **Envelope, flower, shell.** Make a box around the answer. ✓
8. Get ready to check your answers. Mark any item you miss with an **X.** I'll read the words in each row. You tell me if the words name objects or actions, or tell what kind.
9. Row 1. **Motorcycle, ink, lamp.** (Signal.) *Objects.*
10. (Repeat step 9 for rows 2–5.)

━━━━━━━ **EXERCISE 17** ━━━━━━━

ANALOGIES

1. Everybody, touch part C in your Workbook. ✓
- I'll read the analogy. Don't say the answer. Christmas is to **December** as Independence Day is to **blank.**
2. The words you'll choose from are **June, January,** and **July.** Listen to the analogy again and get ready to copy the right word in the blank. Christmas is to December as Independence Day is to **blank.** Copy the right word in the blank. ✓
3. Listen. Christmas is to December as Independence Day is to blank. Everybody, what's the answer? (Signal.) *July.*
4. Everybody, say the whole analogy with me. (Signal.) *Christmas is to December as Independence Day is to July.* Put an **X** next to the analogy if you didn't copy the word **July.**
5. Listen. Christmas is to December as Independence Day is to July. That analogy tells something about those holidays. (Pause 4 seconds.) What does that analogy tell about those holidays? (Signal.) *What months those holidays are in.*

EXERCISE 18
DESCRIPTION

1. Everybody, touch part D in your Workbook. ✓
- Figure out which object I describe.
2. Item 1. This object is a living thing. This living thing is an animal. This animal is carnivorous. Listen again. (Repeat the description.)
- Write the letter for item 1. ✓
3. Item 2. This object needs food. The object is found where it is hot. This is a herbivorous animal. Listen again. (Repeat the description.)
- Write the letter for item 2. ✓
4. Item 3. This object is a living thing. This object is an animal. This animal lives where it is cold. Listen again. (Repeat the description.)
- Write the letter for item 3. ✓
5. Let's check your answers. Mark any items you missed with an **X**.
6. Item 1. This object is a living thing. This living thing is an animal. This animal is carnivorous. Everybody, what letter? (Signal.) *B*. And what does **B** stand for? (Signal.) *A polar bear*.
7. (Repeat step 6 for items 2 and 3.)

Points
(Award points for Workbooks.)

INFORMATION

We're going to work on Information now.

EXERCISE 19
MEMORIZATION: Poem

Say that poem we learned about the mechanic and the astronomer. Get ready. (Signal.) *A mechanic fixes cars; An astronomer looks at stars; A captain has two bars; And a boxer spars and spars.* (Repeat until firm.)

> **Individual test**
> (Call on individual students to say the whole poem.)

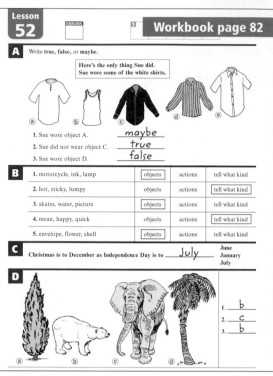

EXERCISE 20
MEMORIZATION: Poem

Say that poem we learned about the beautician and the tailor. Get ready. (Signal.)
A beautician fixes hair;
A tailor can mend a tear;
An exposition is a fair;
And one plus one is a pair.

> **Individual test**
> (Call on individual students to say the whole poem.)

Points

(Award points for Information. Direct the students to total their points for the lesson and enter the total on the Point Summary Chart.)

END OF LESSON 52

Lesson 52

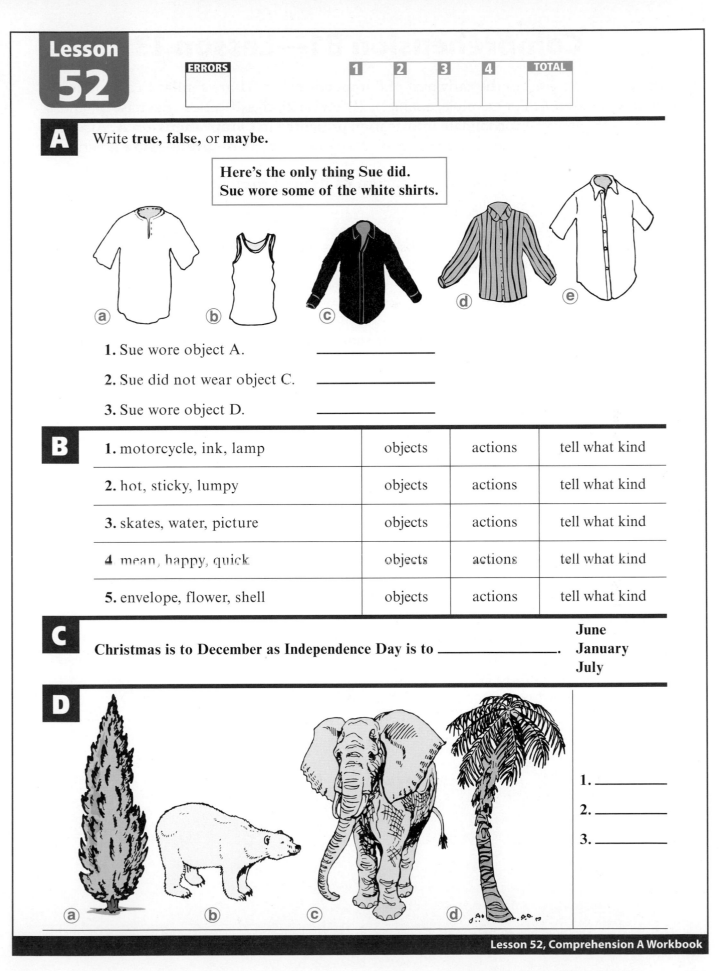

ERRORS

1	2	3	4	TOTAL

A Write **true, false,** or **maybe.**

> Here's the only thing Sue did.
> Sue wore some of the white shirts.

ⓐ ⓑ ⓒ ⓓ ⓔ

1. Sue wore object A. _____

2. Sue did not wear object C. _____

3. Sue wore object D. _____

B

1. motorcycle, ink, lamp	objects	actions	tell what kind
2. hot, sticky, lumpy	objects	actions	tell what kind
3. skates, water, picture	objects	actions	tell what kind
4. mean, happy, quick	objects	actions	tell what kind
5. envelope, flower, shell	objects	actions	tell what kind

C

Christmas is to December as Independence Day is to _____.

June
January
July

D

ⓐ ⓑ ⓒ ⓓ

1. _____

2. _____

3. _____

Lesson 52, Comprehension A Workbook

Comprehension B1—Lesson 13

Some of the activities in the early part of **Comprehension B1** are similar to activities in **Comprehension A.** For example, analogies (Exercise 2), classification (Exercise 3), and inference (Exercise 4) consolidate information presented in **Comprehension A.** Also, the Workbook deductions exercise (Exercise 6) is a variation of a **Comprehension A** activity.

The new material taught in **Comprehension B1** includes the following:

- New definitions (Exercises 1 and 5)

- Parts of speech. By Lesson 13, verbs and nouns have already been taught. Adjectives are introduced in Exercise 7.

- New following-directions tasks (Exercise 8)

- Definitions in which students complete sentences with forms of a vocabulary word (Exercise 9)

- Writing tasks (Exercise 10)

The main difference between **Comprehension A** and **Comprehension B1** is the number of independent activities the students perform. In Lesson 13, students independently do exercises that require them to identify verbs and nouns, use basic evidence to explain why different events happened, answer questions that are based on a statement, and identify parts of a skeleton (using information that had been taught starting in Lesson 3).

Correction Procedures

Follow these steps to correct errors:

1. (Say the answer.)
2. (Repeat the task [the instructions or question].)
3. (Back up in the exercise and present the steps in order.)
4. (Finish the remaining steps in the exercise.)
5. (Repeat the entire exercise if students made more than 1 or 2 mistakes.)

Lesson 13

GROUP WORK

━━━━━ **EXERCISE 1** ━━━━━

DEFINITIONS

1. Complete each sentence by saying **select, selected,** or **selecting.**
2. Listen. The man will **blank** a shirt. What word? (Signal.) *Select.*
   • Say the sentence. (Signal.) *The man will select a shirt.*
3. Listen. The man has **blank** a shirt. What word? (Signal.) *Selected.*
   • Say the sentence. (Signal.) *The man has selected a shirt.*
4. Listen. The man has to **blank** a shirt. What word? (Signal.) *Select.*
   • Say the sentence. (Signal.) *The man has to select a shirt.*
5. Listen. You must **blank** a shirt. What word? (Signal.) *Select.*
   • Say the sentence. (Signal.) *You must select a shirt.*
6. Listen. They are **blank** a shirt. What word? (Signal.) *Selecting.*
   • Say the sentence. (Signal.) *They are selecting a shirt.*
7. Listen. They are not **blank** a shirt. What word? (Signal.) *Selecting.*
   • Say the sentence. (Signal.) *They are not selecting a shirt.*
8. (Repeat steps 2–7 until firm.)

━━━━━ **EXERCISE 2** ━━━━━

NEW ANALOGIES

1. **Analogies** tell how things are the same.
2. Listen to this analogy: A **bird** is to **flying** as a **fish** is to **swimming.**
   • Listen to the first part. A **bird** is to **flying.**
   • Say that part. (Signal.) *A bird is to flying.* (Repeat until firm.)
3. Listen to both parts. A **bird** is to **flying** as a **fish** is to **swimming.**
   • Say the whole analogy with me. (Signal. Respond with the students.) *A bird is to flying as a fish is to swimming.* (Repeat until firm.)
4. All by yourselves. Say the whole analogy. (Signal.) *A bird is to flying as a fish is to swimming.* (Repeat until firm.)
5. That analogy tells one way that a bird and a fish are the same.
   • Everybody, what class are a bird and a fish in? (Signal.) *Animals.*
   • Yes, animals.
6. The analogy tells something about each animal.
   • Listen. A **bird** is to **flying** as a **fish** is to **swimming.**
   • Flying is how a bird **moves.** Swimming is how a fish **moves.** So the analogy tells how each animal **moves.**
   • What does the analogy tell? (Signal.) *How each animal moves.* (Repeat until firm.)
7. Get ready to tell how some other animals **move.**
8. A **bird** is to **flying** as a **fish** is to **swimming** as a **frog** is to . . . (Pause.) Get ready. (Signal.) *Hopping.*
   • As a **horse** is to . . . (Pause.) Get ready. (Signal.) *Running.*
   • (Repeat step 8 until firm.)

┌─────────────────────────────────────┐
│ **Individual test**   │
│ (Repeat step 8 with individual students.) │
└─────────────────────────────────────┘

EXERCISE 3

CLASSIFICATION

1. Name some things that are in the class of **clothing.** (Call on a student. Accept reasonable responses.)
   - Name some things that are in the class of **buildings.** (Call on a student. Accept reasonable responses.)
   - Name some things that are in the class of **living things.** (Call on a student. Accept reasonable responses.)
2. Tell me if the thing I name is in the class of **clothing, buildings,** or **living things.**
   - Garage. (Pause.) What class? (Signal.) *Buildings.*
   - Flower. (Pause.) What class? (Signal.) *Living things.*
   - Shed. (Pause.) What class? (Signal.) *Buildings.*
   - Socks. (Pause.) What class? (Signal.) *Clothing.*
   - Shoe. (Pause.) What class? (Signal.) *Clothing.*
   - Apartment. (Pause.) What class? (Signal.) *Buildings.*
   - Alligator. (Pause.) What class? (Signal.) *Living things.*
   - Cap. (Pause.) What class? (Signal.) *Clothing.*
   - Tree. (Pause.) What class? (Signal.) *Living things.*

EXERCISE 4

INFERENCE

1. Get ready to answer questions about a sentence.
   - Listen. **Nearly all words have a consonant.**
   - Say that sentence. (Signal.) *Nearly all words have a consonant.* (Repeat until firm.)
2. How many words have a consonant? (Signal.) *Nearly all.*
   - Do all words have a vowel? (Signal.) *Maybe.*
   - Do only a few words not have a consonant? (Signal.) *Yes.*
   - Do all words have a consonant? (Signal.) *No.*
   - What do nearly all words have? (Signal.) *A consonant.*
   - What things have a consonant? (Signal.) *Nearly all words.*
   - (Repeat step 2 until firm.)

> **Individual test**
> (Repeat step 2 with individual students.)

EXERCISE 5

NEW DEFINITIONS

1. What word means **guard?** (Signal.) *Protect.*
   - What part of speech is **protect?** (Signal.) *A verb.*
   - What's the noun that comes from **protect?** (Signal.) *Protection.*
   - (Repeat step 1 until firm.)
2. I'll say some sentences. Then I'll ask you the part of speech for one of the words.
   - Listen. He wanted more **protection** from the angry mob.
   - What part of speech is **protection?** (Signal.) *Noun.*
   - Listen. The rubber suit **protected** her from the cold water.
   - What part of speech is **protected?** (Signal.) *Verb.*
   - Listen. Helmets **protect** the players' heads.
   - What part of speech is **protect?** (Signal.) *Verb.*
   - Listen. The goggles were good **protection** for his eyes.
   - What part of speech is **protection?** (Signal.) *Noun.*
   - (Repeat step 2 until firm.)

> **Individual test**
> (Repeat step 2 with individual students.)

Lesson 13

WORKBOOK EXERCISES

> **Note:** Pass out the Workbooks.

——— EXERCISE 6 ———
<u>NEW</u> DEDUCTIONS

1. Open your Workbook to Lesson 13 and find part A. ✓
   - I'll read the instructions. **Complete the deductions.**
2. (Call on a student to read item 1.) *Every person has a skull. John is a person.*
   - Everybody, complete that deduction. (Signal.) *So, John has a skull.*
3. (Call on a student to read item 2.) *Some animals have bones. Snakes are animals.*
   - Everybody, complete that deduction. (Signal.) *So, maybe snakes have bones.*
4. You'll do the items later.

——— EXERCISE 7 ———
<u>NEW</u> PARTS OF SPEECH

Task A

1. What part of speech names people, places, or things? (Signal.) *Noun.*
   - What part of speech tells the action that things do? (Signal.) *Verb.*
   - What part of speech are the words **is, was,** and **have?** (Signal.) *Verb.*
2. The next part of speech is **adjectives.**
   - Here's a rule about adjectives: Any words that come before a noun and tell about the noun are called **adjectives.** Adjectives tell **how many** or **what kind** of noun.
   - What are words that come before a noun and tell about the noun? (Signal.) *Adjectives.*
3. The word **cat** is a noun.
   - Listen. **The cat.**
   - The word **the** is an adjective because it comes before the noun and tells about the noun.
4. Listen. **That cat.**
   - What's the adjective? (Signal.) *That.*

5. Listen. **That fat cat.** There are two adjectives.
   - What's the first adjective? (Signal.) *That.*
   - What's the second adjective? (Signal.) *Fat.*
6. Listen. **Five cats.**
   - What's the adjective? (Signal.) *Five.*
7. Listen. **Five mean cats.**
   - What's the first adjective? (Signal.) *Five.*
   - What's the second adjective? (Signal.) *Mean.*

Task B

1. Find part B. ✓
   - The nouns are underlined in each sentence.
2. Sentence 1. **Six cats played.**
   - What's the noun? (Signal.) *Cats.*
   - What's the adjective? (Signal.) *Six.*
3. Sentence 2. **That dog jumped.**
   - What's the noun? (Signal.) *Dog.*
   - What's the adjective? (Signal.) *That.*
4. Sentence 3. **That big dog jumped.**
   - What's the noun? (Signal.) *Dog.*
   - What's the first adjective? (Signal.) *That.*
   - What's the next adjective? (Signal.) *Big.*
5. Sentence 4. **A big dog jumped.**
   - What's the noun? (Signal.) *Dog.*
   - What's the first adjective? (Signal.) *A.*
   - What's the next adjective? (Signal.) *Big.*
6. (Repeat steps 2–5 until firm.)
7. Sentence 5. **An old black cat ran.**
   - What's the noun? (Signal.) *Cat.*
   - What's the first adjective? (Signal.) *An.*
   - What's the next adjective? (Signal.) *Old.*
   - What's the next adjective? (Signal.) *Black.*
8. Sentence 6. **Ten sheep slept.**
   - What's the noun? (Signal.) *Sheep.*
   - What's the adjective? (Signal.) *Ten.*
9. Sentence 7. **Six men sat.**
   - What's the noun? (Signal.) *Men.*
   - What's the adjective? (Signal.) *Six.*
10. Sentence 8. **A red truck crashed.**
    - What's the noun? (Signal.) *Truck.*
    - What's the first adjective? (Signal.) *A.*
    - What's the next adjective? (Signal.) *Red.*
11. (Repeat steps 7–10 until firm.)

12. I'll read the instructions for part B. **Draw a line over each adjective.**
   - Do the items now. ✓

Task C

1. Let's check your work. Put an **X** next to any item you missed.
2. Read sentence 1. (Call on a student.) *Six cats played.*
   - What did you draw a line over? *Six.*
3. (Repeat step 2 for sentences 2–8.)

> 2. <u>That</u> dog jumped.
> 3. <u>That</u> <u>big</u> dog jumped.
> 4. <u>A</u> <u>big</u> dog jumped.
> 5. <u>An</u> <u>old</u> <u>black</u> cat ran.
> 6. <u>Ten</u> sheep slept.
> 7. <u>Six</u> men sat.
> 8. <u>A</u> <u>red</u> truck crashed.

=========== **EXERCISE 8** ===========

FOLLOWING DIRECTIONS

1. Find part C. ✓
   - I'll read the instructions. **Fill in each blank. Then do what the sentence tells you to do.**
2. Everybody, touch the first blank. ✓
   - What word is under that blank? (Signal.) *Glaf.*
   - Find **glaf** in the list. ✓
   - What does **glaf** mean? (Signal.) *Write.*
   - So write the word **write** in the blank above **glaf.** ✓
3. You'll fill in the rest of the blanks later. Be sure to do what the sentence tells you to do.

=========== **EXERCISE 9** ===========

DEFINITIONS

1. Find part D. ✓
   - (Call on a student to read the instructions.) *Write a word that comes from obtain in each blank.*
2. (Call on a student to read item 1.) *The robber will blank a robe for his back.*
   - Everybody, what word goes in the blank? (Signal.) *Obtain.*

3. (Call on a student to read item 2.) *The ram wants to blank some oats to eat.*
   - Everybody, what word goes in the blank? (Signal.) *Obtain.*
4. (Call on a student to read item 3.) *The man has blank a pig for a pet.*
   - Everybody, what word goes in the blank? (Signal.) *Obtained.*
5. (Call on a student to read item 4.) *Six shoppers are blank ten socks.*
   - Everybody, what word goes in the blank? (Signal.) *Obtaining.*
6. (Call on a student to read item 5.) *Ten socks were blank by six shoppers.*
   - Everybody, what word goes in the blank? (Signal.) *Obtained.*
7. You'll do the items later.

=========== **EXERCISE 10** ===========

WRITING STORIES

1. Find part I.

   - You're going to write a story about this picture of Mrs. Yee and her twin babies.
   - Your story will tell what happened **before** the picture, what happened **in** the picture, and what happened **after** the picture.
2. (Call on individual students.) Tell me what could have happened **before** the picture. (Ideas: *Mrs. Yee gave birth to twin boys. The twins looked alike.*)

Lesson 13

- (Call on individual students.) Tell me what happened **in** the picture. Make sure you tell what **happened,** not what is **happening.** (Ideas: *Mrs. Yee held both twins in her arms. One twin was calm and happy. The other twin was unhappy, so he cried.*)
- (Call on individual students.) Tell me what could have happened **after** the picture. (Ideas: *Mrs. Yee cuddled the twins. Soon, the unhappy twin stopped crying, but then the other twin got unhappy. So he started crying. Mrs. Yee had a hard time keeping both twins happy at once.*)
3. The word box shows some of the words you might use when you write your story.
- Touch the words as I read them: **birth, babies, twins, happy, crying.**
- Remember, if you use any of those words, spell them correctly.
- You'll write your story later. Make sure that each sentence begins with a capital letter and ends with a period.

EXERCISE 11

WORKBOOK AND WORKCHECK

1. (Award points for Group Work.)
2. Do the rest of the Workbook lesson now. Remember to write your story. (Observe students and give feedback.)
3. Get ready to check your answers. ✓
- Put an **X** next to any item you missed.
- (Call on individual students to read each item and its answer. Do not have students read their stories.)
4. (After all the answers have been read, have students record their Workbook points.)
5. (Award bonus points.)
6. (Have students total their points and enter the total on the Point Summary Chart.)
7. (Collect the Workbooks. Mark the stories using this code: **W** for improper wording; **UC** for unclear sentences; **X** for inaccurate sentences.)

Lesson
13

H Fill in each blank.

Workbook page 36

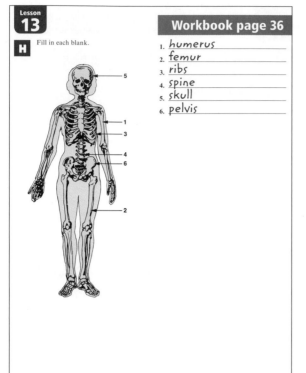

1. humerus
2. femur
3. ribs
4. spine
5. skull
6. pelvis

Workbook page 37

Lesson
13

I Write a story about this picture of Mrs. Yee and her twin babies. Your story should tell what happened **before** the picture, what happened **in** the picture, and what happened **after** the picture.

| birth | babies | twins | happy | crying |

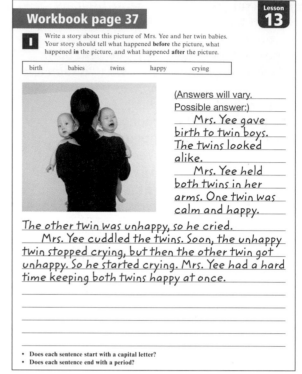

(Answers will vary.
Possible answer:)
   Mrs. Yee gave
birth to twin boys.
The twins looked
alike.
   Mrs. Yee held
both twins in her
arms. One twin was
calm and happy.
The other twin was unhappy, so he cried.
   Mrs. Yee cuddled the twins. Soon, the unhappy
twin stopped crying, but then the other twin got
unhappy. So he started crying. Mrs. Yee had a hard
time keeping both twins happy at once.

• Does each sentence start with a capital letter?
• Does each sentence end with a period?

END OF LESSON 13

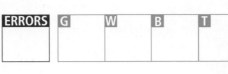
A Complete the deductions.

1. Every person has a skull.
   John is a person.

   _____

2. Some animals have bones.
   Snakes are animals.

   _____

   _____

3. Insects do not have spines.
   Antelopes are mammals.

   _____

   _____

4. John has every kind of bone.
   Ribs are bones.

   _____

   _____

B Draw a line over each adjective.

1. Six cats played.

2. That dog jumped.

3. That big dog jumped.

4. A big dog jumped.

5. An old black cat ran.

6. Ten sheep slept.

7. Six men sat.

8. A red truck crashed.

C Fill in each blank. Then do what the sentence tells you to do.

_____ _____ _____
   glaf   ag   preb

_____ _____ _____
   rop   k   wid

_____.
   hux

ag—the

glaf—Write

hux—line

k—on

preb—word

rop—man

wid—the

D Write a word that comes from **obtain** in each blank.

1. The robber will _____
   a robe for his back.

2. The ram wants to _____
   some oats to eat.

3. The man has _____
   a pig for a pet.

4. Six shoppers are _____
   ten socks.

5. Ten socks were _____
   by six shoppers.

E Circle the verbs.
Underline the nouns.

1. His mom constructed a shed.

2. His mom has constructed that shed.

3. Six men will obtain ten socks.

4. The shoppers will be shopping for hats.

5. A man was mopping with a mop.

6. Three men are mopping floors with mops.

7. A metal ship is rocking in the deep pond.

8. That shop has sold hats and socks.

F Write the letter of the fact that explains why each thing happened.

> A. Lester plays baseball.
> B. Hector plays football.

1. He catches fly balls. _____

2. He catches passes. _____

3. He scores touchdowns. _____

4. He hits home runs. _____

G Read the sentence and answer the questions.

> If it is an insect, it does not have bones.

1. What happens if it is an insect?

_____

_____

2. What do insects not have?

_____

_____

3. Do insects have ribs?

_____

_____

4. Does a bee have bones?

_____

_____

5. What does not have bones?

_____

_____

H Fill in each blank.

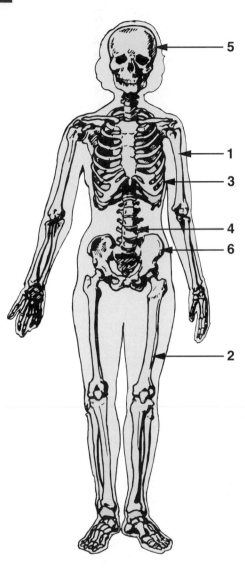

1. _____

2. _____

3. _____

4. _____

5. _____

6. _____

I Write a story about this picture of Mrs. Yee and her twin babies. Your story should tell what happened **before** the picture, what happened **in** the picture, and what happened **after** the picture.

birth	babies	twins	happy	crying

_____

_____

_____

_____

_____

_____

_____

_____

_____

_____

_____

_____

_____

_____

_____

_____

_____

_____

- **Does each sentence start with a capital letter?**
- **Does each sentence end with a period?**

Comprehension B2—Lesson 52

Many of the same tracks that appeared in Lesson 13 of **Comprehension B1** still appear in **Comprehension B2,** Lesson 52; however, new and more complex examples are used in Lesson 52.

■ The Definitions activities deal with three forms of a word—noun, verb, and adjective.

■ The once simple rules have been replaced by basic economics rules, such as "Products that are readier to use cost more."

■ Students have learned eight different ways to combine sentences; the latest way uses the word **however** (Exercise 3).

■ Editing activities focus on basic punctuation errors and identifying redundant sentences.

The independent activities include the following:

■ Using rules as the basis for drawing inferences about the human body, including which tubes are arteries, which tubes are veins, and which gas the blood in each tube carries

■ Using different inflections for verbs

■ Answering questions about a story. This is a variation of an activity that involved a single sentence in Lesson 13. The story presents a new rule. Both literal and indirect questions are used. Note that students indicate whether each question is answered by words in the story or whether a deduction is required.

■ Writing similes based on the sameness of objects

■ Rewriting a paragraph, applying the sentence-combination skills that have been taught

■ Following precise directions to construct a drawing

■ Rewriting combined sentences contained in a passage as separate sentences

■ Reviewing the parts of speech that have been taught—noun, verb, adjective

GROUP WORK

━━━━━━ **EXERCISE 1** ━━━━━━
DEFINITIONS

Task A

1. Tell me the word that means **get**. (Pause.) Get ready. (Signal.) *Acquire.*
   - What part of speech is **acquire**? (Signal.) *A verb.*
2. (Print on the board:)

> **aquisition**

- (Point to **acquisition**.) Here's a noun that comes from the verb **acquire**. **Acquisition.**
- What word? (Signal.) *Acquisition.*
- **An acquisition** is **something you acquire.**
3. I'll say some sentences that have a **blank** in them. Complete each sentence by saying **acquisition** or **acquisitions**.
- Listen. The boat was an expensive **blank**. (Pause.) What word? (Signal.) *Acquisition.*
- Say the sentence. (Signal.) *The boat was an expensive acquisition.*
4. Listen. He made several **blank** at the store. (Pause.) What word? (Signal.) *Acquisitions.*
- Say the sentence. (Signal.) *He made several acquisitions at the store.*
5. Listen. A TV set is a popular **blank**. (Pause.) What word? (Signal.) *Acquisition.*
- Say the sentence. (Signal.) *A TV set is a popular acquisition.*
6. Listen. She protected her one new **blank**. (Pause.) What word? (Signal.) *Acquisition.*
- Say the sentence. (Signal.) *She protected her one new acquisition.*
7. (Repeat steps 3–6 until firm.)

Task B

1. What part of speech is **acquisition**? (Signal.) *A noun.*
- What part of speech is **acquire**? (Signal.) *A verb.*
2. Verbs have different endings. **Acquired** is a verb. **Are acquiring** is a verb. **Acquires** is a verb.

- Is **acquisition** a verb? (Signal.) *No.*
- What part of speech is **acquisition?** (Signal.) *A noun.*
3. I'll say some words. You tell me if what I say is a **noun** or a **verb**.
- **Is acquiring.** Say it. (Signal.) *Is acquiring.* What part of speech? (Signal.) *Verb.*
- **Acquired.** Say it. (Signal.) *Acquired.* What part of speech? (Signal.) *Verb.*
- **Acquires.** Say it. (Signal.) *Acquires.* What part of speech? (Signal.) *Verb.*
- **Acquisition.** Say it. (Signal.) *Acquisition.* What part of speech? (Signal.) *Noun.*
- **Were acquiring.** Say it. (Signal.) *Were acquiring.* What part of speech? (Signal.) *Verb.*
- (Repeat step 3 until firm.)

> **Individual test**
> (Repeat step 3 with individual students.)

WORKBOOK EXERCISES

> **Note**: Pass out the Workbooks.

━━━━━━ **EXERCISE 2** ━━━━━━
ECONOMICS RULES

1. (Print on the board:)

> **Products that are readier to use cost more.**

- Here's a new rule. **Products that are readier to use cost more.**
- Say that rule. (Signal.) *Products that are readier to use cost more.* (Repeat until firm.)
2. A ready-made skirt is readier to use than material and a pattern. Here's why. The ready-made skirt is ready to wear, but material and a pattern aren't.

3. You're going to tell me which is readier to use, a ready-made skirt or material and a pattern. (Pause.) Get ready. (Signal.) *A ready-made skirt.*
• Why? (Call on a student. Idea: *A ready-made skirt is ready to wear, but material and a pattern aren't.*)
• You're going to tell me which is readier to use, a model you have to put together or a model that is already put together. (Pause.) Get ready. (Signal.) *A model that is already put together.*
• Why? (Call on a student. Idea: *A model that is already put together is ready to play with, but the model you have to put together isn't.*)
• You're going to tell me which is readier to use, frozen chicken or cooked chicken. (Pause.) Get ready. (Signal.) *Cooked chicken.*
• Why? (Call on a student. Idea: *Cooked chicken is ready to eat; frozen chicken isn't.*)
• (Repeat step 3 until firm.)
4. Open your Workbook to Lesson 52 and find part A. ✓
• Get ready to answer the questions in part A.
5. What's the rule about products that are readier to use? (Signal.) *Products that are readier to use cost more.* (Repeat until firm.)
6. Which is readier to use, a ready-made skirt or material and a pattern? (Signal.) *A ready-made skirt.*
• So what else do you know about a ready-made skirt? (Signal.) *It costs more.*
• How do you know? (Signal.) *Because it's readier to use.*
• (Repeat step 6 until firm.)
7. Which costs more, a model that you have to put together or a model that is already put together? (Signal.) *A model that is already put together.*
• How do you know? (Signal.) *Because it's readier to use.*
• (Repeat step 7 until firm.)

8. Ms. Anderson obtains five pounds of frozen chicken. Ms. Miller obtains five pounds of cooked chicken. Whose chicken cost more? (Signal.) *Ms. Miller's.*
• How do you know? (Signal.) *Because it's readier to use.*
• (Repeat step 8 until firm.)
9. You'll write the items later.

━━━━━ **EXERCISE 3** ━━━━━
SENTENCE COMBINATIONS

1. Find part B. ✓
• (Call on a student to read the instructions.) *Combine the sentences with however.*
2. (Call on a student to read item 1.) *The man modified his car. His car still did not run.*
• Everybody, say the combined sentence with **however.** (Pause.) Get ready. (Signal.) *The man modified his car; however, it still did not run.* (Repeat until firm.)
3. Let's go over the rules.
• What must every written sentence **begin with?** (Signal.) *A capital letter.*
• What must every written sentence **have?** (Signal.) *An end mark.*
• What mark do you put before **however?** (Signal.) *A semicolon.*
• What mark do you put after **however?** (Signal.) *A comma.*
• Name **four** words that you put commas **before.** (Call on a student.) *Who, which, but, particularly.*
• (Repeat step 3 until firm.)
4. You'll do the items later.

━━━━━ **EXERCISE 4** ━━━━━
NEW **EDITING**

1. Find part C. ✓
• I'll read the instructions. **Underline the redundant sentences. Circle and correct the punctuation errors.**
• A punctuation error occurs when a period, comma, or semicolon is missing or is used incorrectly.

2. I'll read the passage. Say **Stop** as soon as I read a sentence that is redundant or that has a punctuation error.
- **A bell rang. Sam put on his firefighter's hat and his firefighter's coat** *Stop.*
- What's wrong with that sentence? (Call on a student. Idea: *It doesn't have a period.*)
- Everybody, make a circle at the end of the sentence and put a period inside the circle. ✓
3. I'll read more. **He jumped on the fire truck as it roared out of the station. Sam was a firefighter.** *Stop.*
- What's wrong with that sentence? (Call on a student. Idea: *It's redundant because we already know Sam is a firefighter.*)
- Everybody, underline that sentence. ✓
4. I'll read more. **The truck sped down Oak Street and screeched around, the corner of Oak and First.** *Stop.*
- What's wrong with that sentence? (Call on a student. Idea: *You don't need a comma between around and the.*)
- Everybody, circle the comma and then cross the comma out. ✓
5. You'll finish the passage later.

━━━━━ **EXERCISE 5** ━━━━━

WORKBOOK AND WORKCHECK

1. (Award points for Group Work.)
2. Do the rest of the Workbook lesson now. (Observe students and give feedback.)
3. Get ready to check your answers. ✓
- Put an **X** next to any item you missed.
- (Call on individual students to read each item and its answer.)
4. (After all the answers have been read, have students record their Workbook points.)
5. (Award bonus points.)
6. (Have students total their points and enter the total on the Point Summary Chart.)

Workbook page 255

A ECONOMICS RULES

Answer the questions.

1. What's the rule about products that are readier to use?
   Products that are readier to use cost more.

2. Which is readier to use, a ready-made skirt or material and a pattern?
   a ready-made skirt

3. So what else do you know about a ready-made skirt?
   It costs more.

4. How do you know?
   Idea: because it is readier to use

5. Which costs more, a model that you have to put together or a model that is already put together?
   a model that is already put together

6. How do you know?
   Idea: because it is readier to use

> Ms. Anderson obtains five pounds of frozen chicken.
> Ms. Miller obtains five pounds of cooked chicken.

7. Whose chicken cost more?
   Ms. Miller's

8. How do you know?
   Idea: because it is readier to use

B SENTENCE COMBINATIONS

Combine the sentences with **however**.

1. The man modified his car. His car still did not run.
   The man modified his car; however, it still did not run.

2. Vern hurt his quadriceps. Vern won the race.
   Vern hurt his quadriceps; however, he won the race.

3. They had a big supply of tennis shoes. They ran out.
   They had a big supply of tennis shoes; however, they ran out.

4. She concluded her speech. She kept on talking.
   She concluded her speech; however, she kept on talking.

Workbook page 256

C EDITING

Underline the redundant sentences. Circle and correct the punctuation errors.

A bell rang. Sam put on his firefighter's hat and his firefighter's coat. He jumped on the fire truck as it roared out of the station. Sam was a firefighter. The truck sped down Oak Street and screeched around the corner of Oak and First. The truck was going sixty miles an hour; however, it could have gone a lot faster. The truck was speeding along. The truck screamed to a stop at First and Elm. Sam jumped off to look for a fire hydrant which wasn't easy. The fire was at First and Elm.

D PARTS OF SPEECH

Underline the nouns. Draw **one** line **over** the adjectives. Draw **two** lines **over** the articles. Circle the verbs

1. Wind and water were eroding the mountain.
2. That stream has eroded its banks.
3. A large black goat was under a tree.
4. Erosion changes everything on the planet.

E BODY RULES

Draw in the arrows. Write **vein** or **artery** in each blank. Also write **oxygen** or **carbon dioxide** in each blank.

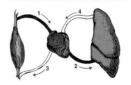

1. *vein, carbon dioxide*
2. *artery, carbon dioxide*
3. *artery, oxygen*
4. *vein, oxygen*

F DEFINITIONS

Write a word that comes from **obtain** or **respire** in each blank. Then write **verb, noun,** or **adjective** after each item.

1. She is trying to ___*obtain*___ new tires. *verb*

2. After you run, your *respiration* is much faster. *noun*

3. Your bronchial tubes are in your *respiratory* system. *adjective*

Workbook page 257 — Lesson 52

4. That country is **obtaining** new jets. __verb__

5. You should **respire** slowly if you feel dizzy. __verb__

G INFERENCE

Read the passage and answer the questions.
- Circle the **W** if the question is answered by words in the passage. Then underline those words.
- Circle the **D** if the question is answered by a deduction.

You know that: **When the demand is less than the supply, prices go down.**

Ms. Thomas runs the only dairy farm near Newton. In July, her cows produce just as much milk as Newton needs, which is 1,000 gallons a month. In August, a big group of people moves out of Newton, and Newton's demand for milk drops to 600 gallons a month. But Ms. Thomas's cows are still producing 1,000 gallons a month.

Ms. Thomas sells 600 gallons at the old price, and then she is stuck with 400 gallons that will soon go bad. She thinks she can get people to buy the 400 gallons if she lowers the price. Her idea works, and she sells all 400 gallons at the lower price.

1. What rule about demand and supply is this passage about?
When the demand is less than the supply, prices go down.

2. What would have happened to the price of milk if a big group of people had moved into Newton in July?
Idea: It would have gone up. — W Ⓓ

3. Was the demand smaller than the supply in August because the demand went down or because the supply went up?
because the demand went down

4. What did Ms. Thomas do to get people to buy the 400 gallons she had left over?
Idea: lowered the price — Ⓦ D

5. What will Ms. Thomas have to do to the demand for milk to sell 1,000 gallons at the old price in September?
Idea: Make it greater. — W Ⓓ

6. Name one way she could do that.
Idea: Tell people they need more milk. — W Ⓓ

7. Did Ms. Thomas lose money in August?
Yes — W Ⓓ

Workbook page 259 — Lesson 52

J SIMILES

Complete the items about the words in the boxes.

| voice   gravel |

1. Tell how the objects could be the same.
Idea: They could be rough.

2. Write a simile about the objects.
Idea: The dog's voice was like gravel.

| lips   cherries |

3. Tell how the objects could be the same.
Idea: They could be red.

4. Write a simile about the objects.
Idea: Her lips were like cherries.

K FOLLOWING DIRECTIONS

Follow the directions.

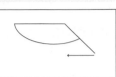

1. Draw a horizontal line in the box.
2. Draw a line that slants down to the right from the right end of the horizontal line.
3. At the bottom of the slanted line, draw an arrow that points to the left.
4. Draw the muscle that will move the slanted line in the direction of the arrow.

Lesson 52 — Workbook page 258

H SENTENCE ANALYSIS

Rewrite the passage in six sentences.

Many great players played for the Los Angeles Dodgers, particularly in the 1960s. One very famous player was Sandy Koufax, who was an amazing pitcher. His style and speed are copied by many pitchers today.

Idea: Many great players played for the Los Angeles Dodgers. The greatest players played in the 1960s. One very famous player was Sandy Koufax. Sandy Koufax was an amazing pitcher. His style is copied by many pitchers today. His speed is copied by many pitchers today.

I REWRITING PARAGRAPHS

Rewrite the paragraph in four sentences. If one of the sentences tells **why,** combine the sentences with **because.** If two sentences seem contradictory, combine them with **although.**

The slaves sang many kinds of songs. The slaves sang mostly work songs and hymns. Most of their music was sung. Some of their music was played on instruments. The music started changing after 1865. 1865 was when the slaves were freed. Sometimes, former slaves played music at dances. Dances were held everywhere.

Idea: The slaves sang many kinds of songs, particularly work songs and hymns. Although most of their music was sung, some was played on instruments. The music started changing after 1865, which was when the slaves were freed. Sometimes, former slaves played music at dances, which were held everywhere.

EXERCISE 6
REVISING STORIES

1. (Have students work in teams to revise their stories from the previous lesson. The teams should give suggestions for improving the stories and should agree on changes.)
2. (After students receive feedback from their team, have them rewrite their stories on a fresh sheet of paper.)
3. (Have 2–3 students read their stories aloud to the class.)
4. (Collect the students' stories. Later, check their work and mark any mistakes. Write comments for parts that are good and for parts with errors.)

END OF LESSON 52

A ECONOMICS RULES

Answer the questions.

1. What's the rule about products that are readier to use?

_____

_____

_____

2. Which is readier to use, a ready-made skirt or material and a pattern?

_____

3. So what else do you know about a ready-made skirt?

_____

4. How do you know?

_____

_____

5. Which costs more, a model that you have to put together or a model that is already put together?

_____

_____

6. How do you know?

_____

_____

Ms. Anderson obtains five pounds of frozen chicken.
Ms. Miller obtains five pounds of cooked chicken.

7. Whose chicken cost more?

_____

8. How do you know?

_____

_____

B SENTENCE COMBINATIONS

Combine the sentences with **however.**

1. The man modified his car.
His car still did not run.

_____

_____

_____

2. Vern hurt his quadriceps.
Vern won the race.

_____

_____

_____

3. They had a big supply of tennis shoes.
They ran out.

_____

_____

_____

4. She concluded her speech.
She kept on talking.

_____

_____

_____

C EDITING

Underline the redundant sentences. Circle and correct the punctuation errors.

A bell rang. Sam put on his firefighter's hat and his firefighter's coat, He jumped on the fire truck as it roared out of the station. Sam was a firefighter. The truck sped down Oak Street and screeched around, the corner of Oak and First. The truck was going sixty miles an hour however it could have gone a lot faster. The truck was speeding along. The truck screamed to a stop at First and Elm. Sam jumped off to look for a fire hydrant which wasn't easy. The fire was at First and Elm.

D PARTS OF SPEECH

Underline the nouns. Draw **one** line **over** the adjectives. Draw **two** lines **over** the articles. Circle the verbs

1. Wind and water were eroding the mountain.

2. That stream has eroded its banks.

3. A large black goat was under a tree.

4. Erosion changes everything on the planet.

E BODY RULES

Draw in the arrows. Write **vein** or **artery** in each blank. Also write **oxygen** or **carbon dioxide** in each blank.

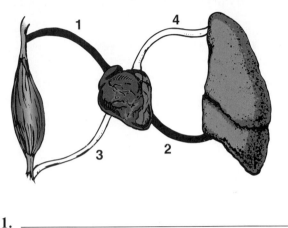

1. _____

2. _____

3. _____

4. _____

F DEFINITIONS

Write a word that comes from **obtain** or **respire** in each blank. Then write **verb, noun,** or **adjective** after each item.

1. She is trying to _____

   new tires. _____

2. After you run, your _____

   is much faster. _____

3. Your bronchial tubes are in your

   _____system.

   _____

4. That country is _____

new jets. _____

5. You should _____

slowly if you feel dizzy. _____

G INFERENCE

Read the passage and answer the questions.
• Circle the **W** if the question is answered by words in the passage. Then underline those words.
• Circle the **D** if the question is answered by a deduction.

You know that: **When the demand is less than the supply, prices go down.**

Ms. Thomas runs the only dairy farm near Newton. In July, her cows produce just as much milk as Newton needs, which is 1,000 gallons a month. In August, a big group of people moves out of Newton, and Newton's demand for milk drops to 600 gallons a month. But Ms. Thomas's cows are still producing 1,000 gallons a month.

Ms. Thomas sells 600 gallons at the old price, and then she is stuck with 400 gallons that will soon go bad. She thinks she can get people to buy the 400 gallons if she lowers the price. Her idea works, and she sells all 400 gallons at the lower price.

---

1. What rule about demand and supply is this passage about?

_____

_____

_____

2. What would have happened to the price of milk if a big group of people had moved into Newton in July?

_____

_____ **W D**

3. Was the demand smaller than the supply in August because the demand went down or because the supply went up?

_____

_____

4. What did Ms. Thomas do to get people to buy the 400 gallons she had left over?

_____

_____ **W D**

5. What will Ms. Thomas have to do to the demand for milk to sell 1,000 gallons at the old price in September?

_____

_____ **W D**

6. Name one way she could do that.

_____

_____

7. Did Ms. Thomas lose money in August?

_____ **W D**

H SENTENCE ANALYSIS

Rewrite the passage in six sentences.

> Many great players played for the Los Angeles Dodgers, particularly in the 1960s. One very famous player was Sandy Koufax, who was an amazing pitcher. His style and speed are copied by many pitchers today.

_____

_____

_____

_____

_____

_____

_____

_____

_____

_____

_____

_____

I REWRITING PARAGRAPHS

Rewrite the paragraph in four sentences. If one of the sentences tells **why,** combine the sentences with **because.** If two sentences seem contradictory, combine them with **although.**

> The slaves sang many kinds of songs. The slaves sang mostly work songs and hymns. Most of their music was sung. Some of their music was played on instruments. The music started changing after 1865. 1865 was when the slaves were freed. Sometimes, former slaves played music at dances. Dances were held everywhere.

_____

_____

_____

_____

_____

_____

_____

_____

_____

_____

_____

J SIMILES

Complete the items about the words in the boxes.

| voice   gravel |

1. Tell how the objects could be the same.

_____

_____

2. Write a simile about the objects.

_____

_____

| lips   cherries |

3. Tell how the objects could be the same.

_____

_____

4. Write a simile about the objects.

_____

_____

K FOLLOWING DIRECTIONS

Follow the directions.

1. Draw a horizontal line in the box.

2. Draw a line that slants down to the right from the right end of the horizontal line.

3. At the bottom of the slanted line, draw an arrow that points to the left.

4. Draw the muscle that will move the slanted line in the direction of the arrow.

Comprehension C—Lesson 45

Some activities presented in **Comprehension C** are extensions or reviews of skills taught in **Comprehension B1** and **B2.** Other skills presented in Level C are new to students.

■ Exercise 1 involves using the words **who** and **which,** a discrimination taught in **Comprehension B1** that is now presented through the student-read script that characterizes **Comprehension C.**

■ Exercise 2 involves analyzing arguments. Students have already been taught the rule regarding faulty causation: "Just because two things happen around the same time doesn't mean that one thing causes the other thing." They now apply the rule to an argument. They are still prompted on the proof for the argument; however, starting in Lesson 48 they will be required to make up their own proof.

■ Exercise 3 is the first presentation of evidence that is irrelevant to a stated rule. Note that the students have already been taught how to determine whether evidence is irrelevant or not. In this exercise, however, for the first time, they indicate whether it is possible to draw a conclusion based on a rule and the evidence presented.

■ Student Book part D is an optional copying task (for students who are mechanically unskilled in writing).

> The star (★) before part E in the Student Book indicates that students work parts E and F independently. The star (★) before part A in the Workbook indicates that students work all parts of the Workbook independently.

■ Student Book part E is a contradictions task that requires the students to compare the information provided by a map with the list of four statements about the map. Students identify statements that are contradicted by the map and indicate what the map actually shows.

■ Student Book part F, a passage to be read for information, is followed by five questions.

■ Workbook part A is a task in analyzing arguments that deals with the rule of faulty causation applied in Exercise 2.

■ Workbook part B involves the use of evidence. Students read the passage, indicate whether the conclusions given are supported or contradicted by the passage, and specify the sentence in the passage that contains the evidence to support or to contradict the conclusion.

■ Workbook part C is an independent variation of the **who-which** skill reviewed in Exercise 1.

■ Workbook part D is a review of two of the facts presented in Student Book part F. The students are responsible for remembering these facts.

Note: The circled letters indicate when you ask a question or when you direct the group to respond.

═══════ **EXERCISE 1** ═══════

SENTENCE COMBINATIONS

1. (Direct the students to find Lesson 45, part A, in the **Student Book**.)
2. (Call on individual students to read part A.)
   ⒜ What word? *Which.*
   ⒝ What word? *Which.*
   ⒞ What word? *Which.*
   ⒟ What word? *Who.*
   ⒠ What word? *Which.*
   ⒡ What word? *Which.*

═══════ **EXERCISE 2** ═══════

ANALYZING ARGUMENTS

1. (Direct the students to find part B.)
2. (Call on individual students to read part B.)
   ⒢ (Call on a student. Idea: *That if Joe taps home plate, he'll hit a home run.*)
   ⒣ (Call on a student. Idea: *Because the last two times that Joe tapped home plate, he hit a home run.*)
   ⒤ Say it. *Just because two things happen around the same time doesn't mean that one thing causes the other thing.*

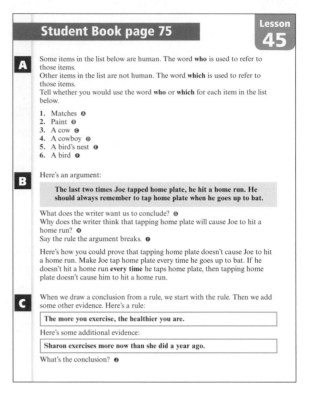

Student Book page 75

Lesson 45

A Some items in the list below are human. The word **who** is used to refer to those items.
Other items in the list are not human. The word **which** is used to refer to those items.
Tell whether you would use the word **who** or **which** for each item in the list below.

1. Matches ⒜
2. Paint ⒝
3. A cow ⒞
4. A cowboy ⒟
5. A bird's nest ⒠
6. A bird ⒡

Here's an argument:

> The last two times Joe tapped home plate, he hit a home run. He should always remember to tap home plate when he goes up to bat.

B What does the writer want us to conclude? ⒢
Why does the writer think that tapping home plate will cause Joe to hit a home run? ⒣
Say the rule the argument breaks. ⒤

Here's how you could prove that tapping home plate doesn't cause Joe to hit a home run. Make Joe tap home plate every time he goes up to bat. If he doesn't hit a home run **every time** he taps home plate, then tapping home plate doesn't cause him to hit a home run.

C When we draw a conclusion from a rule, we start with the rule. Then we add some other evidence. Here's a rule:

> The more you exercise, the healthier you are.

Here's some additional evidence:

> Sharon exercises more now than she did a year ago.

What's the conclusion? ⒥

EXERCISE 3

DEDUCTIONS

1. (Direct the students to find part C.)
2. (Call on individual students to read part C.)
   - **J** Say it. *Sharon is healthier now.*
   - **K** What's the answer? *Irrelevant.*
   - **L** Say it. *There is none.*
   - **M** What's the answer? *Relevant.*
   - **N** Say it. *Carla pollutes the air more.*
   - **O** What's the answer? *Irrelevant.*
   - **P** Say it. *There is none.*
   - **Q** What's the answer? *Irrelevant.*
   - **R** Say it. *There is none.*
   - **S** What's the answer? *Relevant.*
   - **T** Say it. *Frieda doesn't pollute the air as much.*
   - **U** What's the answer? *Irrelevant.*
   - **V** Say it. *There is none.*

EXERCISE 4

INDEPENDENT WORK

1. **[Optional]** (Direct the students to read the instructions for part D to themselves. Then give them exactly two minutes to copy the paragraph. Count as errors any miscopied words and punctuation. Deduct these errors from the number of copied words, and mark the total on the Writing Rate Graph.)
2. Finish the Student Book and do the Workbook for Lesson 45. ✓

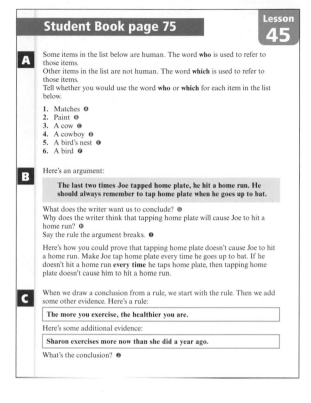

Student Book page 75 Lesson 45

A Some items in the list below are human. The word **who** is used to refer to those items.
Other items in the list are not human. The word **which** is used to refer to those items.
Tell whether you would use the word **who** or **which** for each item in the list below.

1. Matches
2. Paint
3. A cow
4. A cowboy
5. A bird's nest
6. A bird

B Here's an argument:

> The last two times Joe tapped home plate, he hit a home run. He should always remember to tap home plate when he goes up to bat.

What does the writer want us to conclude?
Why does the writer think that tapping home plate will cause Joe to hit a home run?
Say the rule the argument breaks.

Here's how you could prove that tapping home plate doesn't cause Joe to hit a home run. Make Joe tap home plate every time he goes up to bat. If he doesn't hit a home run **every time** he taps home plate, then tapping home plate doesn't cause him to hit a home run.

C When we draw a conclusion from a rule, we start with the rule. Then we add some other evidence. Here's a rule:

> The more you exercise, the healthier you are.

Here's some additional evidence:

> Sharon exercises more now than she did a year ago.

What's the conclusion?

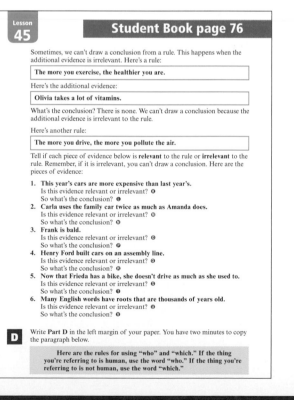

Lesson 45 **Student Book page 76**

Sometimes, we can't draw a conclusion from a rule. This happens when the additional evidence is irrelevant. Here's a rule:

> The more you exercise, the healthier you are.

Here's the additional evidence:

> Olivia takes a lot of vitamins.

What's the conclusion? There is none. We can't draw a conclusion because the additional evidence is irrelevant to the rule.

Here's another rule:

> The more you drive, the more you pollute the air.

Tell if each piece of evidence below is **relevant** to the rule or **irrelevant** to the rule. Remember, if it is irrelevant, you can't draw a conclusion. Here are the pieces of evidence:

1. **This year's cars are more expensive than last year's.**
   Is this evidence relevant or irrelevant?
   So what's the conclusion?
2. **Carla uses the family car twice as much as Amanda does.**
   Is this evidence relevant or irrelevant?
   So what's the conclusion?
3. **Frank is bald.**
   Is this evidence relevant or irrelevant?
   So what's the conclusion?
4. **Henry Ford built cars on an assembly line.**
   Is this evidence relevant or irrelevant?
   So what's the conclusion?
5. **Now that Frieda has a bike, she doesn't drive as much as she used to.**
   Is this evidence relevant or irrelevant?
   So what's the conclusion?
6. **Many English words have roots that are thousands of years old.**
   Is this evidence relevant or irrelevant?
   So what's the conclusion?

D Write **Part D** in the left margin of your paper. You have two minutes to copy the paragraph below.

> Here are the rules for using "who" and "which." If the thing you're referring to is human, use the word "who." If the thing you're referring to is not human, use the word "which."

Lesson 45, Comprehension C TPB-1

Lesson 45

Workcheck

1. Get ready to check your answers starting with Student Book part E. Use a pen to make an **X** next to any item you miss.
2. (Call on individual students to read each item and its answer. Repeat for Workbook items.)
3. (Direct the students to count the number of errors and write the number in the **error** box at the top of the Workbook page.)
4. (Award points and direct students to record their points in Box **W.**)

0 errors	**15 points**
1–2 errors	**12 points**
3–5 errors	**8 points**
6–9 errors	**5 points**

5. (Award any bonus points. Direct the students to total their points and enter the total on the Point Summary Chart.)
6. Show me your work when you've finished correcting it. (When the students show you their corrected work, record their points on your Record Summary Chart.)

Note: Before presenting Lesson 46, present Fact Game 3. You will need a pair of dice for every four or five students. Each student needs a pencil and Workbook.

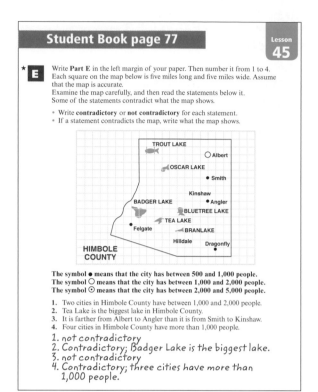

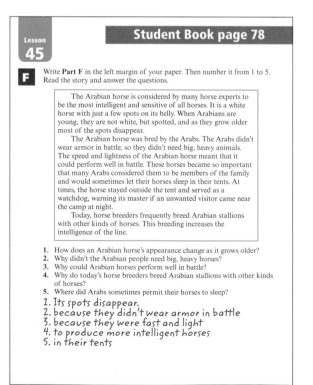

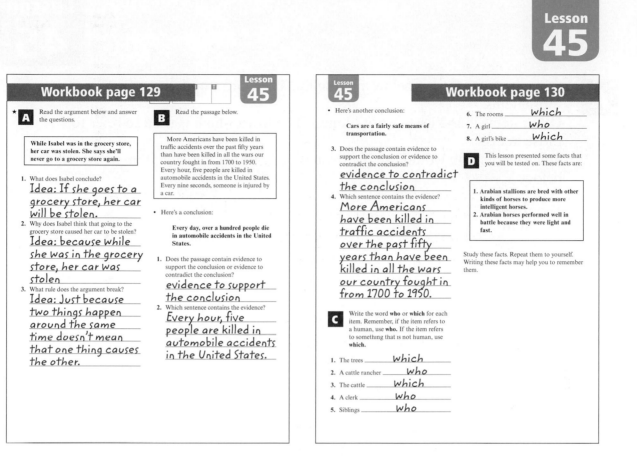

Workbook page 129

★ **A** Read the argument below and answer the questions.

> While Isabel was in the grocery store, her car was stolen. She says she'll never go to a grocery store again.

1. What does Isabel conclude?

   Idea: If she goes to a grocery store, her car will be stolen.

2. Why does Isabel think that going to the grocery store caused her car to be stolen?

   Idea: because while she was in the grocery store, her car was stolen

3. What rule does the argument break?

   Idea: Just because two things happen around the same time doesn't mean that one thing causes the other.

B Read the passage below.

> More Americans have been killed in traffic accidents over the past fifty years than have been killed in all the wars our country fought in from 1700 to 1950. Every hour, five people are killed in automobile accidents in the United States. Every nine seconds, someone is injured by a car.

• Here's a conclusion:

> **Every day, over a hundred people die in automobile accidents in the United States.**

1. Does the passage contain evidence to support the conclusion or evidence to contradict the conclusion?

   evidence to support the conclusion

2. Which sentence contains the evidence?

   Every hour, five people are killed in automobile accidents in the United States.

Workbook page 130

• Here's another conclusion:

> **Cars are a fairly safe means of transportation.**

3. Does the passage contain evidence to support the conclusion or evidence to contradict the conclusion?

   evidence to contradict the conclusion

4. Which sentence contains the evidence?

   More Americans have been killed in traffic accidents over the past fifty years than have been killed in all the wars our country fought in from 1700 to 1950.

C Write the word **who** or **which** for each item. Remember, if the item refers to a human, use **who.** If the item refers to something that is not human, use **which.**

1. The trees _____ *which*
2. A cattle rancher _____ *who*
3. The cattle _____ *which*
4. A clerk _____ *who*
5. Siblings _____ *who*

6. The rooms _____ *which*
7. A girl _____ *who*
8. A girl's bike _____ *which*

D This lesson presented some facts that you will be tested on. These facts are:

> 1. Arabian stallions are bred with other kinds of horses to produce more intelligent horses.
> 2. Arabian horses performed well in battle because they were light and fast.

Study these facts. Repeat them to yourself. Writing these facts may help you to remember them.

END OF LESSON 45

A Some items in the list below are human. The word **who** is used to refer to those items.

Other items in the list are not human. The word **which** is used to refer to those items.

Tell whether you would use the word **who** or **which** for each item in the list below.

1. Matches
2. Paint
3. A cow
4. A cowboy
5. A bird's nest
6. A bird

B Here's an argument:

> **The last two times Joe tapped home plate, he hit a home run. He should always remember to tap home plate when he goes up to bat.**

What does the writer want us to conclude?

Why does the writer think that tapping home plate will cause Joe to hit a home run?

Say the rule the argument breaks.

Here's how you could prove that tapping home plate doesn't cause Joe to hit a home run. Make Joe tap home plate every time he goes up to bat. If he doesn't hit a home run **every time** he taps home plate, then tapping home plate doesn't cause him to hit a home run.

C When we draw a conclusion from a rule, we start with the rule. Then we add some other evidence. Here's a rule:

> **The more you exercise, the healthier you are.**

Here's some additional evidence:

> **Sharon exercises more now than she did a year ago.**

What's the conclusion?

Sometimes, we can't draw a conclusion from a rule. This happens when the additional evidence is irrelevant. Here's a rule:

> **The more you exercise, the healthier you are.**

Here's the additional evidence:

> **Olivia takes a lot of vitamins.**

What's the conclusion? There is none. We can't draw a conclusion because the additional evidence is irrelevant to the rule.

Here's another rule:

> **The more you drive, the more you pollute the air.**

Tell if each piece of evidence below is **relevant** to the rule or **irrelevant** to the rule. Remember, if it is irrelevant, you can't draw a conclusion. Here are the pieces of evidence:

1. **This year's cars are more expensive than last year's.**
   Is this evidence relevant or irrelevant?
   So what's the conclusion?
2. **Carla uses the family car twice as much as Amanda does.**
   Is this evidence relevant or irrelevant?
   So what's the conclusion?
3. **Frank is bald.**
   Is this evidence relevant or irrelevant?
   So what's the conclusion?
4. **Henry Ford built cars on an assembly line.**
   Is this evidence relevant or irrelevant?
   So what's the conclusion?
5. **Now that Frieda has a bike, she doesn't drive as much as she used to.**
   Is this evidence relevant or irrelevant?
   So what's the conclusion?
6. **Many English words have roots that are thousands of years old.**
   Is this evidence relevant or irrelevant?
   So what's the conclusion?

D Write **Part D** in the left margin of your paper. You have two minutes to copy the paragraph below.

> **Here are the rules for using "who" and "which." If the thing you're referring to is human, use the word "who." If the thing you're referring to is not human, use the word "which."**

★ **E** Write **Part E** in the left margin of your paper. Then number it from 1 to 4. Each square on the map below is five miles long and five miles wide. Assume that the map is accurate.

Examine the map carefully, and then read the statements below it. Some of the statements contradict what the map shows.

- Write **contradictory** or **not contradictory** for each statement.
- If a statement contradicts the map, write what the map shows.

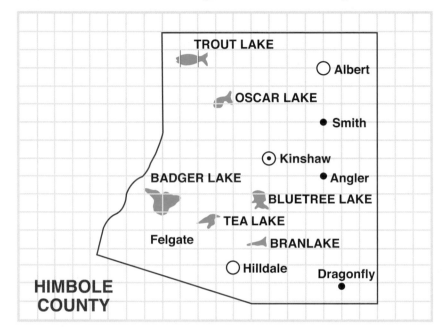

The symbol ● means that the city has between 500 and 1,000 people.
The symbol ○ means that the city has between 1,000 and 2,000 people.
The symbol ⊙ means that the city has between 2,000 and 5,000 people.

1. Two cities in Himbole County have between 1,000 and 2,000 people.
2. Tea Lake is the biggest lake in Himbole County.
3. It is farther from Albert to Angler than it is from Smith to Kinshaw.
4. Four cities in Himbole County have more than 1,000 people.

F Write **Part F** in the left margin of your paper. Then number it from 1 to 5. Read the story and answer the questions.

> The Arabian horse is considered by many horse experts to be the most intelligent and sensitive of all horses. It is a white horse with just a few spots on its belly. When Arabians are young, they are not white, but spotted, and as they grow older most of the spots disappear.
>
> The Arabian horse was bred by the Arabs. The Arabs didn't wear armor in battle, so they didn't need big, heavy animals. The speed and lightness of the Arabian horse meant that it could perform well in battle. These horses became so important that many Arabs considered them to be members of the family and would sometimes let their horses sleep in their tents. At times, the horse stayed outside the tent and served as a watchdog, warning its master if an unwanted visitor came near the camp at night.
>
> Today, horse breeders frequently breed Arabian stallions with other kinds of horses. This breeding increases the intelligence of the line.

1. How does an Arabian horse's appearance change as it grows older?
2. Why didn't the Arabian people need big, heavy horses?
3. Why could Arabian horses perform well in battle?
4. Why do today's horse breeders breed Arabian stallions with other kinds of horses?
5. Where did Arabs sometimes permit their horses to sleep?

A Read the argument below and answer the questions.

> **While Isabel was in the grocery store, her car was stolen. She says she'll never go to a grocery store again.**

1. What does Isabel conclude?

   _____

   _____

   _____

2. Why does Isabel think that going to the grocery store caused her car to be stolen?

   _____

   _____

   _____

3. What rule does the argument break?

   _____

   _____

   _____

   _____

   _____

B Read the passage below.

> More Americans have been killed in traffic accidents over the past fifty years than have been killed in all the wars our country fought in from 1700 to 1950. Every hour, five people are killed in automobile accidents in the United States. Every nine seconds, someone is injured by a car.

- Here's a conclusion:

  Every day, over a hundred people die in automobile accidents in the United States.

1. Does the passage contain evidence to support the conclusion or evidence to contradict the conclusion?

   _____

   _____

2. Which sentence contains the evidence?

   _____

   _____

   _____

   _____

- Here's another conclusion:

   Cars are a fairly safe means of transportation.

3. Does the passage contain evidence to support the conclusion or evidence to contradict the conclusion?

   _____

   _____

4. Which sentence contains the evidence?

   _____

   _____

   _____

   _____

   _____

   _____

 Write the word **who** or **which** for each item. Remember, if the item refers to a human, use **who.** If the item refers to something that is not human, use **which.**

1. The trees _____

2. A cattle rancher _____

3. The cattle _____

4. A clerk _____

5. Siblings _____

6. The rooms _____

7. A girl _____

8. A girl's bike _____

 This lesson presented some facts that you will be tested on. These facts are:

---

1. **Arabian stallions are bred with other kinds of horses to produce more intelligent horses.**
2. **Arabian horses performed well in battle because they were light and fast.**

Study these facts. Repeat them to yourself. Writing these facts may help you to remember them.

Comprehension Fact Game Lessons

The ***Corrective Reading*** Comprehension programs include Fact Games scheduled to occur periodically throughout the programs. In Levels A and B, the Fact Game lessons occur every ten lessons; in Level C, they occur every fifteen lessons.

Most Fact Game items involve recently introduced information and vocabulary. The Fact Games provide an enjoyable format for reviewing program material and assuring that students are learning the various skills on schedule.

In Level A, students work in pairs. One student rolls dice for the whole group and tells what number the dice show. The teacher reads the item that corresponds to the number as the students follow along. One member of each pair of students whispers the answer to the other member. The teacher then tells the answer, and correct responses are tallied. Students earn 1 point for each tally.

In Levels B1 through C, students work in groups of four or five, with one student designated as the monitor. Students take turns rolling the dice, telling what number the dice show, finding the corresponding item number in the printed material, and reading and responding to the item. The monitor judges whether the answer is right or wrong (by referring to the answer key in the back of the Workbook) and awards a point for each correct answer.

The sample Fact Game lesson is presented after Lesson 15 **in Comprehension B1.**

- Item 2 is a Body Systems task that requires the students to identify parts of the skeletal system **(humerus, pelvis, femur)** that are labeled in a picture.

- Items 3 and 8 are Analogies tasks that require the students to say the whole analogy, including the missing word.

- Items 4 and 6 are Deductions tasks that require the students to say the whole deduction, including the missing conclusion. Note that the conclusion in item 4 is "nothing" (the rule does not apply to the evidence), and the conclusion in item 6 involves "maybe."

- Item 5 is a Classification task that requires students to identify class names for groups of objects.

- Items 7 and 11 are Definitions tasks that require the students to name the part of speech of the underlined vocabulary words.

- Items 9 and 10 are Parts of Speech tasks that require the students to identify the adjectives for underlined nouns in given sentences.

- Item 12 is a Definitions task that requires students to say sentences replacing underlined words with vocabulary words they've learned.

Fact Game
2

FACT GAME

> **Note:** Present this Fact Game before beginning Lesson 16. You will need the following materials:
> - One copy of the Fact Game for every student. (Workbook page 45.)
> - One pair of dice for every four or five students.
> - A pencil and a copy of the Fact Game Answer key for each student monitor. (Workbook page 264.)

INSTRUCTIONS

1. (Divide the class into groups of four or five and select one monitor for each group.)
- Open your Workbook to page 45. ✓
- This is the Fact Game for Lessons 6–15.
2. Remember, one player rolls the dice and figures out how many dots are showing.
- Then the player finds the item that has the same number as the dots. The player reads that item aloud and answers it.
3. The monitor looks at the Answer Key on page 264 and tells the player if the answer is right or wrong.
- If the answer is wrong, the monitor says the right answer.
- If the answer is right, the monitor gives the player one point. Don't argue with the monitor.
4. After the player is finished, the dice go to the left and the next player has a turn.
- You have 20 minutes to play the game.
- (Circulate as students play the game. Comment on groups that are playing well.)

5. (At the end of 20 minutes, have all students who earned more than 12 points stand up. Award five bonus points to these players.)
- (Award points to monitors. Monitors receive the same number of points earned by the highest performer in the group.)
6. (Tell the monitor of each game that ran smoothly:) Your group did a good job. Give yourself and each of your players five bonus points. ✓
- Enter your Fact Game points in the box marked **FG**. Then enter your bonus points in the box marked **B**.
- Now enter the total in the box marked **T**.
7. Turn to the inside front cover of your Workbook and enter your total Fact Game points in the box marked **FG2**.

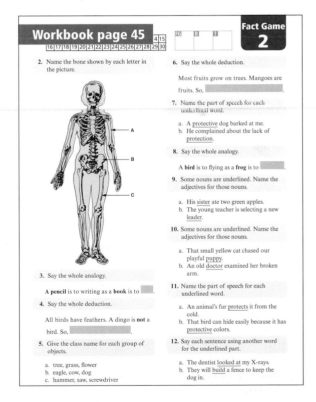

FACT GAME SCORECARD

1	2	3	4	5	6	7	8	9	10	11	12	13	14	15
16	17	18	19	20	21	22	23	24	25	26	27	28	29	30

FG   B   T

**Fact Game
2**

2. Name the bone shown by each letter in the picture.

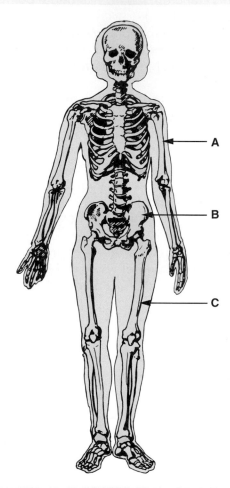

A

B

C

3. Say the whole analogy.

A pencil is to writing as a **book** is to ◻◻.

4. Say the whole deduction.

All birds have feathers. A dingo is **not** a bird. So, ▨▨▨▨▨▨▨.

5. Give the class name for each group of objects.

   a. tree, grass, flower
   b. eagle, cow, dog
   c. hammer, saw, screwdriver

6. Say the whole deduction.

Most fruits grow on trees. Mangoes are fruits. So, ▨▨▨▨▨▨▨▨.

7. Name the part of speech for each underlined word.

   a. A <u>protective</u> dog barked at me.
   b. He complained about the lack of <u>protection</u>.

8. Say the whole analogy.

A **bird** is to flying as a **frog** is to ▨▨▨.

9. Some nouns are underlined. Name the adjectives for those nouns.

   a. His <u>sister</u> ate two green apples.
   b. The young teacher is selecting a new <u>leader</u>.

10. Some nouns are underlined. Name the adjectives for those nouns.

   a. That small yellow cat chased our playful <u>puppy</u>.
   b. An old <u>doctor</u> examined her broken arm.

11. Name the part of speech for each underlined word.

   a. An animal's fur <u>protects</u> it from the cold.
   b. That bird can hide easily because it has <u>protective</u> colors.

12. Say each sentence using another word for the underlined part.

   a. The dentist <u>looked at</u> my X-rays.
   b. They will <u>build</u> a fence to keep the dog in.

FACT GAME 1

2. a. vehicles
   b. containers
   c. vehicles
   d. containers
   e. vehicles

3. a. The dog <u>protected</u> the yard.
   b. The man will <u>obtain</u> lumber.

4. a. obtain
   b. select

5. a. The doctor <u>examined</u> the bone.
   b. She will <u>select</u> a new dress.

6. Every car is a vehicle.
   A convertible is a car.
   So, <u>a convertible is a vehicle.</u>

7. a. a small red car
   b. car

8. a. skull
   b. ribs
   c. spine

9. Some bones are long.
   An ulna is a bone.
   So, <u>maybe an ulna is long.</u>

10. a. containers
    b. vehicles
    c. vehicles
    d. containers
    e. containers

11. skeletal system

12. a. protect
    b. examine

FACT GAME 2

2. a. humerus
   b. pelvis
   c. femur

3. A **pencil** is to writing as a **book** is to <u>reading</u>.

4. All birds have feathers.
   A dingo is *not* a bird.
   So, <u>nothing</u>.

5. a. plants
   b. animals
   c. tools

6. Most fruits grow on trees.
   Mangoes are fruits.
   So, <u>maybe mangoes grow on trees.</u>

7. a. adjective
   b. noun

8. A bird is to flying as a frog is to <u>hopping</u>.

9. a. his
   b. a, new

10. a. our, playful
    b. an, old

11. a. verb
    b. adjective

12. a. The dentist <u>examined</u> my X-rays.
    b. They will <u>construct</u> a fence to keep the dog in.

Decoding Placement Test

Preparation

Reproduce one copy of the test for each student and each tester. A reproducible copy appears on pages 249 and 250 of this guide.

Administration

Select a quiet place to administer the test. Students who are to be tested later should not observe or hear another student being tested. You will need a test form for each student and a stopwatch or a watch with a second hand. When administering the test, sit across from the student. Position the test form so that the student cannot see what you are writing on the form.

Fill out the top lines of the test form (student information). Keep this filled-out test form and hand the student a clean copy of the test.

PART I

Tell the student Read this story out loud. Follow along with your finger so you don't lose your place. Read carefully. Begin timing as soon as the student begins reading the first sentence.

Record each decoding mistake the student makes in oral reading. Mark an X on the filled-out form to show where the student made each mistake.

- If the student omits a word, mark an X above the omitted word.

- If the student adds a word that does not appear in the story, mark an X between two words to show where the word has been added.

- If the student misidentifies a word, mark an X above the misidentified word. Do not count the same misidentified word more than once. (For example, if the student misidentified the name "Hurn" four times, count only 1 error.)

- If the student cannot identify a word within 3 seconds, say the word and mark an X above it.

- If the student makes a mistake and then self-corrects by saying the correct word, mark an X above the word.

- If the student sounds out a word but does not pronounce it at a normal speaking rate, ask What word? If the student does not identify it, mark an X above the word.

- Do not count the rereading of a word or phrase as an error if the word is read correctly both times.

Note: If you wish to use diagnostic procedures, you can use additional code information to indicate the type of mistake the student makes. You may, for example, write **SC** above self-corrections, **SO** above sound-out mistakes, and **O** above the omitted words. You may also wish to write in what the student calls the misidentified words or what the student adds.

After each word-identification error, tell the student the correct word.

When recording the errors, make sure your copy of the story is not visible to the student. The student should not be able to see the marks you are making.

Stop timing as soon as the student completes the story.

Enter the total errors for Part I on the appropriate line at the top of the filled-in test form. Also record the time required by the student to read Part I.

Refer to the placement schedule for Part I to determine placement or whether you should administer another part of the test.

PART II

Part II is a series of sentences that are to be read aloud by the student. You do not need to time this part of the test. To administer, present the section labeled Part II and tell the student Read these sentences out loud. Follow along with your finger so you don't lose your place. Read carefully.

Record each decoding error the student makes while reading. When the student finishes reading Part II, enter the total errors for Part II on the appropriate line at the top of the test form. Then determine the student's placement by referring to the placement schedule for Part II. Fill in the "Placement" blank at the top of the test form.

PARTS III and IV

Each of these sections is a passage that is to be read aloud by the student and timed. To administer, present the appropriate section and tell the student I'm going to time your reading of this selection. Read out loud and read carefully. Record errors as specified for Part I.

When the student finishes reading Part III, enter the total errors and time required at the top of the test form. Then refer to the placement schedule for Part III to determine placement or whether you should administer Part IV.

When the student finishes reading Part IV, enter the total errors and time required at the top of the test form. Then determine the student's placement and fill in the "Placement" blank.

Decoding Placement Schedule

ERRORS	TIME	PLACEMENT OR NEXT TEST
PART I		
22 or more	—	Administer PART II Test
12 to 21	more than 2:00	Level A, Lesson 1
12 to 21	2:00 or less	Administer PART II Test
0 to 11	more than 2:00	Level B1, Lesson 1
0 to 11	2:00 or less	Administer PART III Test
PART II		
41 or more	—	No **Corrective Reading** placement; use a beginning reading program
8 to 40	—	Level A, Lesson 1
0 to 7	—	Level B1, Lesson 1
PART III		
16 or more	—	Level B1, Lesson 1
6 to 15	more than 2:30	Level B1, Lesson 1
6 to 15	2:30 or less	Level B2, Lesson 1
0 to 5	more than 2:30	Level B2, Lesson 1
0 to 5	2:30 or less	Administer PART IV Test
PART IV		
9 or more	—	Level B2, Lesson 1
4 to 8	more than 1:30	Level B2, Lesson 1
4 to 8	1:30 or less	Level C, Lesson 1
0 to 3	more than 1:20	Level C, Lesson 1
0 to 3	1:20 or less	Doesn't need **Corrective Reading** Decoding program

Decoding Placement Test

Name _____ Class _____ Date _____

School _____ Tester _____

PART I	Errors _____	Time _____
PART II	Errors _____	
PART III	Errors _____	Time _____
PART IV	Errors _____	Time _____

Placement_____

PART I

Kit made a boat. She made the boat of tin. The nose of the boat was very thin. Kit said, "I think that this boat is ready for me to take on the lake." So Kit went to the lake with her boat.

Her boat was a lot of fun. It went fast. But when she went to dock it at the boat ramp, she did not slow it down. And the thin nose of the boat cut a hole in the boat ramp.

The man who sold gas at the boat ramp got mad. He said, "That boat cuts like a blade. Do not take the boat on this lake any more."

PART II

Can she see if it is dim?

And it can fit in a hand.

Now the hat is on her pet pig.

I sent her a clock last week.

How will we get dinner on this ship?

The swimming class went well.

When they met, he felt happy.

Then she told me how happy she was.

The tracks led to a shack next to the hill.

They said, "We will plant the last of the seeds."

What will you get when you go to the store?

You left lots of things on her desk.

PART III

Hurn was sleeping when it happened. Hurn didn't hear the big cat sneak into the cave that Hurn called his home. Suddenly Hurn was awake. Something told him, "Beware!" His eyes turned to the darkness near the mouth of the cave. Hurn felt the fur on the back of his neck stand up. His nose, like noses of all wolves, was very keen. It made him very happy when it smelled something good. But now it smelled something that made him afraid.

Hurn was five months old. He had never seen a big cat. He had seen clover and ferns and grass. He had even eaten rabbits. Hurn's mother had come back with them after she had been out hunting. She had always come back. And Hurn had always been glad to see her. But now she was not in the cave. Hurn's sister, Surt, was the only happy smell that reached Hurn's nose.

PART IV

During a good year, a large redwood will produce over twelve pounds of seed, which is nearly a million and a half seeds. And the year that our redwood seed fluttered from the cone was an exceptionally good year. The parent tree produced over fifteen pounds of seed that year, enough seed to start a forest that would be six square miles in size. However, only a few redwood seeds survived. In fact, only three of the seeds from the parent tree survived their first year, and only one of them lived beyond the first year.

Obviously, our seed was lucky. It was a fortunate seed because it was fertile. If a seed is not fertile, it cannot grow, and about nine out of every ten redwood seeds are not fertile. Our seed also had the advantage of landing in a place where it could survive. If it had fallen on a part of the forest floor covered with thick, heavy litter, it probably would not have grown. If it had fluttered to a spot that became too dry during the summer, it would have died during the first year. Our seed landed in a spot where moles had been digging.

Comprehension Placement Tests

The placement procedure for the **Corrective Reading** Comprehension program is designed so that students take two tests. The first (Test 1) is a screening test that requires written responses and is administered to an entire class or group.

Students who make more than 7 errors on the screening test take a second test (Test 2) that places them in **Comprehension A, Comprehension A Fast Cycle,** or **Comprehension B1.** This test is individually administered.

Students who make 7 or fewer errors on the screening test take a second test (Test 3) that places them in **Comprehension B1, Comprehension B1 Fast Cycle,** or **Comprehension C.** This test requires written responses and is presented to an entire class or group.

The battery of placement tests is also designed to identify students who perform either too low or too high for the Comprehension programs.

Test 1

The screening test (Test 1) is made up of 16 multiple-choice items. Students are to complete it in no more than 10 minutes.

Preparation

Reproduce one copy of the test for each student. A reproducible copy appears on pages 256–257 of this guide.

Administration

- Make sure all students have a pencil.
- Pass out the test forms, face down.
- Tell students: Turn your paper over and write your name at the top. You will circle the correct answer for each item. Begin now.
- Do not provide help either for decoding the items or identifying the answers.
- At the end of the 10-minute period, collect the test forms.

Scoring

The Answer Key below shows the correct answers. Count one error for each item that is incorrect. Note that for items 2 and 4, students are to circle four answers. If they don't circle all four correct answers, the item is scored as one error.

Enter the total number of errors in the score blank at the beginning of the test form. Then determine which placement test to administer to each student. Students who make more than 7 errors take Test 2. Students who make 7 or fewer errors take Test 3.

Answer Key			
1.	c	9.	a
2.	a, d, e, h	10.	b
3.	d	11.	b
4.	b, e, h, j	12.	c
5.	d	13.	d
6.	b	14.	b
7.	c	15.	c
8.	d	16.	b

Test 2

Test 2 is administered individually. The teacher or another tester presents the test orally to each student. Students respond orally, and the tester records whether the responses are incorrect. The test contains 22 items, some of which have more than one part. Test 2 requires about 10 minutes per student.

Preparation

Reproduce one copy of the test for each student and each tester. A reproducible copy appears on pages 258–259 of this guide. Each tester should become thoroughly familiar with both the presentation procedures and the acceptable responses for the various comprehension items. Tester judgment is called for in evaluating the appropriateness of responses to many items. (For a discussion of procedures and responses, see pages 254–255.)

Administration

Select a quiet place to administer the test. Students who are to be tested later should not observe or hear another student being tested. You will need a test form for each student.

When administering the test, sit across from the student. Fill out the top lines of the test form (student information). Keep the filled-out test form and position it so that the student cannot see what you are writing on the form.

Start by presenting the following general instructions: I'm going to ask you some questions. Do your best to answer them. There's no time limit, but if you don't know the answer, tell me and we'll move on to the next item. This test is not designed to grade you. It's designed to help us figure out how we can work with you most effectively.

Present the items in order, starting with item 1. If a student responds incorrectly, circle the response number that follows the item. To help you keep track, you may want to draw a line through the number when the item is answered correctly.

Scoring

Total the student's errors by counting every circled response number. Enter the total in the score blank at the beginning of the test form. Then determine the placement of the student.

Placement

The table below shows program placements based on the number of errors made in Test 2.

Errors	Program Placement
31 or more	Place in a beginning language program, such as *Language for Learning*
27 to 30	Provisional placement in Comprehension A, Lesson A*
17 to 26	Comprehension A, Lesson A
14 to 16	Comprehension A, Lesson 1
11 to 13	Comprehension A Fast Cycle, Lesson 1
7 to 10	Comprehension B1, Lesson 1
0 to 6	(Administer Test 3.)

* Some students who perform in this range may perform well on Lessons A through E of Level A. If not, place them in a beginning language program.

Test 3

Test 3 is a written test of 19 items administered to the group. Students underline sentence parts, write answers to questions, and indicate correct responses to multiple-choice items. The test requires about 10 minutes to administer.

Preparation

Reproduce one copy of the test for each student. A reproducible copy appears on pages 260–261 of this guide.

Administration

- ■ Make sure all students have a pencil.

- ■ Pass out the test forms, face down.

- ■ Tell students: Turn your paper over and write your name at the top. You will write the answer for each item. Begin now.

- ■ Do not provide help either for decoding the items or identifying the answers.

- ■ At the end of the 10-minute period, collect the test forms.

Scoring

The Answer Key below shows the correct answers. Each incorrect response counts as 1 error. If students correctly underline only part of the specified group of words in section A or B, score 1/2 error.

Enter the total number of errors in the score blank at the beginning of the test form. Then determine the placement of the student.

Answer Key
1. a. wapdumpos b. (words underlined: *little plants that grow in twinglers*)
2. a. drosling b. (words underlined: *a small kerchief around his wrist*)
3. a. 1,000 gallons b. 1,100 gallons c. Idea: The price of milk will go up.

4.		
a. 7	e. 16	i. 4
b. 1	f. 2	j. 10
c. 15	g. 3	k. 6
d. 5	h. 8	l. 12

Placement

The table below shows program placements based on the number of errors made in Test 3.

Errors	Program Placement
more than 8	Comprehension B1, Lesson 1
5 to 8	Comprehension B1 Fast Cycle, Lesson 1
2 to 4½	Comprehension C, Lesson 1
0 to 1½	too advanced for **Corrective Reading** series

Presentation Notes for Test 2

Items 1–3: Same-Different

These items test the concepts "same" and "different." Present the instructions in a normal speaking voice. Each item has three response numbers. In item 1, for example, if a student names two acceptable ways that a hamburger and an ice-cream cone are different, draw lines through 1a and 1b. If the student does not name a third acceptable way, circle 1c.

You may prompt a student by saying: You've named two ways that they're the same. Can you think of another way? If the student does not respond within 10 seconds after the reminder, circle the response number and go to the next item.

The responses printed on the test sheet are only samples—not an exhaustive list of appropriate answers. A student's response is appropriate if it (a) expresses how the objects are the same (or how they are different), and (b) has not already been given for the pair of objects.

Note that responses are correct for the different items if a student mentions only one of the items. For instance, if the student says the ice-cream cone has a cone, but does not mention the hamburger, the assumption is that the hamburger does not have a cone. Therefore, the response is acceptable.

If you are in doubt about the acceptability of a response, ask the student to give a different one. For example, a student may respond to item 1 by indicating that a hamburger is hot, that a hamburger has a bun, and that an ice-cream cone is cold. The last response is questionable because it is the opposite of the first response. Say: Can you name another way that an ice-cream cone is different from a hamburger? Score the student's response to your question.

Items 4–6: Analogies

Item 4 is an analogy that tells where objects are found (or where the objects typically operate). Any response that accurately tells *where* is acceptable, for example: *lake, stream, fishing hole, ocean, aquarium,* or *under lily pads*.

Item 5 tells which class each object is in. Acceptable responses include *cold-blooded things, animals, food,* and *living things*.

Item 6 deals with parts of objects. Acceptable responses include *fins, tails, gills, scales, eyes,* and *teeth*.

Items 7 and 8: Statement Repetition

These items test statement-repetition skills. The student receives as many as three tries at repeating the statement. You say the statement and tell the student to repeat it. If the student says exactly what you say, draw a line through the response number for that trial. If the student does not say exactly what you say, circle the number. As soon as the student repeats the statement correctly, go to the next item.

For example, if the student correctly says the statement in item 7 on the first try, draw a line through 7a and go to item 8. If the student does not say the statement correctly on the first try, circle 7a and say: Let's try it again. Repeat the statement. Continue until the student has said the item correctly or until you have circled 7c.

Students must say the words clearly so they are not confused with other words. Watch for word substitutions, word omissions, and omission of word endings—for example, saying *twenty-seven* instead of *twenty-seventh* in item 7. On the second and third try, you may emphasize the part of the sentence the student said incorrectly.

Items 9–13: Basic Information

These items test knowledge of general information. For items 9 and 12, there is more than one acceptable response. For the others, however, only one answer is acceptable.

Items 14–17: Deductions

These items assess the student's ability to use deductions. Nonsense words are used in item 17. If students object to the nonsense words, remind them: You can still answer the questions even if you don't know the meaning of some of the words.

Students are not required to use the precise words specified for the items; however, they should give acceptable substitutions.

Items 18 and 19: Divergent Reasoning

These items test the student's ability to use concepts related to true and false. Item 18 deals with descriptions that are true of some things, while item 19 deals with a contradiction (one part must be false if the other part is true).

Blackline Master for Test 1

Name _____ Class _____ Date _____

School _____ Tester _____

Errors _____ Give Test 2 _____ Give Test 3 _____

1. Circle the answer.

> Tom and Jerrit are the same age. Jerrit is 15 years old. So...

   a. Tom is at least 16 years old.

   b. Tom is less than 15 years old.

   c. Tom is 15 years old.

   d. Tom is older than Jerrit.

2. Circle the name of each object that is a container.

   a. bag   e. briefcase

   b. phone   f. ring

   c. book   g. belt

   d. purse   h. dresser

3. Circle the answer.

What is the holiday we celebrate on January 1?

   a. Labor Day

   b. Memorial Day

   c. Thanksgiving

   d. New Year's Day

   e. The 4th of July

4. Circle the name of every season.

   a. Jump   g. September

   b. Spring   h. Fall

   c. July   i. Warm

   d. Monday j. Summer

   e. Winter   k. Tuesday

   f. Pepper

5. Circle the item that is true.

   a. All dogs bark.
      Collies are dogs.
      So some collies bark.

   b. All dogs bark.
      Collies are dogs.
      So all dogs are collies.

   c. All dogs bark.
      Collies are dogs.
      So no collies are dogs.

   d. All dogs bark.
      Collies are dogs.
      So all collies bark.

• Appendix B •

6. Circle the class name for the objects.

a. containers   c. animals

b. vehicles   d. tools

7. Circle the word that means *build*.

a. buy

b. protect

c. construct

d. predict

For items 8–11, circle the word that means the same thing as the underlined part.

8. She <u>resides</u> near New York.

a. visits

b. drives

c. works

d. lives

9. The doctor <u>looked at</u> the patient's arm.

a. examined

b. predicted

c. selected

d. calculated

10. They will <u>modify</u> the plans.

a. support

b. change

c. observe

d. announce

11. She <u>concealed</u> her belief.

a. announced

b. hid

c. explained

d. confirmed

For items 12–14, circle the answer.

12. A **simile** is a statement that tells how things...

a. are different

b. are funny

c. are the same

d. are complicated

13. If information is **irrelevant** to an issue, the information is...

a. untrue

b. hard to understand

c. important

d. unimportant

14. If a passage is **repetitive,** it...

a. introduces many unfamiliar words

b. says the same thing again and again

c. uses no unfamiliar words

d. has long sentences

For items 15 and 16, write the letter of the answer.

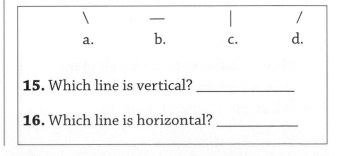

15. Which line is vertical? _____

16. Which line is horizontal? _____

Comprehension—Test 1

Blackline Master for Test 2

Name _____ Class _____ Date _____

School _____ Tester _____

Errors _____ Comprehension Placement _____

(Read to the student.)	**(Circle errors.)**

1. **Name three ways that an ice-cream cone is different from a hamburger.**

   (Ideas: *One is hot; a hamburger has*   1a
   a bun; one is sweet; one has meat; an   1b
   ice-cream cone has a cone; and so forth) 1c

2. **Name three ways that an ice-cream cone is like a hamburger.**

   (Ideas: *They are food; each is bigger*   2a
   than an ant; both have parts; both are   2b
   purchased; you eat them; and so forth) 2c

3. **Name three ways that a tree is the same as a cat.**

   (Ideas: *They are alive; each is bigger*   3a
   than an ant; both die; they reproduce;   3b
   both have coverings; and so forth)   3c

4. **Finish this sentence: An airplane is to air as a fish is to . . .**

   (Ideas: *Water; a lake; an ocean;*
   and so forth)   4

5. **Finish this sentence: An airplane is to vehicles as a fish is to . . .**

   (Ideas: *Animals; food; living things;*   5
   and so forth)

6. **Finish this sentence: An airplane is to wings as a fish is to . . .**

   (Ideas: *Fins; tail;* and so forth)   6

(Read to the student.)	**(Circle errors.)**

I'll say some sentences. After I say a sentence, you try to say it exactly as I said it.

7. **Here's a new sentence: It was March twenty-seventh, nineteen sixty-five. Say it.**

   It was March twenty-seventh,   7a
   nineteen sixty-five.   7b
      7c

8. **Here's a new sentence: Some of the people who live in America are illiterate. Say it.**

   Some of the people who live in   8a
   America are illiterate.   8b
      8c

9. **Listen: It has four wooden legs and a seat and a back. What is it?**

   (Ideas: *Couch; chair.*)   9

10. **Listen: We celebrate this day every year because it's the first day of the new year. What date is that?**

    January 1; the first of January.   10
    (In countries other than the
    United States, substitute a
    comparable local holiday.)

Comprehension—Test 2

(Read to the student.)	(Circle errors.)
11. Say the days of the week. (Students may start with any day of the week, but the days must be recited in order.)	11
12. What is a synonym for sad? (Ideas: *Unhappy; downcast.*)	12
13. One season of the year is summer. Name the three other seasons. *Fall; winter; spring* (can be given in any order).	13
14. Listen: If a dog is green, it has five legs.	
a. Pam's dog is green. What else do you know about it? (Idea: *It has five legs.*)	14a
b. Jim has something with five legs. Is it green? (Ideas: *Maybe; I don't know.*)	14b
15. Listen: Some lobsters are red.	
a. Tony has a lobster. Is it red? (Ideas: *Maybe; I don't know.*)	15a
b. Mary has a lobster. Is it red? (Ideas: *Maybe; I don't know.*)	15b

(Read to the student.)	(Circle errors.)
16. Listen: No brick walls have paint specks. Jerome has a brick wall. What else do you know about it? (Idea: *It doesn't have paint specks.*)	16
17. Here's a rule. The rule has silly words, but you can still answer the questions. Listen: All lerbs have pelps. Listen again: All lerbs have pelps.	
a. Tom has a lerb. What do you know about his lerb? (Idea: *It has pelps.*)	17a
b. What would you look for to find out if something is a lerb? (Idea: *Pelps.*)	17b
18. Listen: It is a farm animal that has four legs, goes "moo," and gives milk. Is that true of only a cow? *Yes*	18
19. Listen to this statement and tell me what's wrong with it. He was fifteen years old and his younger sister was eighteen years old. (Idea: *His younger sister is not younger than he is.*)	19

Comprehension—Test 2

Blackline Master for Test 3

Name _____ Class _____ Date _____

School _____ Tester _____

Errors _____ Comprehension Placement _____

1. They planted wapdumpos, little plants that grow in twinglers.

   a. The sentence tells the meaning of a word. Which word? _____

   b. Underline the part of the sentence that tells what the word means.

2. His drosling, a small kerchief around his wrist, was made of silk and grummicks.

   a. The sentence tells the meaning of a word. Which word? _____

   b. Underline the part of the sentence that tells what the word means.

3. Here's a rule: When the demand is greater than the supply, prices go up.

   Here's what's happening: Digo Dairy sells 1,000 gallons of milk every day. Digo Dairy has orders for 1,100 gallons of milk every day.

   a. How much is the supply of milk? _____

   b. How much is the demand for milk? _____

   c. What is going to happen to the price of milk at Digo Dairy? _____

4. For each word in the left column, write the number of the word or phrase from the right column that means the same thing.

a. currency   _____   1. all at once

b. suddenly   _____   2. silently

c. ambiguous   _____   3. movable

d. hesitated   _____   4. changed

e. exhibited   _____   5. paused

f. quietly   _____   6. plan

g. portable   _____   7. money

h. regulations   _____   8. rules

i. converted   _____   9. general

j. appropriately   _____   10. fittingly

k. strategy   _____   11. clear

l. response   _____   12. answer

13. responsible

14. gradually

15. unclear

16. showed

17. caused

18. slowly

Comprehension—Test 3